Hayden Fry

A High Porch Picnic

Hayden Fry
with
George Wine

SPORTS PUBLISHING INC.

ISBN: 1-58261-033-9
Library of Congress Catalog Card Number: 99-60755

Director of Production: Susan M. McKinney
Dustjacket and photo insert: Julie L. Denzer
Photo section photos courtesy of Southern Methodist University,
North Texas State University, University of Iowa, and
Hayden Fry's personal collection.

SPORTS PUBLISHING INC.
804 N. Neil
Champaign, IL 61820
http://www.SportsPublishingInc.com

Printed in the United States.

*To all of the loyal football players, coaches, and fans at Odessa, SMU,
Arkansas, Baylor, North Texas State, and Iowa.
You were the greatest!!!*

Contents

Acknowledgments

Football is the ultimate team game, and I wish to acknowledge everyone who ever played a role in the teams with which I've been associated.

My genuine appreciation goes to all the coaches and players I've been fortunate to work with throughout the years. Thanks also to the members of the medical and support staffs, as well as the presidents, administrators and faculty who have given us their backing.

Thanks to the fans who have supported our teams. Their loyalty and enthusiasm always made us work and play a little harder.

Finally, special acknowledgment goes to members of my family for their love, devotion, patience and understanding. Without that, my life in football would not have been possible.

—Hayden Fry

Thanks to the sports information staffs at Iowa, SMU, North Texas State, Baylor and Arkansas for the photos and information they provided for this book.

Thanks to the UI Photo Service, as well as Don Roberts, Bob Rasmus and Vince Muzik for their pictures that appear in the book.

Thanks to Mike Pearson of Sports Publishing, Inc. for skillfully guiding the book to its completion.

Thanks to my wife, Barrie, for her encouragement and honest criticism. If she ever leaves her career in medicine, she can always make it as a book editor.

And a special thanks to Hayden Fry for allowing me to work with him on this book and for all the fun we had in doing it.

—George Wine

Foreword

by Jerry Levias

My first encounter with Hayden Fry was when he came to my home to recruit me for a football scholarship to Southern Methodist University. His first question was, "Is that turnip greens I smell cooking?" He ended up looking in all the pots on the stove and having a lengthy discussion with my Mama about how to cook pinto beans.

Hayden was ahead of his time. He saw talented athletes, not black or white, just athletes with potential. He stepped up and did the right thing—he gave black athletes the same opportunities white athletes received. Through my good fortune of having been recruited by Hayden Fry, he became my coach, good friend and mentor for life. Hayden's most profound statement to me was, "Levi, things are going to happen around you and things are going to happen to you, but the most important thing is what's going to happen inside you."

Of all the coaches who recruited me, Hayden was the only one concerned about my education. He was very aware of my performance in the classroom as well as on the field. In my first semester at SMU when my grades weren't up to par, Hayden threatened to call my Mama. From that semester forward, I was always on the Dean's List.

Athletes under Hayden's tutelage graduated and contributed to society. He always believed that if you developed the student, you would get a good athlete. Through him I received an academic, athletic and social education. He helped me to be the understanding person I am today, and taught me how to cope with the inequities of life and society. Hayden Fry, with his West Texas colloquialisms, would always remind me, "Levi, if you don't want 'em to get your goat, don't tell 'em where it's hid."

I'm eternally grateful for Hayden's friendship and guidance. May God bless him always.

Chapter One

EASTLAND, TEXAS

We are all products of a time and a place. Because I was born in 1929—the year the stock market crashed and the U.S. economy collapsed—my formative years coincided with the Great Depression, the decade of the 1930s.

I spent all of that time in Texas, where I lived virtually all my life until I moved to Iowa in 1979. I was born in a little town called Eastland, located in the central part of the state between Fort Worth and Abilene. Later my family moved west to Odessa, which wasn't a whole lot bigger than Eastland.

The Great Depression and small-town Texas did not make a good combination. Although Eastland and Odessa were oil towns, both were hit hard by the economic conditions of the '30s. Money was in short supply, jobs were hard to get, and many folks had a hard time just scratching out a living.

Yet looking back, I remember those days with great fondness. Maybe that's because we had a strong family and generally good health. Most important, perhaps, was that my dad always had a job. Were we poor? I imagine we were, but we never dwelled on it. As a kid growing up, I certainly didn't think about it.

My mother and father were wonderful parents who took good care of me. I was taught to say "Yes, sir," and "No, ma'am," and to wash behind my ears and to keep my hair combed. And I learned one other thing: to always eat every thing on my plate. With my appetite, that wasn't hard to do.

My roots go deep into the Texas soil. The Texas State Genealogical Society has honored me for 150 years of Texas heritage, for which I am very proud. During the Texas sesquicentennial celebration, I was certified as a descendant from one of the Texas First Families, and I am also a member of the Sons of the Republic of Texas. As you can see, I take my heritage seriously.

Benjamin Franklin Fry, my great-great grandfather, was a Baptist minister who moved his family from Georgia to the Texas Territory in 1834. They settled in Jeddo, just east of San Antonio. Reverend Fry stood 6 feet, 9 inches tall, which must have made it easy for him to look over his flock. He was a colorful character who became known as the "Fighting Parson" while serving as chaplain for General Sam Houston, taking part in the Siege of Bexar, the Battle of San Jacinto and the Mexican War. After he died, he was recognized by the Texas Legislature with a historical marker in the Jeddo cemetery.

Great grandfather K.L Fry belonged to Terrell's Regiment of the Texas Cavalry and had 12 children. One of his sons, Richard, heard exciting stories about a military captain named Hayden Arnold. Richard, a member of the Texas Rangers, liked the name Hayden and gave it to one of his sons, John Hayden Fry, my father, who passed the name along to me.

We've got papers that show Grand Daddy Richard went out and caught wild horses and sold them to the army at $5 a head. He signed the sales papers with an X. We don't know if he was joking or not. A lot of people in those days didn't go to school and never learned how to read and write.

Four of Richard's sons, including my father, got interested in the meat business. Two of my uncles, Howard and Claude, had grocery stores in Abilene. Uncle Boyd ran Fry Meat Packing, which operated all the way to New Orleans.

My mother, Cora, was one of eight children and everyone called her "Sister" because she helped raise her seven siblings. Her mother, Ada, outlived four husbands. One of them was named William Hodge, a well-educated and well-to-do man who was my mother's father. I remember my grandmother as a tough little lady and a hard worker. She was part Indian and we called her "Mamaw". So I have enough Indian blood in me to have an instinct for dodging arrows. Maybe that's why as a coach I've managed to dodge most of the bullets fired at me.

My mother and her sisters all had Indian physical characteristics—dark hair, dark eyes and high cheekbones. They were hard workers with lots of stamina. They grew up in the West Texas cotton fields and all had duties and chores to perform as children. They became accustomed to hard work. Most of them stayed in Texas and had lots of children. We used to have Hodge family reunions when I was growing up, and a lot of folks attended.

Both my mother and father, like a lot of youngsters in those days, went to work early in life. Neither had any formal education, and they only went to the eighth or ninth grade. They never attended high school. By the time they were married my dad was a butcher and a grocer. That's what took them to Eastland; he got a job there as a grocery store manager. And that is where I was born on February 28, 1929.

My memories of Eastland are all good. As a little boy growing up, I had good friends and good teachers. One of my boyhood pals was Bill Brashier, who, like me, went into coaching and was my defensive coordinator at North Texas and Iowa for 23 years before he retired following the 1995 season. We are still very good friends.

I have only one sister, Margaret. She is 10 years older than I am, so she finished high school shortly after I started my elementary education. Margaret was a very fine athlete. She could high jump 5-9, which was an exceptional height for a teenage girl in the 1930s. She was also an outstanding softball player on some semi-pro teams that won Texas state championships. Margaret is in good health, and we see each other on a regular basis.

We didn't have a lot of worldly possessions in those days, so it's easy to remember the first and only car my dad ever owned. One day he drove home a shiny, green automobile that caused a lot of excitement in the neighborhood. It was so shiny you could see your reflection in it. We stood around admiring the car until my dad went in the house to get mom.

That's when my pet goat named "Billy" took a look at the car and saw his reflection. Following his instincts, Billy put his head down and rammed the side of the car. Wham! Then he did it again. Bang! And again. Bam! My dad, hearing the noise, came running out of the house and saw the dents Billy had put in his car. He grabbed the goat, dragged him out back and tied him to a tree.

The following day I noticed Billy wasn't around. He was nowhere to be seen the next day, either. In fact, I never saw him again. It wasn't until several years later that I learned what happened. Dad butchered Billy and we ate him! I guess Dad taught that goat a lesson. Anyway, Dad never bought another car, and I never got another goat.

After I finished the second grade in Eastland, my father got an offer for another job. Two brothers who started the Piggly Wiggly grocery chain lived in Eastland, and they offered my dad an opportunity to move out to Odessa and manage one of their new stores. My sister had just finished high school and she was off to college. So my parents packed up our belongings and we headed west to Odessa. To an eight-year-old boy who had never traveled far from home, it seemed like we were headed to the edge of the earth.

Chapter Two

ODESSA, TEXAS

Some folks like to joke that Odessa, way out in West Texas, might not be the end of the world, but you can see it from there. But for a boy growing up there in the '30s and '40s, it was a wonderful town. I loved life the way it was for me in those days. Looking back after all these years, I wouldn't trade it for anything.

Odessa is not a pretty town. It is located in a part of Texas that is desolate and barren. There isn't much rainfall and therefore not much vegetation. The soil is sandy and rocky and it is hard to grow any crops. The terrain is flat, there isn't much grass and there aren't many trees—there is actually a nearby town called "No Trees"—but there are lots of rattlesnakes, windmills and tumbleweed. The summers are hot and the winters are mild enough to play golf every day unless the wind blows and kicks up a sandstorm, which it does on a regular basis.

We used to joke that when a sandstorm whipped up you could see Lubbock and Amarillo blowing by. Sometimes the wind blows so hard and there is so much sand in the air, you can't see and if you are outdoors it burns your face and gets in your eyes. The wind blows sand right through closed windows and doors. My mother used to clean house, and I could write my name on tabletops when I got home from school. Life wasn't easy; you had to be tough to survive.

When we arrived in 1937, Odessa was a rip-roaring oil town. The Depression still had a grip on America, but some people in Odessa were making a lot of money from oil and others were making a decent living. But there was also plenty of poverty. None of the streets in town were paved except Main Street, and there were rows of shacks built of anything that would stand up, including cardboard and tin. That's where the transients lived.

With all the roughnecks brought in to work the oil wells, there were fights all the time. It was a tough place to live, and I had to learn how to defend myself at an early age. We played one game as kids where we drew a big circle in the sand and 12 or 15 of us would get inside the circle. Somebody would holler "Go!" and we'd start beating up on each other. Anything went—kicking, clawing, pulling hair—a real free for all. The last guy left in the circle was the winner. That was our idea of a sandlot game. It was our idea of fun.

Odessa had a great mixture of race, nationality and religion, and a lot of my friends were black and Hispanic. I learned at an early age that we're all pretty much the same, regardless of skin color or religious beliefs. But the schools were segregated, and they stayed that way for a long time after I left town. I always had good teachers and got a good education all the way through school. I liked school and was a serious student; I studied hard and tried to get good grades.

Our first home in Odessa was on the south side of the tracks, which was considered the "wrong side." We lived there long enough for me to make some good friends—many of them what we today call minorities—then we moved a couple of times and eventually bought a house at 503 North Golder. It seemed like one of the biggest houses in Odessa, and I still remember the price: $3,600. My parents needed to borrow some money for the purchase, but they were too proud to ask anyone. So I called Uncle Tom Hodge and told him we needed some money to buy a house. When he loaned us the money, I realized I might become a pretty good salesman someday.

All the homes we lived in had indoor plumbing, but there were still lots of folks without it in Odessa. Outhouses were common in town, and most of them were one-holers, but people with a little bit of money might have a two-holer. I remember the first two-holer I ever saw was on a Halloween night and we turned it over without knowing someone was inside. This guy came flying out the door with his pants down hollering all kinds of things. We took off in the dark and he never caught us.

I learned at an early age there is no such thing as a free lunch, and I was always doing something to make a little money. If I wasn't working at the grocery store for my dad wringing chicken necks and plucking feathers, I was chopping weeds for 10 cents an hour. I also delivered newspapers and had a milk route. I set pins at the bowling alley.

My mother worked outside the home part time, too. One of her jobs was at the local picture show, where she sold tickets for $1 a night. On Saturdays she also worked an 11 p.m. sneak preview for an extra $1.25. So for six nights a week she made $7.25 before taxes. She did that for 19 years! But that wasn't uncommon at that time in Odessa. The town had lots of good, honest, hardworking people struggling to survive.

I never spent much time deciding what to wear to school because I never had a choice. I had two pair of bib overalls. One had blue and white stripes with a place for a claw hammer, a watch and a carpenter's ruler. That pair I wore to Sunday school and church. The other pair was solid blue. I wore those to school. As for shoes, well, if you had a pair of Buster Browns or Thom McCanns, you were big time! I never owned a pair of cowboy boots until I started working in the oil fields.

I grew up a Baptist, and we were regular churchgoers. I once went seven consecutive years without missing Sunday school. I got all kinds of stars and pins for that. We used to joke about "deep-divin' Baptists." They are West Texans who go to East Texas and have mud in their ears after getting baptized in a creek bottom.

There may be some truth in that, because there isn't much rain in West Texas, and water is precious. When it rained, people would catch the water running off their roof and give it to their livestock and other animals. The well water was so hard and full of minerals, it would turn your teeth brown. Sometimes ranchers would dig a well and strike oil. That sounds like a joke, but it actually happened.

World War II began and ended while I was a kid in Odessa. I vividly remember December 7, 1941, the day the Japanese bombed Pearl Harbor. For two days I sold an EXTRA! edition of the local paper. The price was 10 cents, and I kept a nickel. I made more money in those two days than I'd ever made in my life. When the War ended we had two celebrations: one for the end in Europe and one for the end in Japan. Like all towns, Odessa had lots of young men and women in the armed forces.

Midland Army Air Field, 10 miles east of Odessa, had the biggest bombardier school in the military, and that's where I had my first driving job. I drove a truck out to the base at 3 0'clock in the morning to deliver and pick up laundry and cleaning. At 13 or 14 years old I didn't have a driver's license, and I was paid the handsome sum of $1 per round trip.

Odessa had its share of town characters, and the one I remember best is Cesspool Willy, who came back from the War with his brain scrambled. He was a good, hard-working man but he was mentally out of it. He made his living digging cesspools. My dad had been after him to dig a cesspool for us for a long time. Finally, about 3 o'clock one morning, we woke up to a lot of noise outside, and there was Willy digging a cesspool. He was already down several feet. My dad hollered, "Willy, you gotta be crazy diggin' out there in the middle of the night!" Willy came up out of the hole holding a release paper he'd gotten from the hospital and waved it at dad, and said, "I'm not crazy and I can prove it. Can you?" We all went back to bed and Willy went back to work. He'd made his point.

When I was 14, my father came home for lunch one day and died of a heart attack while seated in a taxi in front of our house. He was only 53 years old. He was a trim 6-1 and 170 pounds, and didn't have a history of heart problems. My dad was a good man who had worked hard all his life providing for his family. His sudden death left a real void in our lives.

I started roughnecking in the oil fields when I was 14, and I've been paying Social Security ever since. I had to sign a minor's release, which removed the oil company from any liability in the event I was hurt or killed. My starting wage was 35 cents an hour. I was called "Nubbin," which is a little piece of pipe. Nicknames can be interesting in the oil fields.

One summer, several years later, I worked my way all the way up to $1.10 an hour! I was a motorman, a guy who works on the rigs and tends the motors, and later I worked on derricks. You're real high and strapped in a harness, standing out there supported only by a harness, throwing heavy pipes around. There were no unions when I broke in at the oil fields; I doubt if they hire 14-year-olds today. One of my biggest thrills was putting a big red light on top a derrick. Our rig could be identified at night from five miles away, and that made us special.

A lot of men I worked with were minus a finger or two. Some lost a hand or a whole arm working on the rig. Working with pig iron was especially dangerous. A lot of my friends from school—boys I played football with—worked at the oil fields. We roughnecked during the summers and holidays. We were close and we were tough. We learned how to survive early in life.

I got my first car when I started roughnecking. There were only four or five of us in our entire high school who had a car. Gas was rationed, and we used to siphon it out of each other's cars. I'd siphon Jim's, he'd siphon Bill's, and he'd siphon mine. Took us a while to figure out what was going on. I'd drive my car to work, which sometimes took us to oil fields as far away as Hobbs, New Mexico. That didn't leave much gas to cruise Main Street on Saturday night.

The war had a positive impact on Odessa's economy because it greatly increased the demand for oil. Eighth Street had six or seven taverns in one block, and the roughnecks would walk from one to another carrying beer in their hands. The taverns all had dance halls with sawdust on the floor, and there were always lots of women, mostly wives or girlfriends of the roughnecks. The women would head home just before midnight, because that's when the "evening tower" shift ended in the oil fields, and the women made sure to be home when their men arrived. The "morning tower" shift—midnight to 8 a.m.—brought another group of ladies to the dance halls. The "daylight tower" shift brought still another group of women, and it went on like that around the clock, with new faces arriving every eight hours. If you ever saw the movie "Boom Town" with Clark Gable—well, that was Odessa at that time.

I got in sports at an early age, partly because I loved to play most any game, and partly to stay out of trouble. Like most kids, I started in the sandlots, but by junior high we were in organized programs with good coaches and good teams. In high school we only had three sports—football, basketball and track—and I participated in all three. I liked them all, but football was my best sport, and Odessa was a football town.

The thing I remember about high school is that I had a lot of good teachers and good coaches. I feel very fortunate in that regard. I enjoyed all subjects, even typing, but my favorite was history. I worked hard at being a good student. There were probably 140 students or so in my class, and when I was a senior I was elected class president. I think that because I was a serious student, pretty quiet and a fair football player, I earned the respect of my classmates.

When 13 of us decided to drop senior English to keep from graduating and play another season of football, I was elected class president again. I declined the office because I planned to graduate after the fall semester, when I hoped to receive a scholarship to play college football. But the 13 of us had set a goal to win a Texas state championship, and rules permitted us to return to high school and give it one more shot.

Chapter Three

TEXAS STATE CHAMPIONS

Football has always been a big sport in Texas and it has always been important to the folks in my hometown of Odessa. A recent book called *Friday Night Lights* is precisely about that: the importance of high school football in Odessa. Football is big now, and it was big when I was growing up there more than 50 years ago. Is it overemphasized? Perhaps, but they don't look at it that way now, and we certainly didn't in the years I played.

Our team nickname was Bronchos—that's right, spelled with an "h"—and the Bronchos always had good teams. We played in an eight-team league called the Little Southwest Conference, which was spread over several hundred miles. It included the towns of Abilene, Amarillo, Big Springs, Lubbock, Midland, Odessa, San Angelo and Sweetwater. Odessa was one of the league's smallest towns, but it often had the best football team.

Odessa was further west than any town in the conference, and we traveled to games by bus, which we called "old Yellow Hound." It was just an old yellow school bus. Sometimes we'd have to get up real early in the morning to leave Odessa in time for the game. There were no interstate highways in those days, and the bus trips took hours. We'd play the game and ride back home, sometimes arriving in the middle of the night. Amarillo (275 miles north) and Abilene (200 miles east) were the longest trips, but we never stayed overnight. Sometimes we played games in faraway places like El Paso and Wichita Falls, but we traveled to and from the same day. But we never complained because we didn't know any different. Oh, sometimes when we had a playoff game that was really a long way off, we'd spend the night in a hotel, but it wasn't the Marriott or the Hyatt.

We had sellouts for every home game in a stadium that had been enlarged to 14,000 by the time I finished playing. That was several thousand more than Odessa's population at the time. Everyone in town attended the football games, and we had a lot of fans from the surrounding communities. For the really big games, fans would line up days in advance with their bedrolls and lawn chairs and some reading material. Our fans were blue collar and really loved their Bronchos. Our biggest rival was Midland, only 20 miles up the road. At the time, Midland had more millionaires per capita than any town in America. Midland's fans were white collar.

Odessa businessmen were not bashful about helping our coaches get good players. If they heard about a young, promising player in another town, they'd offer his daddy a job. They didn't see anything wrong with that, and we got some good players that way. The idea came from Wink, Texas, which won a state championship with that kind of recruiting back in the '30s. But nobody ever came into Odessa and offered our parents jobs. That would not have been healthy. Odessa fans took their football very seriously. They didn't just bet money on games—they also bet their wives and girl friends.

We were undefeated three straight years in junior high under Coach Pop Taylor. He really knew how to develop youngsters. I had a lot of teammates who were exceptional players, and we carried our success right on through high school, where I had two great coaches. The first was Clayton Hopkins, who came in from Pecos, Texas—that's where The West begins—and put in the single wing with me playing tailback. Then we got fancy and started lining up in the T, with me at quarterback. We'd either snap the ball, or shift to another formation—the single wing, the double wing or the box. He had us doing exotics.

Then Joe Coleman, who had been the coach before joining the Navy, came back from the war and took over again. The players rebelled, because we really liked Coach Hopkins. But we got over it, of course, and Coleman turned out to be an outstanding coach. He had us running a multiple, diversified offense that was way ahead of its time. We were doing things they'd never seen in West Texas. And our defense was just as good as the offense. Those were the days of two-way football, and I played safety, which I enjoyed as much as playing quarterback.

I had some outstanding teammates, but the best was Byron "Santone" Townsend, the most complete athlete I've ever seen. He's the closest thing to Jim Thorpe who ever lived. He could play anything, do anything, and do it exceptionally well. He was a halfback and went on to play at Texas. They called him "Santone" because he came in from San Antonio. I think he might have been one the businessmen recruited.

Billy and Bobby Moreman were twins who played the ends and later starred at TCU. Fullback Pug Gabrel and halfback Sonny Holderman had fine careers at UTEP. Center Gordon "Jockamoe" Headlee went on to SMU. Tackle Steve "Dog" Dowden played at Oklahoma and Baylor. Other good players were Herman Foster, Harry Pace, Wayne Jones, Pat Evitt, Glen "Jug" Taylor and Clinton "Slim" Hill.

Many of the players had nicknames, and mine was "Crazylegs." I'm not sure how I got it, but it wasn't because I was a dazzling runner. Our squad numbered about 40 players and we had our 50th anniversary a few years ago. Most of those who are still living attended.

We were typical kids growing up—we were full of mischief and liked to have fun—but we didn't drink or smoke or stay out late. We were serious about sports and we wanted to be in good physical shape and do our best. Even if we had wanted to break training, the people in town wouldn't have allowed it. If we'd been seen out late at night, they'd have picked us up and taken us home. One night at the picture show I was eating popcorn, and someone tapped on my shoulder. It was Coach Hopkins, and he took the popcorn. Next day at practice I had to run 1,000 yards with a fat manager on my back.

Our coaches thought that popcorn, soda pop and candy were bad for us. And they didn't allow us to drink water at practice, regardless of the heat. Sometimes at an early morning practice we'd fall down just to lick the dew off the grass. Practice might last four hours, and we'd scrimmage every day. Sometimes after a game in which the coach didn't like the way we'd played, he'd give us a lecture, then we'd go back out on the field and scrimmage.

We maintained training rules and stayed in good physical condition, but we did some of the same, silly, mischievous things that kids have always done. One time at Big Lake we were staying overnight for a basketball tournament. We played two or three games that day and came back to the hotel exhausted, but we couldn't get to sleep because of some strange noise coming from the room next door. We knocked on the door and when nobody answered, we opened it ourselves. The room was full of chickens, all crated up and doing a lot of clucking. So we let 'em out to shut 'em up. The hotel manager frantically chased chickens up and down the halls all night. We lost the next day's game and got out of town.

A couple of my teammates had a teacher they didn't like very much, so one night they took a cow into her classroom and closed the door. You can imagine what the room looked and smelled like when she arrived the next morning. She had a pretty good idea who did it, and asked one of the boys, "Mooch, did you do this?" And Mooch looked at her innocently and said, "Not hardly," while the rest of the guys doubled over to keep from laughing.

The boys' basketball games were played before the girls' games and we had to share the same locker room. One night after a boys' game, some guys left a little crack in a couple of the windows so they could watch the girls change into their uniforms. The girls' coach caught them, but before she could identify anyone, the boys pulled their jackets over their heads and ran off into the dark. The next day the principal announced he wanted to see all the Peeping Toms in his office, but nobody showed up. Nothing ever came of it, but it was the talk of school for a few days. The girls always made sure to keep their windows closed tight after that.

I could have graduated from high school in 1946, but Texas had a rule then that if a boy wasn't 19 by September 1 and hadn't received his diploma, he could play another year of football. It was sort of like a redshirt year, and 13 boys in my class decided to take advantage of it. We all dropped a required English course so we wouldn't graduate and could play again in the fall of '46. It was an unusual situation that produced one of the great teams in Odessa football history.

We won 14 straight games and none of them were very close. I think the closest score we had during the regular season was 12-0 in a game with Big Springs played in a sandstorm. We just smothered people defensively, and we must have shut out at least half of our opponents. Offensively we could either overpower an opponent or hit him with a lot of big plays. Our coaches copied plays from all the good college and pro teams at the time. I remember Illinois had an outstanding team with a star named Buddy Young, and we had plays called "Illinois left" and "Illinois right." Byron Townsend was a great all-around back and an outstanding punter, and Pug Gabriel was our power runner.

As the quarterback, my expertise was faking and ball-handling and keeping the defense off balance. I might fake to three guys and then throw a pass, or I might hide the ball under my jersey and wait for a play to develop. It was legal to do that then, and I was pretty good at it. We didn't throw the ball much because we didn't have to. We scored on a lot of big plays from all over the field.

We just dominated the Texas high school football scene that year. We scored almost 400 points and gave up about 50, but the most amazing statistic was that we never had a turnover. Not one! The few times we fumbled, we always recovered the ball. And I was fortunate not to have any passes intercepted.

For the playoffs that led to the Texas state championship, all the schools were thrown into one bracket and went at it. Now I think they have four or five classes, but then it was only one. So we played some much bigger schools in the playoffs. We had to go through the El Paso district, the Wichita Falls district and the Dallas district to reach the championship game in Austin.

Our opponent was Thomas Jefferson High School of San Antonio, and we played in Memorial Stadium on the University of Texas campus before a capacity crowd of 42,000, which remained a record for years. It was an extremely well-played game by both teams, but I recall that our kickoff man, Bobby Moorman, was so uptight he nearly whiffed the ball, which looked like a squib kick that we recovered. It appeared to be a daring piece of strategy to all those fans in the stands.

We won the game 21-14, beating an outstanding team that had whipped some great competition to get to the championship game. Their coach was Jewell Wallace, and their stars were Kyle Rote, Bubba Wilson, Pat Knight and Sonny Payne. They all became great college players—Rote at SMU in the same fabled backfield with Doak Walker. We got out in front and led all the way in ending a perfect 14-0 season. Eight of our Bronchos made first or second team all-state, and that's when it was two-way football with only 11 players on a team.

After we won the championship, we got on board "Old Yellow Dog" and headed for Odessa, where we had a basketball game the next night. Four basketball starters were members of the football team. We were opening the basketball season and hadn't even practiced. At 6-2 I was our tallest player and played center. At half-time I was the leading scorer for both teams with three points, and at the end of the game I was the leading scorer with five points. We won the game 18-17, and at halftime I recall the coach getting all over me because I only had two fouls. He had the idea that if you didn't have at least three fouls at the half you weren't playing hard enough.

Seventeen players on our state championship team went on to play football in college, a lot of them at major schools. My last basketball season was a short one, because I graduated at mid-year. I was like a lot of my friends—my next big decision would be where to go to college. The search was going to take me to far away, exotic places like Oklahoma and Louisiana. I could hardly wait.

Chapter Four

THE COLLEGE YEARS

When I earned my diploma at Odessa more than 50 years ago, it wasn't too common for high school graduates to go on to college. Most found a job and went to work, got married and raised a family. Many never left town.

But there had never been any doubt that I would attend college. Although neither of my parents were high school graduates, they recognized the value of an education and had always pointed my sister and me in that direction. My sister had attended college and I was also expected to also, which didn't make me unhappy. I liked school and wanted to continue my education in college. It was just a matter of deciding on which one.

I graduated at Odessa after the fall semester of 1946 and started considering my options. Because I was the all-state quarterback on a football team that had won the state championship with a 14-0 record, a lot of schools were interested in me. I had more opportunities than most high school graduates do. I was open-minded as to where to attend college, although I preferred playing football for a school using the T formation. Some were still using the single wing and double wing, and I was not fast enough to be a tailback in that kind of offense.

Recruiting then was a whole lot different. The NCAA was not the bureaucratic monster it is today. It had only a handful of employees and a very small rule book. For one thing, recruiting went on all the time—from the end of one football season to the beginning of the next. There were no restrictions about contacting student-athletes, and there was no national letter of intent. A kid could change his mind and switch schools the day before classes started, and some did.

There was no limit on the number of schools you could visit. Before my decision was made, I visited LSU, Texas, Rice, Baylor, TCU, SMU and Oklahoma. That's two more than today's limit of five. The schools reimbursed travel expenses by the mile, and the recruit could travel any way he wanted to. I often hitchhiked or hopped a freight train, then I'd pocket the travel money. I thought that was a great deal.

My first recruiting trip was to the Cotton Bowl as the guest of LSU. The Tigers were playing Arkansas on January 1 when the Cotton—along with the Rose, Sugar and Orange—was one of the top four bowls in the country. In fact, there weren't many other bowls in those days. I was in charge of getting five of my high school teammates from Odessa to Dallas, and we rode the train. The weather was awful on game day, with snow and ice. We sat on the LSU bench, which would be a NCAA violation today. As I mentioned, things have changed—the rule book is much bigger now.

The coach who recruited me at LSU was Joel Hunt, who had been an all-American at Texas A&M. I later visited the campus at Baton Rouge and had a great time. Y.A. Tittle, who went on to become a great player in the NFL, was the Tigers' star quarterback and showed me around campus. I was really with impressed LSU's hospitality, and especially liked the sorority dance Tittle took me to. I decided the recruiting process might be kind of fun.

Herman Foster, an all-state guard on my high school team we called "Cheese Butt," and I decided to make our visit to Rice at the same time. We hitchhiked, but we told the Rice coaches we were traveling to Houston by train, so we had to hustle and get to the depot in time to meet them. Everything worked out fine, and we had a good visit at Rice. Jess Neeley was making a name for himself as coach of the Owls, and he stayed in the business long enough to become a legend. He was a great man, and 15 years later he was standing across the field in my first victory as a college head coach at Southern Methodist. It's funny how things work out.

Herman and I decided to hitchhike home from Houston through Waco to take a look at the Baylor campus. We'd both been invited to visit there, but hadn't set a date. When we got to town, we called the coaches at Baylor and said, "We're here." They were surprised and happy to see us, and we spent a couple of days visiting the school. I fell in love with the place and decided that it was the college for me.

Baylor had some things working in its favor. Odessa had a lot of Baylor alums who had pushed hard for me to go there. I also had a lot of friends enrolled there. The fact that I was raised in the Baptist Church was a factor. Baylor was and still is the largest Baptist university in the world. But mostly I just liked the environment and feel of the campus and town.

Baylor's head coach was Bob Woodruff, who had played at Tennessee and was a protégé of General Robert Neyland. He had coached at West Point and later at Georgia Tech with Bobby Dodd and was making a name for himself. Woodruff had a young backfield coach named Frank Broyles, who had been a star quarterback at Georgia Tech and was considered one of the bright young coaches in the business. He would later make an impact on my coaching career. After my third year at Baylor, Woodruff moved on to Florida, and my new head coach was George Sauer, who had been at Navy and Kansas. Both men knew the game, and I enjoyed playing for them.

I made my college choice and enrolled at Baylor for the spring quarter in March, 1947. Herman Foster went with me, although he later transferred to Texas Western, now Texas-El Paso. We got there for spring football practice, which was important, because freshmen were eligible and it gave us an early start. It was less than two years since the end of World War II, and there were a lot of veterans coming back to college. Many of them were on the football team.

On my first day of practice, I was listed as the No. 14 quarterback, a real come down for an all-state player. It seemed like everyone ahead of me was a war veteran, much older and much more worldly, and they weren't the least bit impressed with my high school achievements. Some had beards, some had wives and some even had children. I began to think I was in over my head and felt sorry for myself. Then I did what a lot of disillusioned freshmen do: I went home.

My mother was a wise lady, and I'm not sure if she was surprised when I showed up unexpectedly, but I know she was disappointed. She sat me down and gave me a rare lecture. She told me how "the cow eats the cabbage," which is a West Texas expression for "this is how it's going to be!" She told me I couldn't always be No. 1, that sometimes I just had to compete. She told me how she and my daddy had worked hard for me, and that if I never played another down of football I was going back to Baylor to get an education and a degree. She told me she didn't want me working in the oil fields or grocery stores the rest of my life. Then she cooked me a good supper, I spent the night and hitchhiked back to Waco. My coaches never knew I'd left the campus.

Although I had already had a semester of college that included spring football practice, I was chosen to play in two high school all-star games in the summer of 1947. One was the North-South game in El Paso, where my coach was Ray Eliot, whose Illinois team won the Big Ten championship the previous fall. He installed some plays from his T-formation and I was his quarterback. The other game was the Oil Bowl in Wichita Falls, where we played an all-star team from Oklahoma. I was a captain in both games.

I took my mother's advice and did everything I could to become a better football player as well as a college student. By the time Baylor started its season that fall, I had advanced up the depth chart to No. 2 at quarterback and felt pretty good about myself. The guy ahead of me was Jack Price, a war veteran from Johnstown, Pennsylvania, who could really throw the ball.

Throwing the football is what they did best in the Southwest Conference in those days. The sports writers liked to call it an "aerial circus," an accurate description. It was a good league that played wide-open football, and because seven of the eight members were in the state of Texas, it was very competitive.

There were some great coaches in the conference at that time—men like Matty Bell at SMU, Dutch Meyer at TCU and Jess Neeley at Rice. They had creative minds and their teams played exciting football. Star players at other schools included Doak Walker and Kyle Rote at SMU; Bud McFadden, Bobby Layne, Tom Landry and Byron Townsend (my teammate at Odessa) at Texas; Lindy Berry and Billy and Bobby Moorman (two more Odessa teammates) at TCU; and Dave "Hog" Hanner, Pat Summerall and Clyde "Smackover" Scott at Arkansas.

The only pass I ever threw that was returned for a touchdown was at Arkansas. Hanner, who later starred for the Green Bay Packers, hit me as I released the ball and Summerall, who now announces NFL games, picked it off and ran it into the end zone. I tried to jump up and run after him but Hanner held me down. I couldn't move.

My longest road trip as a collegian was the first one I took as a freshman. We flew to Miami to play the Hurricanes in the Orange Bowl, and we won the game 18-7. I have a picture of myself standing outside the airplane, getting ready to fly half way across the country. We traveled to most conference games by bus because the schools in the league were so close. And Miami was an exception as far as a distant intersectional game. The only other one that approached it was at Wyoming my senior year.

We played Mississippi State three times, all on the road at three different cities: Starkville, where the school is located, plus Memphis and Shreveport. The game at Memphis was played at Crump Stadium, built during the depression by the WPA. With quite a few transfers from Army following the cheating scandal at that school, Mississippi State had good teams but we beat them twice and tied them once. I'm not sure why the Army players transferred to Starkville—maybe because West Point, Mississippi, is a nearby town.

A funny thing happened in the Texas game my freshman season. We played at Austin in the same stadium in which Odessa won the state championship less than a year earlier. As I mentioned, it was two-way football in those days—players played both offense and defense—and I was a safety. Following a Baylor punt, Frank Broyles sent me into the game to play defense, and as I trotted on the field, the crowd stood up and gave a mighty roar. I thought, hey, this is pretty nice—they must remember how I helped Odessa win the state title here last year. Then I noticed that Bobby Layne, the great Longhorn quarterback, was coming onto the field from the other side. The cheers were for him, but for just a few seconds I was pretty proud.

Baylor had good teams in the four years I played there. We were 26-13-2 during my time, and we nearly won the Southwest Conference championship in 1949. A loss to Rice in the last game of the season prevented Baylor from taking its first league title since 1924. A year earlier we had beaten Wake Forest in the first-ever

Dixie Bowl in Birmingham. They called that game, "The battle of the Baptists."

In my senior year, we opened a new stadium the Bears still play in. It seats 50,000, about 20,000 more than the old one. Under new coach George Sauer, we had a good team and finished 7-3.

I enrolled at Baylor intending to major in geology. I knew some geologists in the oil fields, and their type of work interested me. But after a year or so I learned there was a glut of geologists on the market and a lot of them were working at gas stations. Many simply couldn't find a job.

I considered going into medicine but when a visit to an operating room made me a little woozy I changed my mind about that. History and German also interested me—I went on to get minors in both—but the course of study I finally settled on for my major was psychology. The more I learned about it, the more interested I got, and by the end of my sophomore year I was really hooked.

I had always been interested in people and studying them from a distance. As a kid I'd sit on main street in Odessa and try to guess a person's occupation by the way he dressed and carried himself. I'd manage to find out and kept track of my success rate. I got pretty good at it. I enjoyed observing people's behavior, and when I found out in college that psychology is a study of that sort of thing, my major was settled.

Experimental psychology really fascinated me. I enjoyed studying rats in a maze and how they went about getting a reward, which was normally food. One of my experiments to see how fast rats learn was published in a professional journal. I timed a rat to see how fast he could run the maze to get his reward, and he became faster and faster. When I placed an obstruction at the 27th entry he slammed into it headfirst. After that, he would race full speed until he reached that entry, then sniff around and creep through it, then resume top speed until he reached his reward at the end of the maze. The experiment proved that rats have memory and the capacity to learn. I felt good about getting my experiment published, but the rat was probably left with a headache.

I was blessed with a lot of good teachers at Baylor. Dr. Schultz in psychology had a big impact on me, as did Dr. Drake in German. I became a friend of Dr. Schultz, who was a good example of an absentminded professor. One time his car came up missing and he was convinced someone had stolen it. A week or so later when I was over to his house he still hadn't located his car. He had some kittens I wanted to use for a study in a psychology class, and he gave his approval. As I was rounding up the kittens, one slipped through a crack into the garage, and when I opened the door, there was the car Dr. Schultz thought had been stolen. He had neglected to look in his garage for it!

I had another psychology professor named Dr. Bean, who had such bad eyes he couldn't see much beyond the first row. As a psych major, I attended every class, but many of my friends did not. When Dr. Bean called roll I'd respond "here" for any of my buddies who were absent. We got away with that for an entire semester.

I had two serious romances as a Baylor student. The first was with Maida Roby, a girlfriend from Odessa who went on to college at John Tarleton, located in Stevenville, Texas. The second, with HueLeita Zachry, ended in marriage after we both finished at Baylor. Her name is a combination of her father's, Huelit, and her mother's, Leita.

I was the last four-year football letterman to graduate from Baylor until freshmen became eligible again in the 1970s. There was one other four-year letterman while I was playing, Hank Dickerson, but he graduated before I did. He kicked off, booted conversions and field goals, and I held the ball for him. We were close friends, and he became very successful in real estate in the Dallas area. He has passed away, as have many of my Baylor teammates.

I was Baylor's No. 1 quarterback from time to time, but I never kept the job very long. I started three games as a junior and thought the job was mine. Then a junior college transfer, Adrian Burk, beat me out. He became an all-American in both football and baseball, and I named my fourth son after him. He's a great guy and a good friend.

As a senior I started a couple of games and played enough during the season to be voted the best ball handler in the Southwest Conference by Texas sports writers. But again I was beaten out by a guy who became an all-American in both football and baseball, Larry Isbell. He was a brother of Cecil Isbell, who starred at Purdue. So my claim to fame as a college football player is—and I told this story to every team I ever coached—if you get beat out, make sure the guy who does it is an all-American!

Chapter Five

BACK TO ODESSA

There was a time in college when I thought I might use my psychology degree by going to work for a big company. I was very interested in some case studies that we had about how large companies negotiated contracts and how they increased production through motivation. The role of an arbitrator was especially interesting to me.

But as my senior year wound down, I realized I wanted to be a coach and teacher, and there were some good starting jobs available for a graduate with the ink still wet on his diploma. I was offered the position of freshmen football coach at Georgia Tech. Frank Broyles had left Baylor to join the staff there, and he wanted me to join him. But I declined and accepted an offer in my hometown.

I joined the Odessa school system in 1951 as a teacher of American history, a counselor and the junior varsity head football coach. But when the varsity backfield coach didn't make it back from the Air Force for practice that fall, head coach Jeep Johnson elevated me to that position.

My starting salary was $3,200, which was good for those days. In fact, it was $400 over the starting pay scale. Then I got a $300 raise when I became a varsity coach. I enjoyed everything about my job, including the teaching, which gave me a good opportunity to stay in touch with the faculty. Many of the teachers thought the coaches were overpaid, so I always made it a point to teach as well as coach while I was working in high school.

I was proud to be one of the first counselors in the Texas high school system. I had barely opened my office and put my nameplate on the door when I got my first counseling job. A young girl who said she was a sophomore came in crying and upset. She finally told me—and it took forever to get this out of her—that she was pregnant and afraid to tell her parents. As a first-time counselor, I was probably as nervous as she was, but after a lot of conversation I convinced her to tell her parents the truth.

She agreed to do that if I would go with her, so we drove to her home, which was in the country, quite a ways out of town. When we got there, I asked her parents to sit down, and she tearfully told them the situation. They took it reasonably well, all things considered. By the time I returned to school I was late for my first football practice, which was embarrassing for a brand new coach. But it was a successful counseling job. The girl's boyfriend was also a high school student. They got married and had the baby, and as far as I know, they're still married today.

My mother was still in Odessa, and I moved in with her. She was still at the same home on Golder Street and was working at the same theater, selling tickets to movies, letting the football players in free. They loved her. Mom had done all right after Dad died. Her health was good and she didn't have many expenses and wasn't stressed financially. She was happy her son had come home to work, and it was good to be with her again. While in college, I had spent the summers roughnecking in the oil fields around Odessa, but it was nice to be back permanently.

HueLeita and I were engaged when I returned to Odessa, but she was still at Baylor and didn't graduate until the fall quarter. We were married December 29, 1951, in her hometown of Corpus Cristi and lived with my mother for a brief time, then rented a home of our own. HueLeita took a job with the Odessa utility company.

My friend, George Bush, who became the 41st president of the United States, was still doing business in West Texas when I went back there to coach. I had gotten to know him a few years earlier when I was roughnecking in the oil fields one summer and he was an oil field supplier following his tour of military duty as a Navy pilot. George was spending so much time in Odessa that he was looking for a place to rent so he could bring his wife Barbara to town, and good rentals were not easy to find in those days.

As it happened, my girlfriend at that time, Maida Roby, had parents with rental property, and I secured George and Barbara a garage apartment, which they greatly appreciated. Both then and after my return to Odessa, George and I went to baseball games together. He really loved the game, which he had played at Yale. He was tall, a good athlete and a regular guy, just like the rest of my friends.

I never heard him express any political aspirations. I certainly never heard him say he'd like to be president some day. He eventually moved on to Midland and started his own oil field supply company. I saw him from time to time during his two presidential campaigns. The Iowa caucuses are important, and he spent quite a bit of time in our state. I've met his sons and both are now governors of big states—George in Texas and Jeb in Florida. Both have been on the Iowa campus.

Before my second year of coaching at Odessa got started, I received my draft notice in the mail. Uncle Sam wanted me in the Army, which I wasn't the least bit thrilled about. It wasn't that I wanted to shirk my military duty, I just wanted no part of the Army. I had been in the national guard four years and I knew the Army wasn't for me.

I had some friends in the Marines who were enjoying that branch of service, and they convinced me the Marines would teach me how to fight and "come back alive". As Harry Truman said, the Marines had a good propaganda machine, and I was buying it. So without acknowledging my draft notice, I hitchhiked to San Antonio and enlisted in the Marines, a decision I have never regretted.

Chapter Six

THE MARINE CORPS

The Korean War had really heated up by the time I got my draft notice in the summer of 1952. I probably would have been drafted in 1946 had I finished high school that year. Several of my buddies were taken then, but when I chose to return to high school for a fifth year, I became exempt. While in college, I joined the National Guard.

I didn't want any part of the army, so I made a beeline to San Antonio and enlisted in the Marines. I had heard a lot of good things about the Corps, and I decided that if I was going to serve my country, that was the branch of the service for me. After being sworn in, I was sent to San Diego for boot camp. I was a "snuffy," the lowest form of enlisted man in the Corps. Despite my college degree, National Guard duty, and teaching and coaching experience, I was at the bottom of the barrel.

I had barely started in boot camp before they found out I was a football player and asked me to go out for the base team. I happily said yes, practiced hard, and worked myself up to second-team quarterback. The guy ahead of me, Ed Brown, was good enough to go on to a professional career.

Then one day, a tech sergeant pulled me aside and said, "Fry, you think you're getting away with something, but you're not! The captain wants to see you." I was scared to death, but when I reported to the captain, he told me that they appreciated the contribution I was making to the football team. But he said I was missing too many drills to complete boot camp. He said I could remain on the football team, but I would have to go back to boot camp following the season.

I saluted and said, "Thank you, sir, but I'm a Marine and I want to drop football and complete boot camp now." That may have been the smartest decision I ever made, even though I again became a "snuffy," the oldest in my platoon.

There are a lot of stories about boot camp in the Marines, and many of them are true. It's a very intense and difficult time for young recruits, and some don't make it. Drill instructors are really tough on snuffies, and you don't realize until later that everything they do is intended to make you a better Marine.

We had an especially tough DI, and one morning after a rugged two hours on the drill field he told us we would stand "junk on the bunk" inspection in one hour. That means everything out of your footlocker neatly lined up on your bunk and the barracks in first-class order. We rushed back to the barracks to find the place trashed—dirt and sand all over the floor and bunks turned upside down. The place was a mess, and no doubt the DI had a hand in it. But we hurried and had it ready for inspection in an hour.

That incident prompted some of us to give the DI a "blanket party," a late-night visit in which the snuffies creep into the DI's quarters while he's sleeping, throw a blanket over him and work him over. Lucky for us he wasn't in his room when we arrived, and lucky for me I never participated in such a cowardly act. I hate to admit I was willing to be part of it. No telling which way my career in the Marines would have gone had the DI been in his quarters. But the story illustrates how angry a person can get when he believes he is being abused by authority.

When they finally let us off the base during boot camp, a bunch of us went to downtown San Diego to celebrate our first liberty. It wasn't long before the military police rounded up every Marine, soldier and sailor in town and herded us to Balboa Stadium, where two service teams were playing in the Poinsettia Bowl. It was raining hard and not many fans were in attendance, but we had to stay and watch the entire game.

I never figured out what that was all about until years later when I was at a function with Lindsay Nelson, the well-known TV sports announcer. He told a story about how he was doing the 1952 Poinsettia Bowl and the weather was so bad nobody showed up. So to make the game look good on television, all the military personnel on liberty in San Diego were rounded up and brought to the game. In other words, I was just a TV prop! I told Lindsay I appreciated his clarification after all those years.

The Marines are big on nicknames, and I picked one up in boot camp that stayed with me as long as I remained a member of the Corps. Boot training included how to deal with live bullets flying overhead while crawling on your belly. One day on this exercise, I came face to face with the biggest rattlesnake I ever saw, and I'd seen some big ones in West Texas. I started crawling backwards and the DI, not seeing the snake, thought I was a coward and started hollering at me. The entire infiltration came to a halt as the DI chewed me out.

When he finally allowed me to speak, I told him about the snake, and we went down and killed the sucker. It was either a timber rattler or a diamond back and had 17 rattlers, which is supposedly a record at Camp Pendleton. At the time I had only one suit, a brown one, which I always wore on liberty. So my buddies took the rattlesnake and the brown suit and came up with a nickname that stuck. From then on I was known as "Rattler Brown."

During boot camp I applied for officer school in both the Marines and the Navy and was accepted by both. I decided to stay a Marine, and was sent to Quantico, Virginia, for officer training. I took a bus to Odessa to pick up HueLeita and we drove an old car all the way to Quantico. We weren't going to see each other during my three months of training, and she rented a small apartment and got a job teaching seventh grade in Fredricksburg, Virginia.

I moved into a Quonset hut out in the boon docks with other officer candidates and started a very intensive three months of training. Every minute of our time was occupied and there was great pressure to keep up both mentally and physically. We not only had to learn a great deal, they also tested our strength and endurance to the maximum. I enjoyed the training because I had always been an enthusiastic student and I was in good physical condition. But a lot of guys were not, and they didn't last long. Men were flunking out every day. Unlike boot camp, I no longer had an age advantage. A lot of the candidates were older and more mature than I was. Many had been in the Marines for several years as enlisted men.

I learned a great many things in the Marines—both in boot camp and officer training and then later on—that helped me as a football coach. I learned that when a group experiences adversity and suffers disappointment, it is brought closer together. You have to endure a certain amount of hardship and stress before something really becomes worthwhile. The Marines train men hard and to do things the right way, just as a football team must train. The Marine Corps does it right, and I took a lot of that training into coaching. I wouldn't take anything for the years I spent in the Corps.

An officer candidate is graded on two things: leadership and test results, or grades. In a class of 486 I finished first in leadership and ninth in grades. That made me the No. 3 man in my class. I was fortunate that athletics had prepared me for leadership, and I had always been a fairly serious student who received good grades. So officer training came easier to me than most, and I enjoyed everything about it, whereas some candidates didn't like it at all.

The men I trained with branched out in many directions. Some went to Korea and were killed in battle. A lot of them became career officers. At least two that I know of became generals. As soon as I was commissioned a second lieutenant I was assigned to Headquarters and Services Company right at Quantico, with a variety of responsibilities in the motor pool, pistol range and chow hall. Oh, and one other thing—my job also included playing football for the Quantico Marines.

The Marines really catered to athletes, as did other branches of the military. Good athletic teams improved morale and increased pride, and if a Marine could play a sport well, that's what he was expected to do. Athletes were identified and sent to a base that had a team. Our Quantico team was coached by Charlie Walker. We played two-way football with a 35-man roster, but only 17 of the players could be officers. As the quarterback, I was one of the few guys in the starting lineup who wasn't all-pro or all-America.

I was, however, one of four Johns in the starting backfield. We used to joke about that because in Texas, where I came from, a john was an outhouse. Besides John Hayden Fry there was John Pettibone of Notre Dame and the Chicago Bears, John Amberg of Kansas and the New York Giants, and John O'Shea of Stanford and the San Francisco 49ers. There were a lot of bad jokes about that backfield. Some said it had a certain odor about it.

We had two ends with all-America credentials—Ken McAffee of Alabama, Frank McPhee of Princeton—plus my old teammate, Bob Trout, who was all-Southwest Conference at Baylor. We had others who had been college stars, such as Buddy Parker of Baylor,

John Mooney of Duke, Rosco Hansen of North Carolina and Bobby Meyers of Stanford. Jackson King, out of the Ivy League, led the nation in punting one year. The talent level on that Quantico team was unbelievable.

I never played with Big Daddy Lipscomb, but I was in line to take immunization shots with him one time. But before he got to the corpsman giving the shots, he passed out. The anticipation of getting the needle stuck in his arm made him faint. But he overcame that, completed his time in the Marines, and went on to stardom in the NFL.

I coached a six-man company team, as well as playing on the 11-man base team. I knew nothing about six-man football, but I got a rule book and put my imagination to work. The game really allowed me to be creative, and I had a lot of plays with deception, using men in motion and reverses. We had a lot of fun, went undefeated and won our league championship.

I got to shake the hand of President Eisenhower while I was at Quantico. He came on the base to play golf one day and said he'd like to meet the officer of the day, which happened to be me. It was a real thrill for a second lieutenant to meet a great general who had led the allies to victory in Europe less than 10 years earlier.

The only year I played at Quantico was 1953, and we were invited to the Poinsettia Bowl after winning the Marine Corps championship. So it was back to San Diego to play a game I'd watched in the rain as a reluctant spectator a year earlier. Fort Ord was our opponent, and the national service championship was on the line. Fort Ord featured some great players like quarterback Don Heinrich and running back Ollie Mattson and won the game.

Some of our players had spent too much time in Tijuana, Mexico, and suffered Montezuma's revenge. But Fort Ord had an outstanding team. I recall a play when Mattson started one way on a sweep, got bottled up, reversed the field and ran 80 yards for a touchdown. I always thought he reversed his field to keep from hurting his average of 12 yards a carry.

After the bowl game, our season was over and we were reassigned. I was among those who received orders to go to Korea, where the war was still going on. We were enroute on a troupe ship when some of us got our orders changed to Japan, where we would play football. (Did I mention that the Marines catered to athletes?) Before getting to Japan, however, we stopped at Iwo Jima, where we simulated the enemy as the Third Marine Division landed on the beaches of that island. For two weeks we had a mock war and we were the bad guys. During the exercises we discovered a lot of caves and tunnels that had been built by the Japanese during World War II. We even found the remains of some Japanese soldiers and discovered some of their tanks and armament in the underbrush. We spent several weeks on the island, and it was an unbelievable experience.

I was stationed in Japan about a year and played the 1954 season with the Marines over there. I also served as an assistant coach to head coach Ted Stawicki. There were a lot of good service teams in Japan and it was big-time football. The Marines played a navy team for the championship in Meji Stadium in Tokyo. The stadium had a capacity of 80,000 and military personnel were brought in from all over to see the game. Many were on R&R from Korea.

When the season ended, the four branches of the service put together all-star teams and held a playoff for the Far East championship. The Marines won the championship game in what was called the Rice Bowl. I played in another all-star game, after which the general took us on a public relations tour of the area. We went to Hong Kong, Singapore, Thailand and the Philippines, spending a few days in each place as goodwill ambassadors. It was a great experience. I never got to Korea, probably because the Marines didn't have a football team there.

My duties included buying and purchasing for the Ninth Marines. As the procurement officer, I got to travel the island, visit all the bases and meet a lot of interesting people. I did some business with a huge department store in Osaka called Dimarui. It was like Neiman Marcus in Dallas, and I bought HueLeita some fine china there for about five percent of what it would have cost back home. The rate of exchange was outstanding for Americans at that time.

I studied four different religions—Shintoism, Buddhism, Taoism and Hinduism—while I was in Japan, taking courses in each. I wanted to know more about the culture of that part of the world, and I met a lot of great scholars and teachers. I didn't have the opportunity to study very long, but I was fascinated by what I learned.

I was very impressed with the intelligence and curiosity of the Japanese. They always treated Americans with great respect, and were friendly and hospitable. If there was resentment lingering from World War II, they kept it concealed. I always thought they were appreciative we didn't use the atomic bomb more extensively.

I've had occasion to go back to Japan several times—mostly coaching in all-star football games—and I continue to enjoy and admire the Japanese.

When my tour of duty ended in Japan, I was sent back to the U.S. with a check. It came from donations taken up by Marines in the Far East to help build a memorial hotel in San Francisco where Marines could stay for a reasonable rate while waiting to be shipped in and out. The check was a welcomed gift that helped build the hotel, and I got to stay around San Francisco for a couple of weeks before processing out of the corps.

I was discharged from the Marines in February, 1955, with the rank of captain and a lot of wonderful memories. It is still the favorite organization I have ever been associated with, by far. Had I not been married, there is no question in my mind I would have made a career of the Marine Corps.

But we had started a family. Our first son, Randy, was born while I was stationed in Quantico. Zach was born in Corpus Cristi while I was in Japan, and some ham radio operators were kind enough to connect me with HueLeita so I could get the news first-hand. That was an exciting way to learn about your second son. So I took my discharge from the Marines and went back to the real world. For me, that was coaching and teaching, and I looked forward to it.

Chapter Seven

HEAD COACH
IN HOMETOWN

When the Korean War ended, the military began downsizing and early releases were offered to Marines who had jobs on the outside or were returning to college. I had taught and coached at Odessa one year before joining the Corps and my job was still there, waiting for my return. When I showed proof of that, I received my release from active duty.

But I didn't go directly to Odessa. When HueLeita and I traveled from Quantico to San Diego a couple of years earlier, we made the trip in a new Chevrolet coupe. When the football season ended in San Diego, we left the Chevy in storage there and I went to Japan and HueLeita to Odessa. So after receiving my discharge in San Francisco, I went to get the Chevy out of storage in San Diego and drove home in what was to me still a new car.

It was the spring of 1955, and I had some time to become reacquainted with my family and get to know my new son, Zach, who was born while I was overseas. That fall I resumed my teaching and counseling duties and was assistant football coach to Cooper Robbins.

The following season Cooper became the athletic director and I was promoted to head coach. I was 26 years old and running the football program at the school that I helped win the Texas state championship less than 10 years earlier. It was a real thrill to be coaching in my hometown with its great football tradition.

Being a native of Odessa had its advantages and disadvantages. I knew everyone in town, and everyone knew me. But some viewed me as if I were the same kid who played quarterback for the Bronchos. I had more than a few people try to tell me what to do and how to run the program. But I tried to understand their attitude and not build any resentment toward fans who really wanted to see our team succeed.

Maybe that's when I decided not to allow fans to get too close to me. As a wise old coach told me one time: "If you listen to the fans too much, you'll be sitting in the bleachers with 'em before long!" Yes, it's probably a little tougher coaching in your hometown, but I went back to Odessa because I wanted to make sure my mother was doing all right after my years away in college and in the Marines. And besides, it was a good job.

I really enjoyed my three years as the head football coach in my hometown, which still had two high schools, one for whites and one for blacks. I coached the same way I did in the Marine Corps, using a multiple and diversified offense, which included enough exotics to keep my players interested and opponents off balance. We had good teams but never won a championship. The power in our league then was Abilene, which won something like 49 straight games and a state title.

One season we were on our way to play at Abilene and I had the school bus stop at the barber shop where I got my hair cut. The shoe shine man, John, and I had grown up together and he had no hair. I had every member of my team rub John's bald head for good luck. Then we went on to Abilene and got beat by 40 points. We really got embarrassed. On the way home one of my players said, "Coach, it didn't do much good to rub John's head, did it?" I looked at him and said, "Son, think how bad it might have been if we hadn't rubbed his head!"

We had college recruiters coming by all the time to visit and take a look at our players. My first week as a head coach, Bear Bryant, who was then at Texas A&M, dropped by with two of his assistants and they stayed for the entire practice. Afterwards, they came by the coaches' locker room, and I asked Coach Bryant if there was anything he had observed that might help us.

"Yes, I think so," he said. "Let's you and I step outside." Then he told me privately, "Coach Fry, I was really impressed with your organization and enthusiasm, but I might make one suggestion. I notice you spend a lot of time correcting your third-string quarterback. That's OK and it will pay off some day, but if I were you I'd devote more of your attention to your first-string quarterback. He's the one who will help you win this season." It was a great lesson for a young coach, one I never forgot. He gave me a lot of other sound advice, too, and I always remembered how a great college coach was willing to spend some time with a coach just breaking in at the high school level. We became good friends through the years.

Odessa might have been the first high school in the country to employ a full-time trainer when it hired Delmar Burt. He went on to Rice at the college level. Bill "Doc" Dayton was the trainer while I was head coach. He employed some chiropractic procedures—he was from the "push and pull" school. He was bald, smoked a pipe and really knew how to rehabilitate players and take care of injuries. We were fortunate to have a highly competent trainer at the high school level in those days, and it illustrates how progressive Odessa was at that time. Dayton moved on to become the trainer at Yale. He was replaced by George Anderson, who later worked for the Oakland Raiders for more than 20 years.

As a high school teacher, I had some talented students, and some of their talents went beyond academics. I taught a course in the history of Texas, and a member of the class was a young man named Roy Orbison, who went on to become one of the most popular vocalists and composers in the country. He was a very nice young man, small and energetic, and wore thick glasses. He was a good student and well liked by his classmates. Roy was well into music when I had him as a high school student. Besides singing, he had a combo called the Wink Wildcats. The name was taken from the town where he lived—Wink, Texas, about 30 miles from Odessa.

Roy was in my home room and one day—I believe he was a junior at the time—I went down to the principal's office on business. When I returned, Roy was standing on my desk leading the class in "The Yellow Rose of Texas." Everyone was singing on key and it sounded pretty good, but I had to do something to discipline Roy, so every day for a week I made him stand in a corner of the room with a wastebasket over his head singing "The Yellow Rose of Texas" to the class. So I take some credit for the unusual high-pitched nasal quality that was in Roy's voice. I used to tell him he would have never developed that characteristic if I hadn't put him under the wastebasket. We used to laugh about that when I occasionally saw him. It was a tragedy that he died at the peak of his professional career.

I taught Sunday school to young adults at the Baptist Church, and my class there included the Gatlin boys, who became famous as country singers known as the Gatlin Brothers. They were good athletes, especially Larry, who wanted to follow me to Baylor when I joined the coaching staff there. A high school quarterback, he accepted an offer from Houston, where he was a good wide receiver. When Amana held its annual VIP golf tournament at the University of Iowa course, the Gatlin Brothers were among the celebrities who played, and I always enjoyed seeing them.

I spent four years at Odessa, the last three as head coach, after returning from the Marines, and the size of my family doubled during that time. HueLeita gave birth to our third and fourth sons, Kelly and Adrian, who joined older brothers Randy and Zach. As you might expect, folks in town joked that I now had my own backfield.

The head coaching position at my alma mater, Baylor, changed after the 1958 season, and John Bridgers was the new man. He had been the defensive coach of the Baltimore Colts, which had just won the won the NFL championship with Johnny Unitas at quarterback. Bridgers was interested in adding a couple of Texas high school coaches to his staff, and I was recommended by Dr. Jim Raynor, our team physician at Odessa. Dr. Raynor was a Baylor graduate who had become acquainted with Bridgers. The fact that I was a Baylor graduate myself probably worked in my favor.

Our 1958 football season at Odessa had just ended when Bridgers called to offer me a job. Although it meant a salary cut, I didn't have to think long before accepting. The opportunity to coach at the college level at my alma mater was too good to reject. I hadn't yet reached the age of 30, and I was making another career move.

Chapter Eight

COLLEGE ASSISTANT COACH

The opportunity to join the coaching staff at Baylor came up unexpectedly and they wanted me on the job as soon as possible. So I threw some personal belongings in my car and took off for Waco, leaving my wife and four sons temporarily behind.

Texas weather can be erratic. As the saying goes: if you don't like the weather now just wait a few minutes, because it will change. The day I left for Waco the weather was awful. We had an ice storm, and I had real trouble getting there. There were many cars in the ditch, and although I managed to keep mine on the road, the going was slow and hazardous. After a couple of hours I began to think the good Lord was telling me something, but I pushed on and finally arrived safely in Waco.

Coach Bridgers put together a good staff in his first year at Baylor. I was hired to coach the defensive backs and felt comfortable doing it because I played safety in both high school and college. Vernon Glass, who was on the all-state backfield with me in 1946, was also on the staff. Other assistants were Walt Hackett, who was later with the Pittsburgh Steelers when they were Super Bowl champs, Catfish Smith, Tom Pruitt, Chuck Purvis, Charlie Driver and Cotton Davidson.

I found out fast that assistant college coaches not only coach, they also recruit. And recruit. And recruit. My last team at Odessa was a good one and Baylor wanted some of the players I had coached there. So I made frequent trips from Waco to Odessa recruiting players I had just finished coaching in high school. The best was Ronnie Goodman, an exciting running back being sought by a lot of other colleges. The national letter of intent was still 10 years away, so I had to recruit him throughout the spring and summer and hope he would enroll at Baylor for the fall term, which he did. We got three other players off that Odessa team, including fullback Buddy White, tight end Jerry Harris and quarterback Gerald "Slick" Erwin.

There was a recruiting area in Texas called the Golden Triangle. At the tips of the triangle were the towns of Beaumont, Port Arthur and Orange, about 20-25 miles apart. It was a big oil refining area that produced an incredible number of major college and professional football players. At one time, the Golden Triangle had 26 players in the professional ranks. Some black players skipped college and went directly to the pros because they had few choices regarding college. Everybody in the Southwest Conference, including Baylor, heavily recruited the Golden Triangle, but we only recruited whites, because every school in our league was still segregated. Had we been taking blacks, too, the triangle would have been platinum instead of golden. Jerry Levias came out of the Golden Triangle, but more about him later.

Schools did things in recruiting then that they would never do today, because there are rules now to prevent such behavior. Because there was no national letter, a prospect had to be recruited —a more appropriate word might be hustled—until he enrolled at your college. As mentioned, I almost lived with Ronnie Goodman for the entire summer before he enrolled at Baylor. That's not fair to the recruit, of course, and today's rules, with specific recruiting periods and signing dates, are make things better for everyone.

When I first started coaching at the college level, some schools had an assistant rent an apartment next door to the recruit and basically live with him all summer. It was not uncommon for a school to intercept a recruit's mail and remove letters from the competition. That, of course, is a federal offense, but the story illustrates how desperate recruiters could be. One way some schools kept a recruit away from other schools was to take him up in a plane and just fly him around for days and days. That kind of stuff actually happened. Fortunately times have changed, and we have rules now to prevent that behavior.

Baylor won only six games in the two seasons before Bridgers became coach, but we had good teams in the two years I was on his staff there. The second season, 1960, we finished the regular season 8-2, losing back-to-back games at midyear to TCU and Texas, both by a touchdown. We won intersectional games against Southern Cal, Colorado and LSU, and had a conference win at Arkansas. We accepted a berth in the Gator Bowl, where we lost by one point, 14-13, to a fine Florida team. Baylor had some outstanding players—Ronnie Bull, Tommy Minter, Goose Gonsoulin and Ronnie Goodman all enjoyed fine professional careers.

As coach of the defensive backs, I put together a secondary that was tough to throw against. We led the nation in pass defense in 1960 and a big reason was Don Trull, who was the scout team quarterback and threw against us every day. Trull went on to become an all-American. Ronnie Stanley and Bobby Ply were two of my best defenders as well as the top two quarterbacks. Stanley became a medical doctor and Ply played with the Kansas City Chiefs.

After my second year at Baylor, I got a call from Frank Broyles, my position coach when I was playing for Baylor. Broyles was by then the head coach at Arkansas, had a strong program underway and wanted me to become part of it. I accepted his offer and became the Razorbacks' offensive backfield coach. HueLeita and I now had five children—our daughter Robin was born in Waco—and we moved our family of seven north to start a new life in Fayetteville, Arkansas.

One reason Arkansas was becoming a big winner in college football was because Broyles had assembled an exceptional coaching staff. Doug Dickey, Jim McKenzie, Wilson Matthews, Dixie White, Steed White and Bill Pace were full-time assistants; Barry Switzer and Fred Akers were graduate assistants. All made their niche as head coaches—Dickey at Florida and Tennessee, McKenzie at Oklahoma, Pace at Vanderbilt, Switzer at Oklahoma and the Dallas Cowboys, and Akers at Texas and Purdue. Dixie White, who was later head coach at Northwest Louiana, invented the "scramble block," a technique that allows small linemen to tie up bigger opponents. When I left Arkansas my replacement was Johnny Majors, who was later head coach at Iowa State, Tennessee and Pittsburgh.

Arkansas had unbelievably talented coaches, but the catalyst was Broyles, a brilliant head coach with a charismatic personality that made him a highly successful recruiter. I have never been around anyone else quite like him. He had a photographic mind that allowed him to sit in the film room, look at a play one time on the screen, turn on the lights and tell his coaches what every player did on both sides of the ball. Then he'd go to the blackboard and diagram the whole thing. And if you asked him about the play 15 years later, he would do it again. I've never known anyone else with that kind of memory. He was just amazing.

Most players on the Razorback roster were from Arkansas, but Broyles, a master recruiter, also attracted talent from Texas and Oklahoma. One of the Texans was nose guard Jimmy Johnson, out of the Golden Triangle near Beaumont. Jimmy has gained fame as the coach who won national championships at the University of Miami, Super Bowl championships with the Dallas Cowboys, and currently coaches the Miami Dolphins.

Another member of the team was offensive guard Jerry Jones, now the owner of the Dallas Cowboys. Johnson was the first coach Jones hired for the Cowboys, luring him away from the University of Miami. When Jimmy returned to Miami to take over the Dolphins, Jones hired Switzer. All of that can be traced to the friendships they developed when they were at Arkansas in the early 1960s. Johnson, Jones and Switzer were all good players for the Razorbacks.

One of the greatest players I ever coached was Lance Alworth, an all-America tailback at Arkansas and an all-pro wide receiver in the NFL. He's the closest thing to a racehorse I've seen on a football field. When he accelerated, turf would just fly. I coined the expression, "When he's even, he's leavin'," which meant the quarterback should throw him the ball when he was even with the defensive back, because the DB wouldn't stay with him long. We told the quarterbacks to just throw the ball where Lance could run under it.

Lance was nicknamed "Bambi" because of his graceful, fluid running style. A little more than six feet tall, he had a powerful build, with big calves and thighs, and ran the 100 in 9.6 seconds. He was a handsome young man with a crew cut, unusually smooth and fair skin and little facial and body hair. He was married to his high school sweetheart all the way through college, earned good grades and was the student body president as a senior. He was as good a person as he was an athlete. I felt privileged to be his coach.

The Arkansas players were special when I was there. They were good young men, tough and hard-nosed. They had great pride and a willingness to work. Arkansas might have had the first out-of-season conditioning program in the country. Wilson Matthews ran it, and the players loved him and responded to him. His program really improved the football team, and a lot of other colleges copied what we were doing.

I've tried to take something with me from everywhere I've been. Under Frank Broyles at Arkansas, I learned the value of work ethic, team effort and toughness, both mental and physical. It was a lot like the Marine Corps. I learned that properly disciplined, football players take to the discipline and are motivated by it. Broyles coached that way, and Matthews was the driving force in creating that attitude with the players. He stayed on the staff all the years Broyles coached at Arkansas, then became head of the Razorback Club.

I also learned from Broyles that a football coach must exercise flexibility to be successful. We opened the conference season with TCU at Little Rock, where Arkansas played some home games. We stayed in Hot Springs the night before the game, and when some of us coaches made bed check, not all players were in their rooms. Some other coaches, who had been out scouting high school games, reported they saw the players at a restaurant down the road.

The coaching staff sat up most of the night discussing whether to allow the players to participate against TCU. Broyles finally decided missing bed check wasn't a felony and allowed them to play. We won, but we wouldn't have without them. That episode taught me it's possible to discipline players without hurting the rest of the team. The players were enrolled in "SC-600" for the remainder of the season. The initials mean Stadium Climb. The numbers mean 6 o'clock in the morning.

I was an assistant at Arkansas only one season, 1961, and one the responsibilities I most enjoyed was meeting with the quarterbacks daily. I soon learned that it was the first time in Broyles' coaching career—as a head or an assistant—in which he, himself, didn't conduct the quarterback meetings. I was flattered that he had that much trust and faith in me. The Razorbacks were nosed out by Texas for the Southwest Conference championship, and accepted an invitation to the Sugar Bowl, where we played an outstanding Alabama team coached by Bear Bryant, the same man who visited my high school practice field at Odessa six years earlier. Alabama and its great all-America linebacker, Leroy Jordan, beat us in a close game.

I recall Leroy making two consecutive tackles on Lance Alworth inside the Alabama five-yard line and deflecting a third-down pass, forcing us to go for a field goal. He convinced me that one inspirational player can stop the other team from scoring. Since that game I always made sure my best player was on the field in critical situations. Some of the "big play" defenders I've had include Larry Station, Mel Cole, John Derby, Mark Bortz, Bobby Stoops, Leroy Smith, Andre Tippett, Devon Mitchell, Lou King, Mike Wells, Merton Hanks, Tom Knight, Damien Robinson, John Harty and Jared DeVries, all of Iowa; John LaGrone, Billy Bob Stewart, Raymond Schoenke and Jerry Griffith of SMU; and J.T. Smith and Beasley Reece of North Texas.

Between the end of the regular season and before the Sugar Bowl game, I got an unexpected phone call from Southern Methodist, which was looking for a coach. The Methodists were interested in hiring a Baptist. I was about to become a major college head coach at 31 years old.

Chapter Nine

SOUTHERN METHODIST HEAD COACH

Southern Methodist, which had recruited me as a player out of high school, was now recruiting me as its head coach. SMU was one of four private schools in the Southwest Conference—the others being Baylor, Rice and Texas Christian—and its football teams had fallen on hard times the past 10 years, with only two winning seasons during that period. It wasn't easy for the private colleges to compete with the state-supported schools in the conference.

SMU did have some tradition and some legendary players of the past. Doak Walker and Kyle Rote were two of the greatest halfbacks the conference had ever seen and spurred the Mustangs to back-to-back championships in 1947 and 1948. The school had also won conference championships in the 1920s and 1930s, but had not done well in the 1950s and had won only 2 of 20 games in the 1960s. It had become increasingly harder to recruit against Texas, Arkansas and Texas A&M, the three schools that had emerged as the powers of the Southwest Conference. SMU had stiffer admissions requirements than almost all other schools in the conference— much stiffer than most— which made recruiting all the more difficult.

But SMU had some things going for it. It was an outstanding academic institution, it had a beautiful campus, and being located in Dallas offered lots of good jobs to its graduates and summer jobs to athletes. Its football team played home games in the Cotton

Bowl—at that time one of the four major bowls in college football —and that was appealing to some recruits.

The call from SMU came while we were preparing our Arkansas team to play Alabama in the 1962 Sugar Bowl, and I was basically offered the job on the phone. Athletic Director Matty Bell had been a successful football coach of the Mustangs, winning two conference championships, and had tried to recruit me out of high school. He had followed my career as a player and assistant coach in the Southwest Conference, I had support from SMU backers with Odessa connections, and the fact that I was coaching with a highly respected Arkansas staff was in my favor. SMU had just fired Bill Meek, who after three decent seasons had fallen on hard times.

I hadn't been looking around for a job as a head coach, so this was a surprising development. After talking it over with my family, Coach Broyles and John Barnhill, the Arkansas athletic director, I decided to accept. The starting salary of $13,000 was less than I was making as an assistant at Arkansas and illustrates the gap between the two programs at that time. But I never made salary an issue. In fact, the only issue I ever raised was racially integrating the football team, which we'll talk about later. I stayed on the Arkansas staff through the Sugar Bowl, and immediately after the game I flew from New Orleans to Dallas to become the eighth head football coach at Southern Methodist.

An unusual incident happened shortly after I arrived. The SMU selection committee wanted to get to know me better, and one of its members had a big boat. He took us all out on Lake Dallas so the committee could quietly get acquainted with its new football coach, away from such distractions as fans and the news media. We were having a nice time out in the middle of the lake when the phone rang and the caller wanted to know if Coach Fry was on board. The caller said it was an emergency. I was shown how to use the ship-to-shore phone—there were no cellular phones then—and took the call, expecting it might be bad news. The caller was Al Davis, who now owns the Oakland Raiders but was then working for the San Diego Chargers. We had become friends when we were both in the military and our football teams played each other. He was calling to solicit my help in signing Lance Alworth to a professional contract. I have no idea how Davis knew I was on Lake Dallas—it was a very private affair and I didn't know myself where we were going—but the story illustrates how resourceful and shrewd he is and why he's been a successful NFL executive.

The first thing I had to do was assemble a coaching staff, and the first assistant I hired was Charlie Driver, who I had coached with at Baylor. Between us, we put together the rest of the staff. I was able to pay my coaches $8,000 to 9,000, considerably less than what assistants were making at Arkansas and some of the other schools in the conference.

Most members of the new coaching staff hadn't brought their families to Dallas yet, so SMU rented us a big, old house near the campus and we all stayed there. Sometimes we ran out of bed linen and towels, but we weren't there much so it didn't really matter. We were gone a lot, mostly on recruiting trips. And we spent so many nights at the office that we finally brought in some cots and often slept there. I had a bunch of young coaches who were willing to work hard. We developed real camaraderie, and I have fond memories of those days.

One of the first things I introduced to the players was a strength and conditioning program. My experience on the Arkansas staff had convinced me of the importance of such a program, which they never had at SMU. In fact, SMU never had one weight, let alone a set of weights. We had no money in the budget to buy that kind of equipment so the coaches made some weights by pouring cement in big tin cans and attaching them to metal bars. Those were our barbells, which sounds farfetched today, but that's what we did in 1962. Then we gutted out an area underneath old Ownby Stadium, where the Mustangs played at one time, and used it for weight and isometric training. My coaches painted it up and made it look pretty good, and the players really took to their new program to improve strength and conditioning.

I knew we had to overhaul a lot of things about SMU football. The image was one of the first things we had to change, and the best way to do that was to change our appearance. We ran a contest for a logo to use on our helmets and came up with a mustang to go along with the nickname of the school's athletic teams. That mustang is probably one of the most identifiable logos in college football today.

The football team wore red jerseys at home before I arrived and I changed them to blue. The helmets were white and stayed that way, but I awarded red helmets to players who performed with distinction. It was a good motivational tool and the players tried hard to earn a red helmet. By the end of my first season we had 13 players wearing the distinctive red headgear, and they took great pride in that. We put little mustang logos on the helmets of players who graded out high after each game—we called them stallion awards—and some of the players accumulated lots of them. I wanted to offer the players something they could win, because they weren't figured to win many games that season.

Another change I made did not go over too well with some fans and members of the news media. I closed practices, because there was too much information coming out of them. Injuries are a part of football, and if all the minor ones are reported daily, it sounds like your practice field has become a war zone. Sometimes players are moved up and down the depth chart for motivational or disciplinary purposes, and there is no reason to report the moves. And, of course, there are lots of times changes are made in the offense and defense, and you don't want your opponent to know about them. The fans and media eventually became accustomed to closed practices, and most understood why we were doing it.

The players on that first SMU team really took to the discipline and new ideas we brought to the program. They were intelligent young men who demonstrated a great willingness to work. Nearly every one of them graduated and became successful in life. To this day they are the finest group of young men I've been associated with. I still hear from a lot of them.

We coached hard-nosed, fundamental football at SMU in 1962. The players had to master the basics before we could get fancy. Our scores that season were low, but the games were close. We were able to hang in most games because we avoided making costly mistakes. We tried not to give anything away.

My defensive coaches were Glenn Gosset, Dudley Parker, Ray Utley and Herb Zimmerman and they did a heck of a job that first year. We used an unusual defense with two monster backs, one on each side who was responsible for run support and short pass coverage. But we varied that up quite a bit to keep the opponents off balance. We tried to confuse the other teams and we did a pretty good job of it. Using the double monster was an equalizer, because our opponent usually had superior personnel. We had used one monster at Arkansas, so I figured, what the heck, let's try two of them.

As a head coach, I spent more time with the defense in the days of two-way football, the way the game was played in the early 1960s. Players had to play both offense and defense. Full teams didn't run on and off the field when the ball changed hands, although there was limited substitution—enough to send plays in by messenger.

I called all the plays from the sideline in my first year as a head coach. I did it for two reasons: it's a part of coaching I really enjoyed, and I have more knowledge and experience in doing it than any of my players or coaches. I called the plays in high school, I called them in college, and I called them as a head coach. I liked developing a game plan during the week and calling the plays on Saturday. It's a part of coaching I greatly enjoyed. I gave the quarterback the option of calling an audible at the line of scrimmage, but he better have a good reason for doing it.

Speaking of quarterbacks, there was a great one on the SMU roster when we took over, but he never played a down for us. Jerry Rhome was going into his junior year, and his presence on the team was one reason the job was attractive to me. He had been a great high school player in the Dallas area and had exceptional potential. When SMU changed coaching staffs, some other schools talked to him about transferring, which was a common practice in those days. Because our approach was so basic during spring practice, he became convinced that we weren't going to open up the offense and allow him to throw the ball, and he transferred to Tulsa, where Glenn Dobbs had established an excellent passing game. Jerry teamed up with an outstanding wide receiver, Howard Twilley, and became the nation's passing leader. He was an exceptional quarterback who would have really helped us in starting our program at SMU. We would have had a much more diversified attack and been a much better offensive team. But I never blamed him for leaving. My coaches and I didn't do a good job of convincing him to stay.

Losing our starting quarterback was a big blow, and then we experienced two more personnel setbacks. We lost center and linebacker Mike Kelsey to an untimely death and end Happy Nelson was forced to quit the team due to a serious illness. Kelsey collapsed and died on the practice field while standing in line during a defensive recognition drill. With that kind of tragic news coming from a football team that wasn't supposed to be very good anyway, the Mustangs were picked to finish in the conference basement again.

We opened with three intersectional games—Maryland, Southern Cal and Air Force—before we hit the Southwest Conference schedule. Matty Bell believed it was necessary to play tough

non-conference opponents to sell tickets to home games. We were
competing with the Dallas Cowboys for fans and media attention,
and the Cowboys were one of the best teams in the NFL. We played
at Maryland and Air Force at home and lost both games by a touchdown, but we got blown out at Southern Cal, which went on to
win the national championship. I had turned down an opportunity
to join the Southern Cal coaching staff a few years earlier and they
wound up hiring John McKay, who was their head coach in 1962.
That was the only game all season in which we weren't competitive.

We opened the conference schedule on television by beating Rice in the Cotton Bowl, 15-7, giving me my first victory as a
head coach. The Rice coach was still Jess Neeley, the same man
who recruited me after I finished my high school career at Odessa.
He was by that time a legend, and his presence made the victory all
the more meaningful. We followed that with a 14-0 shutout at Texas
Tech the next week, making an SMU team with a 32-year-old rookie
head coach a very surprising 2-0 in the conference. But we couldn't
win another game, although our five losses were by a combined
total of only 22 points. I couldn't have asked an outmanned football team for a greater effort.

Playing Baylor and Arkansas was difficult for me that season,
and not just because both had good teams. Because I had coached
so recently at the two schools, I knew the coaches on each staff
and most of the players on each team. John Bridgers was still the
head man at Baylor and he had given me my first opportunity to
coach at the college level. We played his team a good game but
eventually lost, 17-13.

Arkansas was an even bigger game for me than Baylor, because the Razorbacks were a power in the conference, and Frank
Broyles was considered one of the top coaches in college football.
Late in the game we trailed by only two points, 9-7, and put together a nice drive. We got down around the Arkansas 20-yard line
and I decided to use the element of surprise and kick a field goal
on third down. Arkansas had a defensive field goal unit that had
blocked several kicks that year, and I didn't want to give Broyles
time to get that unit on the field. So on third down we broke huddle,
lined up and tried a field goal. It surprised them, and the scheme
would have worked, but one of my guards stepped out instead of
in, and the Arkansas nose guard had an easy path up the middle to
block the kick. He was the same nose guard the Razorbacks had

when I was there a year earlier—Jimmy Johnson, now coaching the Miami Dolphins. Had the field goal been successful, I would have had one of my all-time coaching upsets. As it was, Arkansas hung on to that two-point advantage and won the game, 9-7.

We finished the season with a 2-8 record, but the competitive nature of the ball club and the gritty determination it displayed all season against superior opposition won me coach of the year honors in the Southwest Conference. It was the first and last time a coach with only two victories was given that honor, which really belonged more to the players and my coaching staff than it did me. We lost one close game after another and the morale could have easily caved in. Instead, the players came out every Saturday and gave a maximum effort. Although we didn't win a lot of games, my first season as a head coach had been rewarding.

Chapter Ten

EARLY YEARS AT SMU

SMU had its share of influential alumni who were football fans. One was Lamar Hunt, organizer of the American Football League and founder of the Dallas Texans, now the Kansas City Chiefs. As a member of the Hunt family in Dallas, he had a lot of clout and was very helpful to me, lending support to the program I was building at SMU.

His father was H. L. Hunt, thought to be the richest man in the world at that time. I mentioned to Lamar that I'd like to meet his dad sometime, but I was still a bit surprised when Mr. Hunt's secretary called to say Mr. Hunt would be happy to meet the SMU football coach. As directed, I arrived at his office, located in a big building in downtown Dallas, at noon a few days later.

I walked into the reception area and the secretary said, "You must be Coach Fry. Mr. Hunt is expecting you." She escorted me into his office, which looked nothing like it belonged to the world's leading capitalist. It didn't suggest great wealth; it was about as disheveled as mine. In fact, Mr. Hunt looked somewhat disheveled himself. He appeared to need a haircut and a shave, and his clothes were a little rumpled.

He graciously introduced himself and was pleasant and friendly, with a good sense of humor. He asked me if I'd like to have lunch. I said yes, expecting him to take me to the executive dining room. Instead, he pulled a brown paper bag from his desk and removed a sandwich, which he cut in two with a letter opener.

Then he handed me half a sandwich and said, "I hope you like peanut butter and jelly."

As a matter of fact I do, so after we had munched the sandwich and visited for a few minutes, he asked me if there was anything in particular I had in mind. I told him I'd like to know his secret for success. He paused a moment, then looked across his cluttered desk and said, "My advice is to set a goal, develop a plan on how to reach it, then put all your energy into achieving it." He simplified his answer so a young football coach could understand it, and I followed his advice throughout my coaching career. I was only in his office 15 or 20 minutes, but when I walked out I felt like a million dollars.

When we opened the 1963 season at Michigan, I unexpectedly met another captain of industry. The Michigan coach was Bump Elliott, who would become the Iowa athletic director and hire me as his football coach. But that is getting ahead of the story. Bump's Michigan team had us physically outmatched, but my kids gamely hung in there and played a competitive game before finally losing 27-16.

After the game I was talking to my team in our dressing room when one of my managers interrupted to say there were some men from the Ford Motor Company outside who wanted to see me. He said they were persistent. So I went the door and met Lee Iacocca, Ford's CEO, and some of his aides. He said he had an important announcement for my football team, and asked to come in.

He climbed on top of a training table—he's a big man so he really towered over the group—and told the team that Ford was about to introduce a new sports car that was small, sleek and fast, with great acceleration and maneuverability. He said that several names for the car were under consideration—among them Cougar, Bronco, Cheetah and Colt.

"But today, after watching the SMU Mustangs play with such flair, we reached a decision," he announced. "We will call our new car the Mustang. Because it will be light, like your team. It will be quick, like your team. And it will be sporty, like your team." He said we should be proud that Ford had selected the SMU nickname.

My players were proud and happy with Iacocca's decision. His announcement was a real mood elevator after the loss to Michigan. It was a great tribute to the SMU players that of all the names he could have picked for the new sports car, he chose ours. When Ford began producing Mustangs, I received one of the first to come off the assembly line. And, of course, we had it painted in SMU colors—red, white and blue.

The SMU football team wasn't expected to go anywhere in 1963, and the loss at Michigan didn't do anything to change the expectations. But we went home and played a solid game against Air Force, and that 10-0 triumph set the stage for one of the greatest upsets I have ever been associated with.

Navy brought a team to the Cotton Bowl that was contending for the national championship and was expected to crush the Mustangs. The Middies were led by Roger Staubach, the great quarterback who went on to win the Heisman Trophy and star for the Dallas Cowboys. He was the main reason Navy was ranked No. 4 in the nation and was an overwhelming favorite to beat us.

The week of the game I took a sophomore sprinter off the track team and installed him at running back. His name was John Roderick, who we had used some at wide receiver, but never as a running back, so this was going to be a real experiment. He was from Highland Park High School in Dallas and had 9.4 speed in the 100, but he was so thin I called him my pipe cleaner. He was a real good kid, a bit of a character, and we really hit it off.

John had a phenomenal game against the Middies, who must have been in shock. They just weren't ready for him. I'm sure the Navy coaches were asking each other, "Who is this guy?" He ran 11 times for 145 yards and scored two touchdowns, one on a spectacular 45-yard dash. What John did to Navy that day you only see in movies made in Hollywood. But he did it, and kept us in contention in a high-scoring game.

We did our best to contain Staubach, who was not only a fine passer but an excellent running quarterback. His scrambling style really put pressure on the defense. On one of his scrambles he reversed his field and was greeted by one of our defensive ends, John Maag, who put a tremendous hit on the quarterback. It was the biggest defensive play of the game and sent Staubach to the bench with a shoulder injury. He returned, only to get knocked out of the game again.

We trailed 28-26 late in the game when Roderick broke loose for 23 yards and Billy Gannon scored the go-ahead touchdown on a short run. Staubach took Navy down the field one more time, but on Roger's final pass of the game, Tommy Caughran preserved a great victory for SMU by making a diving interception in the end zone. The Mustangs had a 32-28 upset over a great Navy team that didn't lose another game and finished second, behind Texas, who we were scheduled to play in three weeks.

People who question the value of college football need look no further than the 1964 SMU-Navy game. In one afternoon my players gained more pride, confidence and self-respect than many college students ever have an opportunity to achieve. They were heavy underdogs, given virtually no chance to win, but they set a goal, followed a game plan, and fought hard to achieve victory. Does that sound a little like the advice Mr. Hunt gave me?

We opened the Southwest Conference campaign with three straight losses by a total margin of 18 points to Rice, Texas Tech and Texas. Just as the previous season, we were playing competitive football but losing close games. The score of the Texas game, played before the largest crowd of the season at the Cotton Bowl, was 17-12. After the Longhorns won the national championship that year, Coach Darrell Royal noted, "SMU gave us more trouble defensively the past two seasons than any other team. They stopped us on their own, not because of our mistakes." I appreciated his remarks, as I always do when a coach takes time to compliment my team.

In the next two weeks we beat Texas A&M on the road, then came home to get a win over Arkansas, the first against my old boss, Frank Broyles. We found ourselves with a 4-4 record and being mentioned for a possible bowl game. Everyone was all revved up, but the excitement was about to turn another direction. An unexpected event right in our own town was going to get world-wide attention.

On November 22 in downtown Dallas, President Kennedy was shot to death while riding in a motorcade. On that particular day, some of my coaches and I went to lunch at a barbecue place not far from where the shooting took place. But we didn't know about it until we drove back to the SMU campus and Bob Pruitt, an assistant basketball coach, told us the news as we got out of the car. He said he'd just heard the news on the radio.

Shell shock is the most accurate description I can use to describe the reaction in Dallas. The most awful thing imaginable had happened right in our town. To compound everyone's churning emotions, the suspected assassin, Lee Harvey Oswald, was shot to death by Jack Ruby, a big sports fan and a well-known SMU supporter. Ruby ran a night spot called the Century Club in downtown Dallas frequented by a lot of our players. I wouldn't be exaggerating much to say that everyone knew Jack Ruby.

The aftermath of the assassination lingered a long time throughout the entire country, especially in Dallas. But we had a season to complete and were forced to turn our attention to football. The president was assassinated on Friday and many games were scheduled around the country the following day. Some games were played, some were postponed, and some were cancelled. (Iowa, for instance, cancelled its game with Notre Dame.)

We were slated to play TCU at nearby Fort Worth, but school officials decided to postpone the game until November 30. So we had an unexpected Saturday off, then lost at Baylor and TCU. Our season was over and the last two defeats gave us a record of 4-6, but to the surprise of many fans, and to the anguish of some teams who thought they were more deserving, we were chosen to play in the Sun Bowl. It was, and still is, the only time a team has gone to a bowl with that kind of record. Now, of course, a bowl participant must have six wins against Division I opponents.

We were selected because we had an exciting team, most of our losses had been by small margins, and our victory over a powerful Navy team had created a lot of national attention. It was the first bowl in which SMU had participated in 15 years, and our team and fans were excited about the opportunity to play Oregon, which coincidentally had been SMU's opponent in the Cotton Bowl 15 years earlier.

We had a talented quarterback duo of Mac White and Danny Thomas who both turned in a good performance. White was the bowl game's leading rusher, Thomas the leading passer. But turnovers put us in a 21-0 hole at intermission and we had a big deficit to overcome in the second half. We nearly pulled off a big comeback, but fell short and lost 21-14. We had more total yards and more first downs, but couldn't overcome our first-half fumbles.

Neither could we overcome "Montezuma's revenge," which ravaged our team following a visit to Jaurez, Mexico. Sixteen of our starters had upset stomachs on game day and were running to the toilets faster than they were running on the field. They couldn't hold onto the ball and they couldn't hold anything on their stomachs. After getting the poison out of their system, they played much better in the second half.

Some of the sports writers in Texas had a little fun with the SMU program receiving nice recognition the past two seasons without having a winning record. One columnist wrote, "Fry had two wins last year and was named coach of the year. This season he won four and got a bowl bid. Makes you wonder what will happen when he finally produces a winner at Ponyland." I hoped to soon find out.

Chapter Eleven

SMU ATHLETIC DIRECTOR

N ot long after the 1963 football season ended, Matty Bell decided to retire after 30 years at SMU. He had won four Southwest Conference championships as the school's football coach, had taken the 1935 Mustangs to the Rose Bowl, and coached the legendary SMU teams of 1947 and 1948 that featured Doak Walker and Kyle Rote. He had been the school's athletic director the past 19 years, and it was his retirement from that role that impacted me.

When President Willis Tate offered me the dual role of athletic director and football coach, I was somewhat surprised because I was only 34 years old and had little administrative experience. The president assured me I would have his full support, and after thinking it over, I accepted. The opportunity to run a major college athletic program at my age was too good to pass up.

In announcing my appointment to the press, President Tate said, "Mr. Fry has revitalized our football program and won the admiration of the administration, faculty, staff, student body, alumni and general public by the manner in which he has conducted his program." I appreciated those kind words, but I would rather have seen him decrease the superlatives and increase the salary, which only went up $2,000.

Matty Bell officially retired at the end of June, 1964, and for the next eight and a half years I was both the AD and football coach at SMU. I promoted sports information director Lester Jordan to assistant athletic director. A wonderful man, he had been at SMU for nearly 20 years in various capacities and knew the school inside out. He is the founder of Academic all-America teams that honor athletes who excel in both the classroom and on the playing field. Today, GTE is the national sponsor of those teams. I later brought Jim "Hoss" Brock over from TCU as assistant AD, and he and Lester handled many of the administrative chores which I couldn't give my full attention because of my duties as head football coach. Brock later became executive director of the Cotton Bowl.

SMU had a good overall athletic program during my years as athletic director. We had some fine coaches, led by Red Barr, whose swimming teams almost always won the conference championship and ranked high nationally, and Doc Hayes, whose basketball teams were usually among the best in the league. In the 1966-67 school year, SMU won football and basketball championships, a rarity in the Southwest Conference.

Shortly after I was named SMU's athletic director, my football program received a setback when the Southwest Conference hit us with a two-year probation that included no bowl games. One of my coaches had bought a recruit some gas and a meal—the total cost was about $35—and someone found out about it and turned us in. Some other schools in the conference were jealous because we had brought SMU football back from the dead. Then when we got verbal commitments from 14 of the top 22 prospects in Texas things really got bad, and some other schools tried digging up dirt on us. They went after anything they could find.

Although this was a conference and not an NCAA probation, it was a setback to our program and made us look like cheaters. So we decided to fight fire with fire and turned in quite a few conference schools for violations we knew they had committed. We blew the whistle on them like someone had on us, and our report had quite an impact. Jess Neeley told me it was like we had fired a shotgun around the league to see how many schools we could hit.

Some schools we reported were put on probation, just as we had been. None of the penalties were severe. But the message had been sent, and what we did cleaned up the conference for many years. Hard feelings lingered for a long time, and I was not the most popular coach in the league. But I think some of the other coaches recognized that although I was young, I couldn't be pushed around. I wasn't going to allow a double standard to exist in the conference. If SMU was going to be penalized for a minor violation, other schools would be, too.

We opened the 1964 football season with back-to-back road games at Florida and Ohio State, two of the toughest places to play in college football. We had the lead at Florida, then started losing quarterbacks. Before the game was over we had our top three on the bench with injuries. I had a sophomore defensive back named Larry "Moon" Mullins who had played quarterback in high school but never in college. But we were desperate for a quarterback and asked him to play the position. I remember how we warmed him up, having him take snaps and make handoffs on the sideline. Not surprisingly, we lost the opener, but it was an even game until the fourth quarter.

We got a couple of our injured quarterbacks cleared to play at Ohio State the following week, but Donnie Oefinger got his jaw broken right off the bat, and then his replacement, Mac White, went out with back ailment. We were again desperate for quarterbacks. It was an unbelievable turn of events, and the beginning of the worst year for injuries in my coaching career. We were always patching up this position or that one, and could never put a healthy team on the field. It was a nightmare.

The 1964 season convinced me that it's suicide to over-schedule your team in non-conference games. You not only lose the games, you get your ball club beaten up and weakened for the remainder of the season. But Matty Bell believed in tough schedules, and I had to play the teams he contracted. Opening at Florida and Ohio State is not the way to build momentum and confidence in a football team.

We limped through the remainder of the season, winning only one game. With such a serious problem at quarterback, it was a struggle for our offense every week. We went four straight games without scoring a point, but I was proud of the way my players hung in there and battled and kept the games close. At Texas, for instance, we were only beaten 7-0.

We rebounded and had a decent season in 1965. The opener was played at Miami in the Orange Bowl, and it rained so hard before the game, we skipped the warm-ups and went to the dressing room. The rain stopped, but the heat and humidity both went up and we just wilted during the game. But we hung on to win, 7-3, to get our season off on the right foot.

We faced another difficult non-conference schedule, losing at Illinois the following week before coming home to play our home opener against Purdue. The Boilermakers had an outstanding team featuring Bob Griese, the Big Ten's best quarterback, and were coming off a tremendous upset of Notre Dame, ranked No. 1 in the country at the time. Griese went on to a great professional career with the Miami Dolphins and now does color commentary for ABC-TV.

We installed a spread formation during the week and it surprised Purdue. Our little red-haired quarterback, Mac White, had a terrific game, and we controlled the ball, keeping it away from Griese and the potent Purdue offense. We had a trick formation in which we moved our tight end, Bob Goodrich, to tackle and made him an eligible pass receiver. He got wide open in the end zone, and White threw him a touchdown pass to tie the score at 14-14. Goodrich is now an executive producer for ABC sports.

Late in the game we put together a drive that gave us the ball inside the Purdue 15-yard line. We went for a winning field goal, but my kicker got uptight and took out a yard of turf and the ball never got off the ground. Although we were in a position to win and pull a big upset, we felt pretty good about tying one of the best teams in the Big Ten.

We had some momentum going into the conference season, and we started strong, winning at Rice 17-14 before losing by two to Texas Tech, 26-24. Then we put together two outstanding games, beating Texas 31-14 and Texas A&M 10-0. It was my first win as a head coach over Texas and my second straight victory at A&M, which is a hard place to win.

Texas had an all-America linebacker in Tommy Nobis, who could really chase down opposing running backs, so we decided to run right at him. We came out in a spread formation with an unbalanced line and one running back, and on the first play ran right at Nobis. Jim Hagle, our big running back from Corsicana, Texas, took the handoff and went about 90 yards for a touchdown. Texas never recovered from the shock, and we won by the surprising score of 31-14.

With a 4-2-1 record, we were in a position to finish strong, but we went to Arkansas the following week and not only lost the game, but some key players as well. We ended with close losses to Baylor and TCU and a winning season escaped us, but I felt good about my football program and the direction it was headed.

Although the two years of probation had a negative effect on recruiting, it was amazing we were able to bring in the caliber of players we did, especially since SMU also had such high admission requirements. I was finally given permission to bring in five players each year who had SAT scores under 1,000, while most schools were routinely admitting prospects with scores in the 700-750 range. The strict admission standard was another reason winning non-conference games against the opponents we were playing was very difficult. You're putting your football team at a real disadvantage when you ask it to play schools with lower academic requirements.

But despite those disadvantages, we had recruited pretty well and were looking forward to the future. Freshmen still were not eligible at that time, and we had one player on our freshman team who would change the face of the Southwest Conference and the recruiting policies of every other school in the league.

Chapter Twelve

INTEGRATING THE SOUTHWEST CONFERENCE

When SMU called me to discuss its head coaching job, our conversation was fairly routine. They did most of the talking and I did the listening, with an occasional question here and there. It was clear that they wanted me as their head football coach, but when I asked about racially integrating the team our discussions hit the wall. The question obviously surprised them, and they told me there was no chance of that happening. They said nobody in the Southwest Conference had an integrated athletic program, and SMU was not going to be the first. I told them in that case, I wasn't interested, and our conversation ended on that note.

My attitude about race was developed early in life. I had black friends while growing up in Eastland and Odessa who I played with and worked with. We spent a lot of time together. They lived on the "wrong side" of the tracks, but I had lived there for awhile, too, so I could identify with that. When they had to sit in the back of the bus or in the balcony at the picture show, I often sat with them. By the time I reached junior high, I was genuinely bothered by the way my friends were treated. We went to different schools because the color of our skin was different, which never seemed fair to me.

By the time I was in high school, when my black friends were playing football at Dunbar instead of with me at Odessa, I made a commitment that if I was ever in a position to change that, I would.

So when SMU called, I raised the possibility of integrating the school's football team, because I wanted to do it. SMU was certainly not a great head coaching opportunity, with its low salary and 10 years of bad football teams. If I became the SMU football coach I wanted permission to recruit black players, and I knew I would have to negotiate that before accepting the job, not afterward.

Although I was disappointed by SMU's response, I wasn't surprised. It's the way things were at that time. Some southern schools were talking about integrating their athletic programs, but nobody seemed willing to do it. Nobody wanted to be first, even though it was the right thing to do. Racial attitudes ran deep among influential alumni and fans. It was a difficult issue—far too controversial for most college administrators.

I then put the opportunity for a head coaching job out of my mind and went back to work as an Arkansas assistant, preparing the Razorbacks for the Sugar Bowl. But a couple of days later, I got another call from SMU telling me they were considering my request to integrate the football team, and wondered if I was still interested in the job. I told them I was if I could recruit black players. They said they'd get back to me.

The key people at SMU—those making the decision—were President Willis Tate, who was an all-Southwest Conference tackle on SMU's Rose Bowl team of 1935; athletic director Matty Bell, who had enjoyed success as the school's football coach; and faculty representatives Harold Jesky and Ed Mouzon. I was pleasantly surprised by their reversal in attitude on my request, but I knew better than to get my hopes too high.

It wasn't long before I got a third call with their decision: I could recruit one or two black players with the understanding that they would not only be good players, but also good students and fine citizens. In fact, they preferred them to be outstanding students and citizens. They made it crystal clear that I would have to do some careful screening, and it would take time, perhaps a year or more, to find a young man who qualified as a player, student and citizen. And even when I found this gem, he would have to be willing to be the first black player in the Southwest Conference. They emphasized that this would be a historic step for SMU, that it would be met with resistance, and they did not want it to fail.

They didn't ask for my immediate answer. They said that this was a very important decision and I should think it over carefully.

But I didn't have to think long; I knew what I wanted to do. The opportunity to open the Southwest Conference door to black athletes really excited me. I knew there were a lot of great black high school players in Texas and I thought they should have the opportunity to stay home. I was tired of seeing them go north to the Big Ten and west to the Pac-10. I was convinced I could find a black youngster who could meet the high standards set forth by SMU, and I believed once he proved himself others would follow. Was I putting my coaching career on the line? Perhaps, but that never occurred to me.

When I got settled in at SMU and hired a staff, I told my coaches about the administration's willingness to integrate the program. But we kept it among ourselves and never made it a big story. Besides, there were so many things that demanded our attention that we had to put finding a black recruit on the back burner. The football program was in bad shape and we had a lot of work to do if we were going to be competitive our first season. But we quietly started to survey some of the black high schools of Texas, looking at their top players. I didn't care how long the search was going to take, I just wanted to make sure we found the right youngster.

We had been on the job about a year when assistant coach Charlie Driver came into my office one day and said he might have found the black high school player we were looking for. Jerry Levias was his name, and he played at Hebert High School in Beaumont. Yes, that's in the golden triangle I mentioned earlier. Jerry still had two years of high school football left, but he had great speed and versatility and did about everything for Coach Clifton Ozan at Hebert. He played quarterback, wide receiver, running back and returned kicks.

As we learned more about Jerry, he seemed to be everything we were looking for. He wasn't very big—only 5-8 and 160—but he was a great player, an exceptional student, mentally tough and came from a strong family. His parents and grandparents were outstanding people and very influential in his life. He was so deeply committed to his religious beliefs that he carried a Bible in his pocket. He had never been in any kind of trouble on or off the field.

When I saw Jerry perform on the field I decided he was the most exciting high school player I'd ever seen in Texas, and we actively started recruiting him. The whole staff was involved, and it took a real sales job. We talked about the pitfalls as well as the advantages and didn't attempt to gloss over anything. We told him that just as Jackie Robinson had broken the color line in Major League Baseball, he would be doing the same thing in the Southwest Conference. We took great pains to explain that there would be some difficult times for him just because of the color of his skin. We told him there would be times when he would have to summon all of his intelligence, patience and mental toughness to survive.

We had plenty of competition in recruiting Jerry, all of it from schools out west or up north. Our biggest competitor was UCLA and Coach Tommy Prothro. UCLA had a connection because Mel Farr, a former star at UCLA, was Jerry's cousin. They really went after him and it was a fierce recruiting battle. I'd like to think it was our brilliant recruiting efforts that won Jerry over, but in the end I believe he was motivated to be the person who opened the door for other black athletes in the south. He was a quiet and introspective young man, but he was also a trailblazer.

When Jerry enrolled at SMU as a freshman in the fall of 1965, I was proud to be his coach and elated that we had integrated major college football in our part of the country. To their credit, President Tate and his administrators had never waffled on their commitment to me and stood by me when I was personally attacked for recruiting a black player at SMU. I got hate mail, anonymous threatening phone calls, and confrontations at social functions. If Jerry had failed on the field or in the classroom, I probably would have been run out of town.

But as unpleasant as those episodes were for me, I never dreamed what Jerry would have to endure. He experienced racial taunts, threatening letters, even bomb threats. He was spit on and cussed at. Over a period of time, as the threats persisted, law enforcement got involved, including the FBI. They told us not to reveal the threats to the public because it would bring on more of the same. Jerry was a pretty depressed young man for awhile. Some of his own teammates were unkind to him initially, and there must have been times when he felt like quitting SMU and going to a college where he wouldn't experience such awful racism.

We screened his phone calls, mail and interview requests that came though our office. We tried to put a reasonably tight security blanket around him, but we couldn't walk him to class and be with him all the time. Freshmen were not eligible for the varsity, which was a good thing because Jerry had enough to deal with without worrying about football. As his teammates and classmates got to know him, they found out he was a great young man, and racial barriers were broken down.

Jerry was especially popular with the young kids and always gave them his time. He was their No. 1 target for autographs. They liked his friendly smile and enjoyed talking to him. Some just wanted to touch him. Don't kids have great instincts?

Chapter Thirteen

SWC CHAMPIONSHIP AND THE LEVIAS YEARS

By the time Jerry Levias completed his freshman year, the SMU students and faculty generally accepted, respected and liked him. Oh, there might have been some holdouts, but I never knew anyone who, after he or she got to know Jerry, didn't genuinely like him. So the first phase of integrating Southwest Conference football was completed—we had broken down the barriers on our own campus. Now came the next phase—we were about to take Jerry to enemy stadiums at other campuses. Few players in our league had ever competed against anyone who wasn't white. Playing against a black like Jerry would be a first for almost all of them.

Our first three games were all against non-conference teams from the north, which was a break, because Jerry was just another player in those games. It gave him a chance to get his feet on the ground as a college football player. We used him as a wide receiver and kick returner and occasionally gave him the ball on a reverse. Our quarterbacks were not especially good passers, so we weren't able to get him the ball as much as we'd have liked. But his speed and presence on the field made him a threat that drew the attention of the other team.

We opened the 1966 season at home against Illinois, which had blanked us 42-0 at Champaign the previous season. We hadn't been able to cross midfield in that game against a team coached by

Bump Elliott's brother, Pete Elliott. But it was a different story this time. We got out in front early and played strong defense. We won the game 27-6 and looked good doing it. Jerry's college debut had attracted considerable attention but was somewhat overshadowed by our impressive victory against a good team from the Big Ten. He made some nice plays, but nothing special.

We turned in another solid defensive performance the following week in beating Navy 21-3 and began to think we might have a pretty good ball club. This was the first SMU team composed entirely of players recruited by my staff. We went into the season thinking we should be an improved team from a year ago, but nobody, including our coaching staff, expected us to contend for the conference championship.

We wound up our non-conference campaign at Purdue, which had a great quarterback in senior Bob Griese, and a budding star at running back in sophomore Leroy Keyes. The game produced a lot of points, but the Boilermakers won it, 35-23. We couldn't have known at the time, of course, but Purdue would go on to represent the Big Ten in the Rose bowl, and SMU would get the Cotton Bowl berth as the Southwest Conference champion.

Although he had done nothing spectacular, Jerry Levias had performed well in the first three games against strong competition, and there had been no racial incidents. By the time we were ready to open the conference season, a couple of the league coaches had assured their fans and alumni that they would never recruit black players. Others were saying the same thing privately. That kind of talk irritated me because I knew that the coaches who were still around in a few years would be recruiting blacks actively as whites. It's amazing how their attitudes changed after they saw what Jerry Levias was doing for the SMU program. I can laugh at it now, but it gave me a lot of anguish then.

Our conference opener at Rice was indicative of how the season would go, with a lot of close games. We had a high-scoring game that went down to the wire. Rice went ahead late in the fourth quarter, 24-21, and after Levias made a good return of the kickoff, we put together a drive and came up to fourth down at the 21. We had a very good kicker, Dennis Partee, who later played professionally for the San Diego Chargers, and I decided Rice might take the bait on a fake field goal.

Levias was our holder, and the play was designed for him to run the ball. Jerry took the snap, spun out of his crouch and sprinted around the left side for 11 yards and a first down. A couple of plays later, with only nine seconds remaining, he caught a touchdown pass from Mac White that gave us a 28-21 victory. Earlier that quarter, Levias had thrown a 47-yard TD pass to Larry Jernigan on a trick play. So in a period of about seven minutes, he had thrown for a TD, made a key run on fourth down and caught the winning TD pass. He made a lot of clutch plays for us during his career, but those three stand out as three that won a game.

Following a convincing 24-7 victory at Texas Tech the following week, we played at Texas in the most physical game of the season and came away a 13-12 winner. Partee got two teeth knocked out on the opening kickoff, then things really got rough. Mac White, Inez Perez and Mike Livingston were our quarterbacks, and all three sustained injuries. White and Perez were small, and none were classic T-formation quarterbacks, but all were hard-nosed competitors.

We won two of our next three games, because Texas A&M and Baylor got careless and made late-game kickoffs straight to Levias. The Aggies tied the game 14-14 with only a few minutes left, but instead of kicking off away from Jerry, they kicked the ball right to him. He made a great runback, which gave us the field position and momentum to go on and score the deciding TD in a 21-14 win.

Two weeks later Jerry had the greatest kickoff return day of his career. Baylor went ahead 22-17 late in the game, then kicked off to Levias, who had already run a kickoff back for a touchdown. He made another long return and our offense again took advantage and scored, and we pulled out a 24-22 victory. Jerry ran back three kickoffs for 160 yards that day, still an SMU record. In between those two games, we lost our only conference game at Arkansas.

TCU was the only opponent remaining between SMU and its first conference championship since 1948. Early in the week of the game, TCU announced it was closing its practices. That wasn't normal procedure at TCU, and I wondered what was going on. What didn't they want us to know? Then I recalled the success TCU had enjoyed with the spread formation used by Dutch Meyer, so I had our defense work against the spread that week. And sure enough, on Saturday, TCU came out with an offense spread across the field. But we were ready for it, and more than up to the challenge. We won 21-0, and a shutout has never been more pleasing in my coaching career.

It was a magical season for the Mustangs, with four games won in the final minute of play. We were the conference champions and on our way to the Cotton Bowl. League titles are usually won by teams that win close games, stay reasonably healthy and have a little luck. That was certainly the case with my SMU team of 1966.

Jerry Levias had a fine rookie year—especially so considering the scrutiny under which he played—and attracted fans everywhere we went. Our attendance increased by more than 30 percent, which led the nation that season. He led the conference with a 26-yard average on kickoff returns. Because we didn't have a good passing quarterback, Jerry didn't catch a great number of passes, but he averaged more than 23 yards per reception, still an SMU record, and seven were for touchdowns. He scored twice more on punt and kickoff returns.

As the target of racial slurs and taunts, Jerry proved his mental toughness. He never complained to me about them; I got the reports from his teammates and other witnesses. And he never lashed back at the perpetrators, which must have taken amazing restraint on his part. There were other racial incidents. Returning by bus from one of our road games, we heard on the radio that a sniper had been at our game that day intending to shoot Levias. We didn't know anything about it, but we stopped and called Jerry's family to tell them he was fine. I don't, however, recall any serious problem we ever had with lodging or at restaurants.

Levias was recognized for his play by being selected to the all-conference team. So were six other Mustangs: linebackers Jerry Griffin and Billy Bob Stewart, defensive linemen John LaGrone and Ron Medlen, offensive guard Lynn Thornhill and quarterback Mac White. The seven players are more than SMU ever had on an all-conference team in one season. To the victors go the spoils.

Once-beaten Georgia was our assignment in the Cotton Bowl. The Bulldogs had an outstanding team and were favored to win, but we thought we had a reasonable chance. Our weather in December was bad, however, and we had poor preparation for the game. We finally went over to the fairgrounds and worked out in what was essentially an indoor cattle lot, but that didn't do us a lot of good. We just didn't have any bounce or spring in our legs for the game. Georgia scored on the first play and we played catch up all day, finally losing 24-9.

We ranked No. 10, in the final Associated Press college football poll, SMU's best finish in 18 years. It was a wonderful achievement for my coaching staff. In five years we had brought Mustang football back from the dead by winning a conference championship and breaking into the Top 10 nationally. More importantly, we had proved that racial integration could work in the Southwest Conference. The first season for Jerry Levias had not been without incident, but it was an unquestionable success.

Instead of starting the 1967 season with a non-conference game, we opened at Texas A&M for television reasons. TV didn't manipulate schedules then the way they do today, when you're asked to start games morning, afternoon and night. But TV wanted to air SMU's game at A&M and they wanted it early in the season. The Aggies were delighted to play us early. They were still sore that we had beaten them the previous season and wanted to kick our butt on television. And, of course, we were delighted to get the TV exposure.

Things didn't look good for the Mustangs when our top quarterback, Mike Livingston, suffered a broken leg in the first half. We replaced him with little Inez Perez, who responded with a terrific passing game. It was a wonderful game for TV because the lead kept changing hands and we found ourselves behind 17-13 on A&M's seven-yard line and only four seconds remaining. We called a pass play—Perez to Levias—and Perez responded by doing a nice piece of scrambling before he launched the ball to Jerry in the back of the end zone. Jerry made one of his spectacular catches and scored the winning touchdown. A&M's big stadium fell silent as the scoreboard showed we had pulled out a 20-17 victory.

The result of the game really hurt the diehard Aggie fans, who had just seen their team lose its third straight to SMU. I knew how badly they wanted to win, but I was still taken aback by an incident outside our dressing room after the game. A prominent member of the Aggie booster club stopped me and said, "You should feel great, Coach Fry. You beat us, but it took a Mexican and nigger to do it!" I wanted to hit him in the mouth, but instead I took a deep breath, remembering how many times I'd told Jerry to restrain himself in these kinds of situations, and walked away.

Our seasons went in different directions after that. A&M went on to win the Southwest Conference championship and beat Alabama in the Cotton Bowl. Livingston's broken leg was indicative of how our season would go. Injuries mounted and we lost our next seven games. I know fans and the news media get tired of hearing coaches say it, but injuries play a huge roll in a team's success, or lack of it. When a team gets a lot of players hurt, it's usually a disaster.

In the third game of the season we were at Minnesota, and we had to play Eddie Valdez at quarterback when injuries wiped out that position. Eddie was a wonderful young man but when he got excited, which he did while playing football, he wanted to communicate in Spanish. We had another kid on the team who seldom played but spoke Spanish, so we put him in the game to serve as Eddie's translator. He took the plays we sent in from the sideline and gave them to Eddie in Spanish and the rest of the team in English. Then he would line up at wide receiver—just stand there and never do anything. We used that ploy when I was in the Marines and I dislocated my shoulder and couldn't throw the ball. But I stayed in the game to call the plays and lined up at wide receiver. And in both games the defense had a man covering a wide receiver who was never going to get the ball thrown his way.

We got healthy enough to end the year with victories over Baylor and TCU, which sent us into the 1968 season on a positive note with a two-game winning streak. Despite our 1967 record, Levias led the conference with 57 pass receptions, seven for touchdowns. He also had an excellent year returning kickoffs and punts and again made the all-conference team, the only Mustang selected.

With some good players returning—Levias for his senior year —and a fine passing quarterback coming off the freshmen team, we thought we could rebound with a decent team in 1968. The quarterback was Chuck Hixson, and although he had great potential, he had no college experience and we didn't put needless pressure on him. Besides, our first two opponents were Auburn and Ohio State, both on the road.

As the players were warming up on the field before our season opener, one of Auburn's assistant coaches, Paul Davis, came over and handed me a plaque. He said, "Hayden, you ought to read this." The inscription said some nice things about SMU and its football team. But it also said no Negro had ever played at War Eagle Memorial Stadium because they were banned from doing so. It was obviously a direct reference to Levias, and Davis thought it was funny. It was his idea of a joke.

I took the plaque, said nothing, and carried it to our dressing room. When I was talking to the team I realized I still had it in my hand, and decided the players should hear what it said. I told them where I got it, then read it to them and tossed it in a trash barrel. They were stunned, with disbelief written on their faces. By that time Jerry Levias was recognized as an outstanding college football player and a team leader for whom everyone had great respect. We also had our second black recruit, nose guard Rufus Cormier, with us that day.

I said nothing after I read the message on the plaque. I just led the players out to the field and watched them jump all over Auburn. Chuck Hixson made his debut at quarterback for SMU by throwing for nearly 300 yards and three TDs. We got a big lead against a team coached by Shug Jordan and quarterbacked by Pat Sullivan, winner of the Heisman Trophy. Heavily favored to win, Auburn made a big rally late in the game, but we had already put too many points on the board and won 37-28. I still consider that victory one of the most satisfying of my career.

I later became good friends with Paul Davis. He is a decent man and didn't give me the plaque as a racial gesture. He probably never thought about the consequences. But what he did reflected the attitude in the South at that time, and I'd like to think I played a small role in changing it.

At Ohio State the following week, we played a team loaded with a lot of talented sophomores, including quarterback Rex Kern and cornerback Jack Tatum. They were so good, in fact, that they led the Buckeyes to a perfect season and the national championship that year. Two hours before the game I was walking around one end of the field when Keith Jackson, the TV announcer who did the game for ABC that day, wandered by and asked me what I was doing. I told him I wanted to see what the end zone looked like at Ohio Stadium because I wasn't sure we were going to get there during the game. The Buckeyes outweighed us by more than 50 pounds along the line of scrimmage according to the game program and were a big favorite.

Because Ohio State was so big, we couldn't run the ball but we had no trouble throwing it. SMU launched an NCAA-record 76 passes that day, 69 by Hixson and seven by Gary Carter, a big left hander we had to put in the game when Hixson's arm got tired.

Levias caught 15, still a school record. We moved the ball up and down the field, but shot ourselves in the foot by throwing interceptions deep in their territory. Tatum had two TD saves in the end zone. Teams often exchange films for scouting purposes, but Woody Hayes, the longtime boss of the Buckeyes, wouldn't trade with us. He probably wished later that he had.

We had a big statistical advantage, outgaining the Buckeyes by 115 yards. We even made the longest run from scrimmage against them all year, a 38-yard gain on a fake punt we called the Bumerooski, named after Bum Phillips, one of my assistants who later enjoyed success as a head coach of the Houston Oilers in the NFL. Ohio State won the game 35-14, but I could tell Coach Hayes was really upset when I shook hands with him after the game. Angry because we had made his defense look so bad, he made his coaching staff— which included Lou Holtz, Bill Mallory and Lou McCullough— stay around after the game and review the film. Normally, he gave them Saturday night off to be with their families, but not that evening.

Our first home game of the '68 season against North Carolina State was highlighted by another extraordinary performance by Jerry Levias, who caught nine passes for 213 yards, an SMU yardage record that still stands. Three were for touchdowns, which tied the school record he had set the previous season against Texas. Jerry is still the only SMU player who has twice made three TD receptions in a single game. We beat N.C. State 35-14.

At TCU the next week we had a racial incident on the field. After Jerry caught a pass, a defensive back stopped him with a good, hard tackle. As the two hit the ground, the defender rolled over on Jerry and spit in his face. I didn't see it happen, but I did notice that when Jerry came off the field he had his head down and seemed to be beside himself with emotion. When I got a chance to talk to him he was all choked up and told me what had happened.

By that time TCU was about to punt the ball back to us, and I asked Jerry if he felt like going back in the game to return the kick. He nodded his head and took a few steps on the field before he stopped and said, "Coach, I'm going to take this one back all the way." I smiled and told him he'd first better get his helmet, which he'd tossed behind the bench in frustration.

Like Babe Ruth, he called his shot, making the most spectacular punt return I've ever seen. He reversed his field several times, giving some defenders more than one chance to tackle him, but none could do it as he zig-zagged 89 yards to the end zone. His dazzling run broke a 14-14 tie with 13 minutes left, and our defense made his TD stand up to give us a 21-14 victory.

Behind Levias and Hixson, SMU became a potent offensive team in 1968. But that team wasn't just one-dimensional. It also had the school's first 1,000-yard rusher, Mike Richardson. We finished the regular season 7-3, with losses to three outstanding teams: Ohio State, Texas and Arkansas. We scored more than 30 points in six of our victories and nearly hit that total in losing to Arkansas, 35-29. Hixson led the nation in passing, throwing for more than 3,000 yards and 21 touchdowns. Levias ranked second in pass receiving with 80 catches for more than 1,000 yards and eight TDs. We were an exciting team anxious to take our explosive attack to a bowl game.

We got a bid to the Bluebonnet Bowl to play Oklahoma, a Top 10 power out of the Big Eight. The bowl had several "firsts", including the first bowl game played on New Year's eve and the first bowl game played indoors. The site was Houston's Astrodome, then only a few years old, and the game drew a capacity crowd of 53,543, a record for an indoor football game. And it was another first for me: I'd never seen a football game played indoors, let alone coached in one.

The game got plenty of hype, with Oklahoma featuring all-America Steve Owens and its powerful running game against our aerial attack led by Hixson and Levias. Owens had not been thrown for a loss the entire season, but we put in a special split-six defense, stacking my No. 2 fullback, Daryl Doggett, behind nose guard Rufus Cormier, our second black recruit. We tackled Owens behind the line of scrimmage several times, but the Sooners led 14-6 after three periods, setting up one of the wildest fourth quarters in bowl history.

Ray Scott, who announced the game for television, told me that it was the most exciting game he had ever broadcast. After we scored two touchdowns to take a 21-14 lead, the teams traded TDs to leave us with a 28-21 advantage. Oklahoma then drove the field and scored again with barely a minute left to make it a one-point game. The Sooners took time out to talk it over, then went for two points and the win, but we cut down a running play short of the goal line to earn a thrilling 28-27 victory.

In my post-game press conference, I noticed Dizzy Dean, the old baseball pitcher, in the room. I have no idea what he was doing there. As the winning coach, I was all revved up, and I asked him,

"Diz, am I laying it on too thick?" He took a puff of his cigar and said, "Son, if you done it, you ain't braggin'." I still have people tell me that they were on their way to a New Year's eve party that night but got caught up in watching our exciting football game on TV and were late for the party.

The Jerry Levias era was over at SMU, and integration of the Southwest Conference was a success. There was already a sprinkling of other black players in the league and there would be many, many more. We had certainly chosen the right person to integrate the conference. As a football player, he never missed a game; as a student, he may have never missed a class. He became an all-American football player as one of the best pass receivers and kick return specialists in the country. More important, he excelled as a student, ranking near the top of his class and graduating with honors.

Jerry took both mental and physical beatings just because of his race, but he never complained. I frequently asked him how things were going and he always had the same response: "Pretty good, Coach." I know there were some bad times for him, but I can't be fully aware of his feelings because I am not black. And I'm sure he experienced abuse that I was unaware of. Jerry went on to a fine professional career with the Houston Oilers and San Diego Chargers. He now lives in Houston, where he has experienced success in business, as he has everything in his life. I admire Jerry Levias more than any player I have ever coached.

Chapter Fourteen

FIRED FROM SMU

With the Jerry Levias years over, Chuck Hixson stepped up to become the best quarterback in the Southwest Conference and one of the best in college football. After leading the nation in passing as a sophomore in 1968, he finished second in '69 and fourth in '70. A lot of years have passed since he played, but he still holds most of the SMU passing records, including career marks for touchdowns, yardage and completions. He threw for more than 300 yards in eight games, more than any Mustang quarterback.

Had Hixson and Levias played together for three seasons there's no telling what kind of numbers they'd have put up. It would have been awesome. As it was, Chuck's favorite target in his final two years was Gary Hammond, who we used as a wide receiver in '69 and a running back in '70. He led the conference in receiving both years, with more than 100 catches in the two seasons, and twice made all-league.

We were still playing rugged non-conference opponents, and lost back-to-back road games at Georgia Tech and Michigan State in '69. The following season, we suffered consecutive losses to Oklahoma and Tennessee. That got us off on the wrong foot both years and we were unable to break even in either season.

College football teams started playing 11 games in 1970, which gave us an additional non-conference opponent. We played at Northwestern, which had a strong team that finished second in the Big

Ten that year. Hixson scored a touchdown late in that game on an option, a play we hadn't shown before because he was not a good runner. But it surprised Northwestern and worked. Trailing 20-19, we called the same play for a two-point conversion. It fooled 'em again—Chuck faked a handoff and ran over the goal line to give us a 21-20 victory.

With Hixson having graduated, we featured more of a running game in my final two seasons at SMU. Alvin Maxson became the school's second running back to break the 1,000-yard barrier, and he did it in both 1971 and '72. He led the Southwest Conference in rushing as a sophomore in '71 and made all-league both seasons.

We got off on the wrong foot again in '71, losing our first two games to Oklahoma and Missouri, and failed again to have a winning season. But the following year, which turned out to be my last, we opened with victories over Wake Forest and Florida and finished with a 7-4 record.

The game with Florida was played at a new stadium in Tampa and put me across the field from Gator Coach Doug Dickey. We were old friends, having been on the Arkansas staff together in 1961. Interestingly, we had both played for the same head coach in college, Bob Woodruff. I had played for him at Baylor, and when he left there to go to Florida, he became Dickey's head coach. Years later, as the athletic director at Tennessee, Woodruff hired Dickey as his football coach, but more on that shortly.

In preparing to play Florida in '72, I noticed on their films that they sometimes used an unusual defensive stunt. We were talking about it in a staff meeting, and Bum Phillips, my defensive coordinator, suggested we try a play that was successful against his defense when he used the same stunt. It was an off-tackle play that required a special blocking scheme.

Florida used the stunt three times against us, and each time our quarterback called an audible to run our special play. One resulted in a touchdown, and the other two produced long runs that set up scores. It's interesting that we won the game, 21-14, as the result of a play suggested by one of my defensive coaches.

We were getting pressure from some of our fans—especially some big donors—to move our home games from the Cotton Bowl to recently built Texas Stadium. Some of our biggest contributors had purchased skyboxes at the new stadium and wanted to use them for our games. But there was also a large number of fans who wanted us to stay at in our traditional home, the Cotton Bowl, known as "the house that Doak Walker built." As both the athletic director and football coach, it was my call, and I came up with the compromise of playing our non-conference games at Texas Stadium and our league games at the Cotton Bowl. It was the dumbest call I ever made. In trying to please both sides, I managed to get them both mad at me.

We played two games in Texas Stadium in '72, and my team responded well in its new surroundings, rolling over Wake Forest and New Mexico State by huge margins. SMU hadn't scored 50 points against an opponent in 23 seasons, and we did it twice in consecutive home games! Those two victories, plus the one at Florida, got us off to a good start. Our only non-conference loss was at Virginia Tech, 13-10.

We won our conference opener against Rice to make our record 4-1, but when we lost our next three games, rumors began circulating that my job was on the line. Initially I didn't pay much attention to them. I felt I had done a good job in my 11 seasons as SMU's football coach and nine years as its athletic director. I had two years remaining on my contract and assumed the University would honor the agreement. Besides, we had a 4-4 record with three games remaining, with an opportunity to finish strong and get a bowl invitation.

We went to Arkansas and won convincingly, 22-7, but that didn't stop the rumors and the media picked up on them. There was even speculation about who would succeed me at SMU. The names of Johnny Majors, then at Iowa State, and Barry Switzer, Oklahoma's offensive coordinator, were suggested in one news report. The president who hired me at SMU, Willis Tate, had recently retired and been replaced by Paul Hardin. Although I didn't know the new president well, he seemed like an honest and decent man and had never told me my job was on the line.

When we beat Baylor the following Saturday, our record was 6-4 and we were in line for a berth in the Liberty Bowl. That should have ended the rumors about my getting fired, but it didn't. With one game remaining and a bowl invitation in the balance, the stories continued to swirl about my status. I still hadn't gone to our new president to discuss them. I assumed that if the rumors had substance he would do the professional thing: summon me to his office and tell me face to face. That was a mistake on my part.

The day before we ended the season with TCU, I heard on my car radio that SMU had announced I was fired as its football coach and athletic director. I was stunned. I drove straight to the office to be with my coaches, who were in a state of shock. We would coach the Mustangs one more game, then pack our bags.

After getting my emotions together, I went to the president's office to confront him. I wanted to know why I was getting fired. I was a little surprised that he was in and willing to see me, but the meeting was short. When I asked him for an explanation he simply said he was sorry, that the decision had been made. He choked up and cried a little bit. I left his office with the feeling that the decision had not been his.

My players were very supportive of my coaches and me. They were angry and hurt, but more than anything, they were puzzled. Why would SMU officials pull the rug out from under their season? A bowl berth was no longer possible. A football team can't go to a bowl game without a coaching staff. But the players put aside their anger and frustration and beat TCU 35-22 the following day. We had finished the season strong by winning our final three games, and with a 7-4 record, we should have been on our way to the Liberty Bowl. Instead, my coaches and I were on our way out.

Because SMU never made it clear why I was fired, the fans and media were left to speculate. The racial issue even came up again. Earlier that year, the *Fort Worth Star Telegram* reported that "as many as 15 of the state's best Negro high school football players are banding together to form a 'super team' at SMU." It was a false report, of course, but some of our fans were unsettled by the rumor that we were putting together "an all-black team" at SMU. I never learned the source of the rumor or why it was started.

It didn't take me long to decide on the reason for my dismissal. For several years some of SMU's big contributors had been trying to get me to buy players. They wanted me to use their money to recruit illegally, and I refused to do it. Every time I was approached on the matter I told them absolutely no. I believe they used a new president who wasn't strong enough to stand up to them to get me. Paul Hardin was a nice man who caved in when big contributors put pressure on him. I think he agreed to fire me after we lost three straight games and it appeared we were on our way to a losing season.

About a year later, Hardin himself was fired. And after that, SMU began buying players, got caught, and paid a heavy price. It is the only school that has ever been given the so-called "death penalty" by the NCAA. There would be no more cheating to get football players because there would be no more football team. Not for a few years, anyway. It's not surprising that SMU has not recovered from that penalty.

The Mustang boosters who wanted me to buy players were many of the same ones who promised financial support when Tennessee offered me its coaching job a few years earlier. The Tennessee athletic director was Bob Woodruff, my coach at Baylor. Because Woodruff had coached at Baylor, he appreciated how hard it was for the private schools to succeed in the Southwest Conference. He liked what I was doing with the SMU program and wanted me to take over at Tennessee. He made an attractive offer that included a lump sum of money I could split up any way I wanted in coaching salaries.

But the SMU supporters got wind of what was going on and made me a counter offer. I talked it over with my coaches, who all enjoyed working at SMU and living in the Dallas area, and we decided to stay put. That was a mistake on our part, because we never saw any of the money the SMU boosters had promised us. But by the time we realized the SMU supporters didn't intend to keep their word, Tennessee already had a football coach. Woodruff hired Doug Dickey, who played for him at Florida.

I had a lot of reasons to be angry about the way SMU treated my coaches and me. We had worked hard and done a good job. Our 7-4 record the year we were fired was third best in the Southwest Conference. In my final seven seasons, playing with teams recruited entirely by my coaching staff, our record against the three other private schools in the league—Baylor, TCU and Rice—was 18-3. SMU competed in a metropolitan market dominated by professional teams, and we had to fight hard for fan support and media attention. Yet as athletic director, I had reduced the athletic budget by 10 percent in the last two years.

I was really concerned for my coaches. SMU not only cut off their salaries, they also cut off all benefits, so my immediate concern was trying to help them find jobs. One member of my staff, Dudley Parker, had been with me for my entire 11 years with the Mustangs. That's a long time for a football coach to stay at a Division I school. The only two coaches who outlasted me at SMU were Darryl Royal at Texas and Frank Broyles at Arkansas.

It didn't take me long to find out that SMU didn't intend to honor the two remaining years on my own contract. I never received any kind of settlement. My attorney looked over the contract and told me that the way it was written, there wasn't anything I could do. That's when I lost faith in contracts. I haven't read one since. All I knew about my contract at Iowa is what I read in the paper. I have always tried to keep my end of an agreement, and I believed my employer should do the same. That seems reasonable to me, but SMU didn't keep its end of the bargain and I was looking for work.

Chapter Fifteen

NORTH TEXAS STATE

There's an old saying that every coach should be fired once just to toughen him up and test his love for the game. There may be some truth in that, but it's unlikely the person who said it had five kids to buy presents for a Christmas time. Being out of work during the holiday season is no fun, as I found out in 1972. My ouster from SMU left me deeply disturbed and scarred. The school's refusal to honor the terms of my contract and its unwillingness to tell me why I had been fired had me wondering about the people who run our universities.

Especially disturbing was the manner in which my coaches had been treated—fired without notice and cut off without salary or benefits. Unfortunately, that was a rather common practice in those days. I later urged the American Football Coaches Association to do something about it and won the support of such coaches as Darryl Royal, Frank Broyles, Charlie McLendon and John McKay. With pressure from our Association, most universities now give assistant football coaches one-year appointments beginning July 1. If the school fires them at the end of the football season, the coaches have some time to find a job and get their lives in order without worrying about salary and benefits.

My firing sparked quite a response from all kinds of folks. I heard from the clergy, elected officials, teachers, kids and even grandmothers. They all offered support, but if I didn't find work soon, someone would have to offer a loan. I wanted to stay in coaching, although I was getting offers in other fields. One of the most un-usual came from Colonel Byrd. I never knew his first name—ev-eryone just called him Colonel, probably because he was a brother of Admiral Richard Byrd, the arctic explorer and the first man to fly over the north and south poles.

Colonel Byrd was a huge Texas fan. He even had longhorns—the Texas logo—painted on the sides of his airplane. And he owned a lot of property in the state, including the Texas Book Depository in Dallas, the building from where Lee Harvey Oswald was accused of shooting President Kennedy to death. Colonel Byrd wanted me to sell the building for him, then go to Argentina and sell some property he owned down there. So I had an opportunity to go into real estate, but I declined and looked at some coaching jobs.

When SMU let me go, our family home was on Lake Ray Hubbard in Rockwall, just east of Dallas. We had been there for a couple of years, we were nicely settled and really liked our home on the lake. So when North Texas State University contacted me about a job just up the road in Denton, I was interested. I thought it was close enough to our home on Lake Hubbard that I could commute and my children wouldn't have to be uprooted from their friends and schools, at least not right away.

North Texas had just fired Rod Rust. He was the football coach there for six years and enjoyed success his first three seasons, with a 22-6-1 record. The last three seasons, however, his teams slipped to 7-26, including 1-10 the past year. The school was a member of the Missouri Valley Conference but did not have much football fol-lowing or tradition. Gate receipts and financial contributions were both at a low level, and the entire athletic program was under study, with the emphasis on football. There was speculation that North Texas might de-emphasize football, maybe even drop it. But it didn't seem likely that school officials would want to talk to me if they were headed in that direction. Besides, taking over programs in trouble is a challenge to me. I inherited a football team at SMU in bad shape, and would later do the same thing at Iowa.

Dr. Bill Miller, the chairman of the North Texas athletic coun-cil, set up a meeting with me and his selection committee at a marina on Lake Dallas, halfway between Dallas and Denton. I'll al-ways remember the name of the café where we met—the Duck Inn. Unlike most men in his position, Dr. Miller had played college football himself and had a good understanding of the game. He did a great job of convincing me to meet with the selection committee the next day. A freak ice storm hit the area that evening, and my good friend C.Q. Smith was kind enough to drive me to the meeting.

We were well into the meeting when the door popped open and a big man appeared in the doorway and said something like, "If you people hire Hayden Fry you can count on my financial support." Then he left as abruptly as he had appeared. I knew I had seen his face before, but I couldn't put a name to it. Everyone in the room was startled and taken aback. It was the strangest thing that ever happened to me in a formal interview.

During that meeting, and some discussions that followed, the North Texas officials convinced me that they wanted to have a good football team. They liked my background in marketing the sport at SMU, and some of the things I did to generate interest there, and were willing to try some of the same things. Football at North Texas was hurting for attention, and they were turning to me for help. But I did get the feeling that if I couldn't win some games and stimulate gate receipts and financial contributions, they might not give another coach the opportunity.

Just before Christmas, North Texas held a press conference at Texas Stadium, where we would play some home games, to introduce me as its new football coach. The press reported that President C.C. Nolen "beamed" when making the announcement, which made the new coach feel good. I was also hired to be the athletic director, although that announcement wouldn't be made for another month. They had internal candidates for that job and it was a delicate matter that created an awkward situation for me for a brief time.

I soon learned the identity of the man who barged into my interview and why I recognized his face. He was Bo Adams, an assistant football coach at Mountain Home, Arkansas, when I was on the staff at Arkansas. He coached with one of my good friends, Howard Cissell, president of the Arkansas High School Coaches Association at that time. Adams was sincere in his offer to support me if I became the coach at North Texas.

He had left coaching and made a lot of money with his own mail-order insurance business. He eventually took over A.L. Williams Insurance in Atlanta.

A few days after I got the job, Adams and I and a fellow named Rex Cauble were soliciting financial support for North Texas football. Cauble was an old rodeo performer who had ridden a horse named Cutter Bill in cutting contests, then went into the oil business and made a fortune. Adams and Cauble were real characters who could open doors. They were invaluable in helping me build the North Texas program. Within a week, we had 16 courtesy cars for the athletic department staff and coaches, and we were able to raise money to hire some good assistant coaches for me.

Bill Brashier, a boyhood pal from my early years in Eastland, had also gone into coaching and was a member of the previous staff. I retained him on my original five-man staff that also included Andy Everest from SMU; Mike Crocker, a successful high school coach in Texas; Bob Lee, a winner in the junior college ranks; and Howard Cissel, a well-known Arkansas high school coach. Crocker and Cissell gave us recruiting connections with Texas and Arkansas high schools, and Lee knew his way around the junior college circuit.

I immediately started to work on changing the football image, just as I had at SMU. The North Texas colors were green and white. Kelly green had been used in the past and we changed that to lime green. We promoted the nickname Mean Green instead of Eagles, although we selected a modernized eagle as the logo on our helmets. Mean Green came from Mean Joe Greene, who played at North Texas and was a star defensive lineman for the Pittsburgh Steelers. He was helpful to me in recruiting. North Texas football teams still call themselves the Mean Green, wear lime green jerseys and helmets with the modernized eagle logo.

I inherited a hard-working group of players who were eager to learn and anxious to improve. They were a little short on talent, but they laid the foundation for my later years at North Texas. My first team finished 5-5-1, a big improvement over the previous year that produced only one victory. The next year we took a step backward before we broke through in 1975 to start a run of four successful seasons.

We gave up our home on Lake Hubbard—the commute got to be too much—and I moved the family to Denton in time for the children to start school there in the fall of 1973. We enjoyed living in a smaller community, which I found much more relaxing than the metropolitan area where I had worked the previous 11 years. But because of the size, we had a small support base and had to work hard at selling our program.

As athletic director, I was in charge of a marketing program that had to fund itself. In other words, we had to raise money before we could spend it on things like new uniforms for the band and flashy halftime entertainment. We worked hard making people in the area aware that North Texas was dedicated to having a good football team. When the Mean Green started to win, people became believers, and we led the nation in increased attendance.

We held some fundraisers that featured some big names from the entertainment world, including Willie Nelson and Bob Hope. We sold out the concerts and made money for our athletic program—and we got an unexpected gift when Willie Nelson came to town. At a reception after his performance, he came over to me and asked who was in charge of the evening. I told him that as the athletic director, I was. Fine, he said, then maybe I could give him his check. I was surprised by his abruptness, but reached in my pocket and handed him a check for $40,000. Then he asked me for a pen, which I gave him, and he signed the check over to the North Texas athletic department and gave it back to me. I learned that is typical behavior for Willie Nelson. He has a big heart and lends a hand to people who need help. For years he's held an annual celebrities golf tournament near Houston that raises money for charity. One of the kindest things he ever did was helping the farmers during their financial crisis of the 1980s. But what he did that night in Denton made a huge impression on a football coach/athletic director scrambling to fund a program.

Two victories punctuated our breakthrough season of 1975. It was our third year, and we beat defending Southwest Conference champ Houston 28-0 at Texas Stadium, then after losing at Mississippi State 15-12, we won at Tennessee 21-14. Those two wins got people's attention and served notice that North Texas could play with the big boys. The victory at Tennessee probably cost Bill Battle his coaching job—he was fired after the season—and it definitely cost us the opportunity to play the Vols again.

We had a two-game agreement with them, with a clause that they could buy out the second game if they wanted to. After we whipped 'em, they definitely wanted to. They agreed to play North Texas because their athletic director, Bob Woodruff, had been my coach at Baylor, and because my assistant AD, DeWitt Weaver, had been an all-American at Tennessee. Those connections were good enough to get the two-game agreement but not strong enough to keep it after we beat them the first game.

My former employer, SMU, was willing to play us, mostly because my successor as athletic director there was Dick Davis, who had been my broker when I was coaching the Mustangs. We were good friends and we both thought the game was a natural, so we played three times in my six years at North Texas. All three games were played at Texas Stadium, and they were exciting and hotly contested. I knew that if we were going to attract attention in the area we were going to have to play some area teams, so I really appreciated the willingness of Davis to schedule us.

In 1976 we lost to Mississippi State, Texas, SMU and Florida State by margins from one to seven points. Those were the only teams to beat us that season and we had our second straight 7-4 record. I had letters out all over the country trying to get games with high-profile schools. Most wrote back and said they weren't interested. Some didn't bother to answer my letter. We were willing to play at their place because we would have a nice payday and we needed the money. Texas gave us $125,000 to play in Austin, and that was a lot of money to us at that time. I still have a soft spot in my heart for the schools who were willing to play us.

After winning the Missouri Valley Conference championship my first year, North Texas dropped out of the league because we didn't believe it served our best interests. It was a basketball league that paid little attention to football, and we were in a football state. But we weren't interested in being an independent—we wanted to belong to the Southwest Conference and we were vocal about it. Rex Cauble got us a couple of old Model-A Fords, we painted them green and drove them to every town in a 75-mile radius. We took along the Mean Green Dollies, a campus co-ed support group, trying to stir up attention and support for North Texas' bid to join the SWC.

We thought the Dallas-Fort Worth area should have a state school in the conference, and we got no objection from SMU and TCU. Texas and Arkansas supported us, as did Houston, a new member of the league. There were ongoing discussions about our possible membership, but someone always brought up academic standards and admission requirements, areas where North Texas was thought to be lagging by conference standards. The talks continued and the interest was always there, and I think North Texas had a chance to be accepted had I stayed. But it never came to a vote, and after I left nobody pushed it.

As it turned out, had North Texas been admitted to the SWC it wouldn't have been a member very long, anyway. The league started to crumble when Arkansas left to join the Southeastern

Conference. Some of the other schools began looking around, getting ready to save themselves if the conference fell apart. When Texas, Texas A&M, Texas Tech and Baylor got together with the Big Eight to form a new league called the Big 12, the Southwest Conference was history. Having played and coached in the SWC for 14 years, it made me sad to see that happen. I have many fond recollections about my time in the old conference. But there was increasing concern about poor attendance at the private schools, just as there was for a long time in the Big Ten about fan support at Northwestern. Fortunately, that has improved in recent years.

One of our biggest concerns at North Texas—the thing that finally caused us to leave—was not being rewarded with a bowl bid following a good season. We were 7-4 in both 1975 and '76 and waited for the phone to ring. It never did. In 1977 we were led to believe the Independence Bowl would give us a bid if we beat Louisiana Tech in the last game of the season, but we had to win convincingly. Tech was one of the national leaders in scoring defense and total defense and we were going to play them right in Shreveport, where the Independence Bowl is located. I told my players that to ensure a bowl bid we had to score more than 40 points.

Late in the game we scored a touchdown to give us 39 points, then went for a two-point conversion, which was successful. We won the game 41-14. It was probably the worst thing I ever did as a coach. The Tech coach was Maxey Lambright, a good guy, and I felt terrible about running up the score. I've never liked that kind of thing, but we were desperate for a bowl bid and wanted to score more than 40 points. We went home to wait for an invitation. When the phone rang it was the Independence Bowl telling us that they were taking Louisiana Tech as the home team, and because we had beaten them so badly they didn't want a rematch. With a 9-2 record, we got no bowl bid. That's when my coaches decided it might be time to move on.

We had a soccer-style kicker that season—an Iranian named Iseed Khoury—who we recruited out of the student body. He was a great soccer player who could kick the football where he wanted to. We had an on-side kick play that we used when we caught the receiving team in the right alignment. When Iseed saw it he would holler "pink" —which he pronounced "peenk" —and kick the ball to a spot where he would run to and recover it himself. In the Louisiana Tech game he saw the alignment, yelled "peenk" and kicked. He and a Tech player dove for the ball at the same time and cracked helmets. Iseed was knocked cold and carried from the field on a stretcher. But he recovered and later returned to the bench. When we scored again I asked him if he felt like kicking off. "Only if I don't have to yell peenk!" he responded. He was a great young man who became a successful soccer coach.

Three of my sons played for me at North Texas. Randy and Kelly were defensive backs. Zach was a running back. Randy took a shot in the NFL with the Houston Oilers, then played for Shreveport in the old American Football League. It was a great experience having my sons on my team. We all enjoyed it and had a good time. Adrian, my youngest son, was an extremely good all-around athlete.

We had some good players at North Texas, many who went on to play professionally. Bernard Jackson was the school's first running back to gain 1,000 yards. He ran for 1,453 my last year. Michael Jones scored 98 points, still a school record, in 1977. Ken Washington was a fine quarterback who could both run and throw the ball. Quarterback Jordan Case played a long time in the Canadian League. J.T. Smith returned kicks for years in the NFL. Defensive back Beasley Reece played with the Dallas Cowboys and is now a TV commentator for NFL games. Defensive end Bernard West played in Canada. Defensive tackle Reginald Lewis and defensive back Hurles Scales went on to the NFL.

Title IX became a law about the time I went to North Texas. As athletic director, it was up to me to implement it. I hired an associate AD for women's sports and we put together a program for women. It was a difficult thing to do because of the financial strain we were already under to upgrade the football team. But we worked hard and got it done, and by the time I left we had competitive women's teams. The administrative load, already substantial, got to be an even bigger burden, and I began to wonder what I was doing as both the football coach and athletic director.

In 1978, we again went 9-2 and once again received no bowl invitation. It became frustrating for the players and coaches. In the past four seasons we had a record of 32-12 and no bowl wanted us. It usually came down to one of two reasons: either the bowl didn't think North Texas had enough fan support to sell tickets, or the other team in the bowl didn't want to play us.

I had received job offers from time to time, but we were having a great time building a program at North Texas, and I always found a reason to say no. Oklahoma State, Purdue, Ole Miss and Miami were among the schools that talked to me. Purdue might have interested me at some point, but the timing of its offer wasn't good. I took a good look at Miami, where Pete Elliott was athletic director, making a visit to its campus. But there were certain things about the job that didn't appeal to me and I rejected it. Miami had just fired Carl Selmer, who I wound up hiring on my staff at North Texas.

Following a 9-2 record and no bowl offer in 1978, the timing was right when Iowa called me. After getting rejected by the bowls four straight years, I was ready to listen. Bill Brashier surveyed the coaches, who voted to explore the Iowa offer. They knew the Big Ten champion was guaranteed the Rose Bowl berth, and that other good teams in the league were courted by other bowls. I had never set foot on the Iowa campus or been in Iowa City. I only knew one thing about the Hawkeyes: Bump Elliott was the athletic director, and I was ready to listen to what he had to say.

Chapter Sixteen

IOWA, 1979-1980

Iowa had one thing in its favor as far as I was concerned: Bump Elliott was its athletic director. Bump had a reputation as being a fair, honest and well-liked administrator. He was a football man, a Michigan all-American who was head coach at his alma mater for 10 years. And there was another thing I admired about Bump. He was a Marine, serving in the Corps as an officer at the end of World War II. The Iowa job had an additional appeal to me. I could shuck my duties as athletic director and devote full time to coaching football, which I hadn't been able to do in 15 years.

After being contacted by two major universities about their head coaching jobs, I received a third call, this one from Bump Elliott. Bump's brother, Pete, who had once tried to hire me at Miami, recommended me. Bump and Ed Jennings, a vice-president in charge of athletics at Iowa, flew to Dallas for a meeting. I got a room at an airport hotel and paid for it myself, which I kidded them about later. Jennings was along to represent President Willard Boyd, who had the reputation for not caring much about football. After we visited awhile and touched on several things, they told me the job was mine if I wanted it. Jennings assured me that I would have Boyd's support, and that the president was committed to having a good football team. I told them I was very interested but I wanted to visit with my coaches and check out some things.

My coaches and I tried to analyze why Iowa had been a loser for so long. The Hawkeyes hadn't had a good football team since the days of Forest Evashevski and had gone 17 years without a winning season. During that time the school had fired four coaches. Bob Commings was the most recent after his 1978 team finished 2-9. Films of that season revealed the stadium was generally full, indicating strong fan support. The newspapers we looked at showed Iowa got good press coverage, suggesting good interest from the media.

It was hard to figure out why the Hawkeyes weren't winning. Iowa was a Big Ten university with strong financial support. It had a great athletic director in Bump Elliott and a president who said he was committed to winning football. It was The University in a state that didn't have competition from professional teams. That was because the state had a small population, of course, which meant it had a small recruiting base, which was about the only negative we could find. After looking at the whole picture, my coaches were ready to make the move, and so was I.

On December 8, I flew up to Iowa to meet the president and athletic board, and unless I ran into something that turned me off, I would be introduced as the Hawkeyes' new football coach the following day. It was a very cold and icy day, not one conducive to giving me a favorable impression of the Iowa campus, which I had never seen. But the people were warm and friendly, and that evening I was given a nice reception at the president's home, where I met the members of the athletic board.

Bump told them that I would be the last football coach he would ever hire, and that puzzled me. A little later I got a chance to talk to him privately and asked him what he meant by that comment. "Simple," he said. "I don't think they'll give me a chance to hire another coach, so if you don't make it, neither will I."

I was especially interested in meeting President Boyd. I told him the thing I was most concerned about was the University's commitment to have a football team as good as its academic program. I told him I couldn't compete in the Big Ten with a short stick; I needed the same things the winners had. I told him that because Iowa was already at a disadvantage in recruiting, it was important the school didn't put itself at a disadvantage in other areas, such as facilities and staff. He assured me I had his full support and that he would do everything he could to help me win within the rules of the Big Ten and NCAA.

It was even colder the next morning when I was taken to the Iowa Fieldhouse to be introduced at a press conference as the school's sixth football coach in 20 years. That rate of turnover would scare off a lot of people in my business, but I had faced the same thing at SMU and North Texas, so it was old hat to me. For some reason, rebuilding football programs has always fascinated me and was one of the things that drew me to the Iowa job. Considering the weather, I was surprised by the large contingent of reporters and television cameras that awaited me at the press conference. Their numbers were encouraging. If the news media could show that kind of interest in a losing football team, how would they react to a winner?

My North Texas coaching staff came to Iowa pretty much intact. Bill Brashier was my defensive coordinator, Bill Snyder my offensive coordinator. I also brought along Howard Cissell, Don Patterson and Clovis Hale. I interviewed the coaches from the previous Iowa staff who were interested in joining me and hired Dan McCarney, Bernie Wyatt and Tom Cecchini. The final spot went to Barry Alvarez, who had just won a state high school championship at Mason City. Because most of the coaches had been with me at North Texas, continuity was not a problem. And having had only five assistants at North Texas, I was delighted to nearly double the size of my staff at Iowa.

The Iowa players had been losing and been kicked around for a long time. None of them knew what it was like to be a winner at the college level. Not surprisingly, they were a disillusioned group of young men. So the first thing we had to do was inject some enthusiasm and confidence into the program. We tried to be positive about everything, negative about nothing. At the same time, we had to provide discipline and leadership. We made sure they went to class, dressed properly, and were prompt for meetings. All of those things relate to how a player conducts himself on the field, but it's not easy to convince youngsters of that when they have never experienced success.

Some of our first meetings with the players were stormy sessions. Some guys sat with their legs up on the tables, their shirts out and their hats on. They saw nothing wrong with that. One night at training table I had to separate two players from fighting. We had to correct that kind of behavior and be firm in what we were doing. We treated everyone the same, regardless of how they had been perceived by the previous coaching staff. Eventually, the players realized we were running a tight ship and began to appreciate what we were doing. As I've said before, players want discipline whether they know it or not, and we were giving it to them in heavy doses.

We never tried to run anyone off, and we had very few defections. Initially, John Harty didn't want to be part of our program, but over time he understood what we were trying to accomplish and wanted to be part of the team. We were glad he made that decision, because he played for us two years and became an all-American defensive tackle. Then he had a long and productive career in the NFL.

My biggest initial disappointment about Iowa football was the facilities. They were woefully lacking in most areas, far behind most Division 1 schools. We had no place to conduct a squad meeting, so we had to go to the Pharmacy Building. (Imagine pharmacy students having to hold meetings in a football building.) There were no facilities for weight training, other than those used by the wrestling team, which might explain why the Hawkeyes had been getting pushed around on the field. The offices were inefficient. They were small and there weren't enough of them.

But those things could be corrected, and I had the president's commitment they would be. In the meantime, we went to work cleaning things up. We were amazed with some of the stuff we found tucked away in the deep recesses of the stadium, such as blocking sleds, tackling dummies and old equipment. Things that had just been ignored through the years. Some of it must have been there since Nile Kinnick's days. I put paint brushes in my coaches' hands, just as I had at SMU and North Texas, and we painted almost everything black and gold, which is taken for granted now. At that time, however, it was almost like the Iowa colors were being kept a secret.

One thing we didn't paint black and gold was the stadium's visitor's locker room, which we painted pink. It's a passive color, and we hoped it would put our opponents in a passive mood. Also, pink is often found in girls' bedrooms, and because of that some consider it a sissy color. It's been fun to get the reaction of visiting coaches to the color of their locker room. Most don't notice it, but those that do are in trouble. We've had some coaches—Bo Schembechler of Michigan and Mike White of Illinois to name two —who had their managers cover the walls with white paper so their players couldn't see the pink paint. When I talk to an opposing coach before a game and he mentions the pink walls, I know I've got him. I can't recall a coach who has stirred up a fuss about the color and then beaten us.

Despite the lack of adequate weight-training facilities, we conducted an out-of-season conditioning program, and the players really put themselves into it. They were beginning to understand that we where there to help them become better players. In looking at the game films of the previous season, it was obvious that the level of ability wasn't very high, which disappointed us but didn't surprise us. I recall being especially impressed with Joe Hufford in looking at films. But he finished in 1978 and never played for us. We were fortunate to recruit his two brothers, Paul and Mike, in later years and both were fine players.

After being on the job at Iowa about a month, two major events took place in my personal life. HueLeita and I had been going though divorce proceedings, which were finalized in January. She was still living in Denton with our daughter, Robin. Our four sons had all finished college and were on their own by then.

Also that month, I got word from Denton that my mother had passed away at age 83. She always gave her family a great deal of love and worked hard until she was 78 years old. She went without many things to provide good meals and decent clothes for me. She was a wonderful woman and I loved her very much. She was my hero.

By the time spring practice started we had convinced the players that we were serious about helping them win, and they demonstrated they were willing to work. The weather was pleasant in Iowa that spring and we had good practices. We left the gates open—the only time we would do that at Iowa—because we wanted the fans and the press to see how we conducted workouts and how we treated the players. We also wanted to stimulate interest in our program and get people talking about our football team. Some of our practices attracted good-sized crowds. I was especially encouraged by the large turnouts for scrimmages on Saturday mornings, when several thousand fans were in the stands and often cheered when we made good plays.

Dennis Mosley had an especially fine spring and did a lot of exciting things at running back. He had been one of the previous coaching staff's prize recruits, but he hadn't done much in his first three years, partly because of injuries. We had to convince him that he could play a full season, even if he had to play through some aches and pains. We worked at toughening him up mentally and he responded. I was amazed that Iowa never had a player rush for 1,000 yards, so I went out on a limb one day and predicted Mosley would become the first to do it. That was a bigger attention grabber than I ever anticipated, and the press ran with it. I would look foolish if Dennis failed. But it gave Hawkeye fans something to talk about during the summer months, and I believe Mosley was inspired by my confidence in him.

Every chance I got during my first year, I put President Boyd in a position where he would have to publicly support my program and commit to winning. I knew I might be alienating faculty members and others, but I had to get his support on the record, because there were still people who doubted he was sincere. I don't know what Boyd thought of football before I arrived, although I realized he had fired three of my predecessors. But I tried to be open and honest with him and tell him what we needed at Iowa to compete in the Big Ten, and I think he listened to me.

Before Boyd left for the Field Museum directorship following my second year, his wife came to my office and thanked me for making her husband aware of what a football could mean to a major university. She said her husband realized that football, conducted and played in the right way, is a major asset. I appreciated her observations, and I'm sorry the Boyds weren't around when we started to win.

Recruiting is difficult for a staff in its first year, especially when taking over a program that hasn't been winning. Recruiting is basically selling, and it's much easier to sell an established, successful program. One of the top recruits in the country in our first year at Iowa was Reggie Roby, a tremendous punter in Waterloo. We needed a punter badly, and we wanted to make a statement that we could land a top in-state recruit, so we really went after Reggie. Dan McCarney was our chief recruiter in the Waterloo area and he did a good job, but a lot of schools were after Roby and he didn't commit to anyone.

The night before the signing date, we took our whole coaching staff to Waterloo to show Roby how much we wanted him. I don't know if that was the deciding factor, but the next day he signed with us. I was never so happy to sign a punter. Getting Reggie helped us convince Iowa kids that playing for the Hawkeyes was the thing to do. And he helped give us one of the best kicking games in college football for the next four years.

Before the season started my personal life took another turn when I married Shirley Griffin, who I had met about a year earlier at a North Texas fundraiser. Shirley has two children. Her son, Bryan, is now in the computer business and has a daughter named Hayden Michelle. Her daughter Jayme is a veterinarian. Both live in Texas.

We opened the 1979 season against Indiana, a Big Ten opponent. It was the first time I had coached a game at Kinnick Stadium, and I'll never forget the fans' reaction when we came out and lined up in a spread formation. We got a standing ovation. When we completed a pass we got another one. That appreciation didn't go unnoticed to my coaches and me.

We really played well the first two quarters and led 26-3 at halftime. Dennis Mosley had run for more than 100 yards and tied the Iowa record with four touchdowns. He was making my prediction look good, and it was only halftime. When we got to the dressing room, the players were celebrating like the game was over, and I knew we were in trouble. We tried to convince them there were 30 minutes left to play, but we couldn't get that across to them. They weren't accustomed to 23-point halftime leads.

Indiana made some halftime adjustments and played much better the final two quarters. We were still leading 26-23 with less than a minute remaining when we had a breakdown in pass coverage, and the Hoosiers hit a 66-yard touchdown bomb. The final score was 30-26, and we were on the wrong end of it. It was very painful for my team, but at the same time it was a real learning experience. They found out what Yogi Berra meant when he said, "It ain't over 'til it's over."

As it turned out, that defeat kept us from getting Iowa's first winning season in 18 years. My good friend Lee Corso was Indiana's coach at the time. After the game he said, "Coach, you have a five-year contract. I needed this win more than you did!" He was joking at the time, but he was fired a few years later.

The next two weeks we had to play the two best teams in the Big Eight, Oklahoma and Nebraska. We went to Norman and played the Sooners off their feet. They had the 1978 Heisman Trophy winner in Billy Sims, but we did a good job of containing him. We were only down one point after three quarters, then Oklahoma got two late touchdowns and won 21-6. When it was over, Iowa fans were slapping our players on the back and congratulating them like they had won the game.

I was really angry, and told the players that I would bust the first guy in the mouth I saw smiling. A Chicago paper took that quote and ran with it, making me sound like I abuse my players, which I would never do. I was just trying to drive home a point that we weren't playing to look good, that we were playing to win. The days of moral victories were over at Iowa. I had to break down that kind of thinking.

The next week at home against Nebraska, we went ahead 21-7 in the third quarter and might have pulled off a huge upset had Andre Tippett not gotten hurt on the kickoff. Tending to his injury on the field caused a long delay in the game that took the wind out of our sails and the Cornhuskers rallied to win 24-21.

My first victory as the Hawkeye coach came the following week when we beat a pretty good Iowa State team, 30-14. It was meaningful for me, because it came against a worthy opponent before our fans at Kinnick Stadium. We finished the season winning four of our seven remaining Big Ten games and earned a first-division spot in the conference standings, giving us something to build on. Overall, with the talent we had, our final record of 5-6 was pretty good.

Three Hawkeyes made the all-Big Ten team: Mosley, linebacker Leven Wiess and center Jay Hilgenberg. Three members of our freshmen class played important roles. Roby had a solid season punting, kicking placements and kicking off. Two other freshmen, defensive tackle Mark Bortz and defensive back Bobby Stoops worked their way into the starting lineup, with Stoops leading the team in interceptions.

And I didn't get the limb sawed off in predicting Dennis Mosley would become Iowa's first 1,000-yard rusher. He stayed healthy, played every game and finished the season with 1,267 yards, a total that led the Big Ten. He made the old coach look like he knew what he was talking about.

In the spring of 1980, I started a marketing program, much as I had done at North Texas, trying to change the image of Hawkeye football and increase pride in the program. My aim was to get it off the ground and running smoothly, then let the University take it over. It was never my intention to realize any personal financial gain, although some of the news media suggested that was the case.

My partners were Bill Colbert, an artist, and Jim Quinn, a salesman. Colbert, who created the Tiger Hawk we have worn on our helmets since my first season at Iowa, designed the clothing and merchandise. My wife, Shirley, and son, Zach, ran the business end of the company. We called ourselves Hawkeye Marketing and everything we sold was black and gold and displayed the Tiger Hawk logo. Penney's, with 60 stores in Iowa, agreed to be our major outlet. Things really took off and the results were obvious at Hawkeye football games, basketball games and tailgate parties. Everyone was wearing black and gold clothing that displayed the Tiger Hawk.

I always wanted to put the Tiger Hawk on the big water tower across the street from Kinnick Stadium, but I never got it done. I thought it would look great on game day, in full view of 70,000 fans and all the television cameras. Most of our football games are on TV, and a big Tiger Hawk on that water tower would be wonderful exposure for Hawkeye athletics, which the logo has come to symbolize. Maybe we'll get it done someday.

The University eventually took over the marketing business, established Hawk Shops as outlets and began a licensing program. The program has generated hundreds of thousands of dollars for the Iowa athletic program through the years and employs a number of people. It is an important part of the athletic department now and taken for granted, but when we started it in 1980, some people questioned what we were doing. It's an illustration of how difficult it often is to do something new and different.

We opened the 1980 football season with a 16-7 victory at Indiana, then had some serious offensive problems and only scored 10 points in our next three games. One of the losses was to Arizona 5-3, which looked more like a baseball score than a football score. We were having trouble running the ball without Dennis Mosley and several offensive linemen who had also graduated.

We were looking for players anywhere we could find them, including the junior college ranks. Several JC players really helped us in our early years, including defensive end Andre Tippett , wide receiver Keith Chappelle, quarterback Gordy Bohannon, and offensive linemen Brett Miller and Ron Hallstrom. We actually brought in Hallstrom to play defense, then converted him to offense and he had a fine career in the NFL after leaving Iowa.

We lost four straight before we got enough offensive punch to win three of our last six. Pete Gales, considered a better running quarterback than a passer, set an Iowa record at Purdue by throwing for 321 yards. He was throwing because we couldn't run, and when that happens you generally lose, which we did. Gales' school record set in 1980 has since been bettered 16 times, which illustrates how far our offense has come since those early days.

After Purdue, we lost to Ohio State and were the underdog in the final game of the season at Michigan State. Reggie Roby kicked two first-quarter field goals to give us a 6-0 lead, and with a fourth-and-four at the Spartans' six-yard line, everyone expected us to try another one. But I was tired of kicking field goals and wanted to give my offense some confidence, so we ran J.C. Love-Jordan on a statue-of-liberty play that scored a touchdown to go up 13-0. That seemed to inspire my team and deflate the Spartans, and we went on to an unexpectedly lopsided 41-0 victory.

The decisive win at Michigan State was a real shot in the arm for our program. It gave us another first-division finish in the Big Ten and it put everyone in a positive frame of mind during the off-season. Keith Chappelle caught 64 passes for 1,037 yards in 1980, totals that are still Iowa records. He finished his career, but we had a number of good players returning and we were hopeful that 1981 might be the year we broke through and had a winning season.

Chapter Seventeen

Iowa, 1981 Big Ten Championship

I've always been amused at the old coaching axiom that it takes five years to turn around a football program. That's silly. There are too many variables from school to school, program to program, to put a time on it. For me at SMU, five years was right on the button. At my next stop, North Texas, it took three. I hadn't advertised a specific time when I arrived at Iowa, and I didn't have any in the back of my mind. You just do the best you can each year, try to make some progress, and see what happens. If you're doing the right thing, you should eventually break through.

By 1981, the facilities for football had improved some, but not greatly. The coaches had new offices, and the players had better weight training, but we still had inadequate meeting space and we had no place to practice when the weather was bad. We got a new president that year when Willard Boyd left for the Field Museum in Chicago. He was replaced by James Freedman, and I made sure Freedman was aware of the University's commitment regarding football facilities. He had come from the University of Pennsylvania, which as a member of the Ivy League never put much emphasis on football. But he realized that sports are important at a Big Ten university and said we had his support.

We had excellent practices that spring and suspected we might be pretty good in the fall if we could overcome a wicked non-conference schedule and go into the Big Ten reasonably healthy.

We had home games with Nebraska and UCLA, both preseason Top Ten teams, and went to Iowa State, which had beaten us the previous season. We had no illusion about contending for the Big Ten championship, we just wanted to win more games than we lost. It had been 19 years since Iowa had a winning season, and those kind of things begin to wear on the coaches and players, even though they're not responsible for most of the losing seasons.

Our defense and kicking game looked especially good during spring drills, and when you're strong in those two areas, you have a decent chance for a good season. We had a mix of players who were brought in by the previous coaching staff and players we had recruited out of both high school and junior college.

We had a lot of experience on defense. Seven starters were seniors who were on campus when we arrived at Iowa and had matured and worked hard at becoming better football players. They included linebackers Mel Cole and Todd Simonsen, noseguard Pat Dean, end Brad Webb and defensive backs Lou King, Tracy Crocker and Jim Frazier. End Andre Tippett, all-Big Ten in 1980, tackle Mark Bortz and safety Bobby Stoops were also important cogs in the defense and players we had brought in.

Reggie Roby, going into his junior year, had developed into one of the best punters in college football. Offensively, we had no stars at the skill positions. Pete Gales, the returning starter, and Gordy Bohannon, a JC transfer, were the quarterbacks. We spent the spring sorting out the candidates at running back and wide receiver, trying to make decisions at those positions. Our best lineman was tackle Ron Hallstrom, another JC product who had come to us as a defensive player. Our aim was to go into the season with an offense that played sound fundamental football and wouldn't beat itself. We weren't going to do anything very fancy.

Preseason predictions had Iowa as a middle-of-the-pack team in the Big Ten. That's where we had finished the past two seasons, and to the experts, that looked like where we would finish again. Pretty good defense and kicking game, but a lot of question marks on offense, they said. I couldn't disagree with that. But I did believe we would play a lot of close games and if our offense could score enough points to win most of those, we could surprise people.

Nebraska came into Kinnick Stadium with great confidence for the season opener. The Cornhuskers were ranked No. 6 in the polls and had blown us away in Lincoln the previous year. We came out in an unbalanced line, which surprised them, and by the time they figured out what we were doing we had a 10-0 lead. That was the score after three quarters and our defense wasn't about to let this one get away. Nebraska got a touchdown from Roger Craig, who we had recruited hard three years earlier. He was just down the road in Davenport, but Nebraska already had him wrapped up when we arrived. The final score was 10-7, with Lou King's pass interception in the last minute icing the victory for us. Nebraska gained only 234 yards against our defense, and Reggie Roby averaged 54 yards on five punts. Our game plan had worked perfectly.

We couldn't maintain the momentum at Iowa State the following week and lost 23-12 when our penalties kept their two touchdown drives alive. That brought UCLA to Kinnick Stadium for our last non-conference game. The Bruins were unbeaten, ranked sixth nationally and were favored to make us their third victim. But our defense turned in another superb performance, allowing only 121 yards, and got a touchdown when Mark Bortz recovered a fumble in the end zone. Pat Dean had 10 solo tackles. Our ball-control offense ran 80 plays compared to the Bruins' 48 and we won the game 20-7, my 100th career victory.

In the first three weeks of the season we had beaten two Top Ten teams and our achievements hadn't gone unnoticed. For the first time in 20 years Iowa had a nationally ranked football team. People were beginning to notice the Hawkeyes. We were No. 18 in the country and proud of it.

At Northwestern the following week, we bulldozed the home team, scoring 30 first-quarter points on our way to a 64-0 victory. Our two leading rushers were young players who would have a bigger impact in future seasons, Eddie Phillips and Owen Gill. Also, a quarterback named Chuck Long saw his first action as a Hawkeye and completed the only pass he threw. Northwestern gained a meager 71 yards against our defense. The 64-point margin is still Iowa's largest over a Big Ten opponent, but I felt badly about the lopsided score because the new Northwestern coach was Dennis Green, a former Hawkeye player. He is now the successful coach of the Minnesota Vikings in the NFL.

Our offense kept it going at home against Indiana, building a 35-14 halftime lead in a 42-28 Iowa Homecoming victory. Gordy Bohannon threw three touchdown passes, two to Mike Hufford, and Norm Granger returned a kickoff 99 yards for another score. By now we were up to No. 12 in the national polls, pretty heady stuff for a program that hadn't experienced a winning season in 19 years. Our players were feeling good about themselves and gaining confidence, which they would need for their next game.

Michigan wasn't on our schedule my first two years at Iowa, so when we went to Ann Arbor for a game October 17 it was my first time inside the 100,000-seat stadium since taking my SMU team there in 1963. The Wolverines were good then, but had become even better under Coach Bo Schembechler, who had established one of the best programs in college football. His teams had won or shared Big Ten championships four of the last five seasons. Bo and I had never coached against each other before but over the next decade our teams would play a lot of close and exciting games.

For the third time the 1981 season we were facing a team ranked No. 6 in the nation. First it had been Nebraska, then UCLA and now Michigan. Our game plan was simple and Bo probably guessed what it was. We were going to play error-free, ball-control offense, and we were going to make Michigan start each possession a long way from our goal line. Roby's punting would be a crucial, because we didn't think Michigan could sustain long drives against our defense.

Tommy Nichol, only a freshman, had become an important factor for us by that time. Twice in the first quarter we drove into Michigan territory and he kicked field goals of 20 and 36 yards. All-American Anthony Carter caught a 17-yard touchdown pass in the second period for the Wolverines, giving them a 7-6 lead at half-time. Nichol booted another field goal, this one from 30 yards, giving us a 9-7 advantage early in the third quarter, and that's the way the game ended.

Our defense did a marvelous job in limiting Michigan's potent attack to 273 yards, and our offense controlled the ball with a good mix of running and passing. A critical moment in the game came late in the third quarter when the Wolverines faced a third and goal at our 12-yard line. They threw a pass, which Mel Cole intercepted in the end zone. Tracy Crocker made sure he didn't try to run it out by tackling him. That was the only scoring chance Michigan had in the second half. Had Cole not intercepted the pass, the Wolverines probably would have kicked a field goal and gone ahead 10-9, and we might not have won the game.

We not only beat the Wolverines, we took over their No. 6 spot in the Associated Press poll. It was Iowa's highest national ranking since 1960, the first time Iowa had won at Michigan since 1958, and the first time Iowa had won without scoring a touchdown since beating Purdue with two safeties in 1939.

The following week Minnesota did to us what we did to Michigan: the Gophers won without scoring a touchdown. Jim Gallery made four field goals, the last with two minutes left, to hand us a 12-10 defeat. At Illinois the next game, we uncharacteristically turned the ball over six times—once in our own end zone to give the home team an easy touchdown—and lost the game 24-7.

We needed to inject some life in our offense, which had gone stale, scoring only one touchdown the past three games. So against Purdue we came out in a shotgun and our crowd loved it, especially when we began hitting some passes and scoring some points. Gordy Bohannon scored twice on quarterback draws out of the shotgun and Tracy Crocker recovered a Purdue fumble in the end zone for another a TD. Purdue's Scott Campbell came into the game as the nation's leading passer, but our defense smothered him and we won impressively, 33-7.

The victory insured us of Iowa's first winning season in 20 years, and ended a string of 20-straight losses to Purdue. In my early days at Iowa I told people we had to plow up some snakes and kill 'em. Beating Purdue that day killed a couple more snakes.

Wisconsin was leading the Big Ten when we played at Madison November 14 and as we bussed to Camp Randall Stadium from our motel, it was obvious Badger fans were thinking Rose Bowl. Roses were everywhere in the streets. Wisconsin fans were smelling roses and thinking of playing in Pasadena New Year's Day. With two games remaining on our schedule, we were just hopeful of getting a bowl berth some place. No one thought of the Hawkeyes as a Rose Bowl contender.

The dreams Wisconsin fans had of the Rose Bowl turned into a nightmare for them in the first half, when our defense allowed the Badgers only one first down and 29 total yards. Meanwhile Bohannon kept the Badgers off balance, hitting 10 of 13 passes for 123 yards, which set up two short touchdown runs by Phil Blatcher. Tommy Nichol added a field goal, giving us a 17-0 halftime lead, and we turned the game over to Reggie Roby and our defense, which tackled Wisconsin ball carriers behind the line of scrimmage 12 times. The final score was 17-7, with Andre Tippett, Brad Webb, Mel Cole and Lou King starring for the defense.

We found ourselves with a 7-3 record going into the final game of the season and the Liberty Bowl wanted us. They had representatives in the press box ready to offer us a bid, win or lose, as soon as our home game with Michigan State was over. We were thrilled. Not only had we broken through and had a winning season, but we were going to a bowl game! But to our great surprise, we didn't end up in the Liberty Bowl.

The scenario on the final Saturday of the Big Ten season was this: Michigan had the inside track to the Rose Bowl. The Wolverines were hosting Ohio State and were favored to win. If they did, they were Big Ten champions. Nobody expected them to blow the title and the Rose Bowl berth. They had already lost once at home —to Iowa—and Bo Schembechler never allowed his team to lose twice at home in one season.

Michigan State came into our game with a 5-5 record and a chance for a winning season, but we jumped on them with 16 points in the first quarter. Then our attention was diverted by scores coming in from Ann Arbor, where Ohio State was giving Michigan fits. A fan behind our bench had the Michigan game on the radio and was passing information along to our players, who relayed it to me. By halftime of our game we had the final score from Ann Arbor. Art Schlichter had scored on a quarterback keeper in the final minute to give Ohio State an upset over Michigan. The crowd at Kinnick Stadium roared when the final score was announced. Our fans were aware of the circumstances. If we could hold on to our 16-7 lead over the Spartans, we were going to the Rose Bowl, hard as that was to believe.

That was the basis of my whole halftime message to our players. If they beat Michigan State they would share the Big Ten championship with Ohio State. But because the Buckeyes had been to the Rose Bowl more recently than Iowa, we would be the Big Ten's representative in Pasadena. The players were excited and I emphasized to them that they had to stay calm and focus on the second half of our game, which they had to win to earn a Rose Bowl berth.

After Tracy Crocker intercepted a pass in the end zone early in the third quarter, we blew the Spartans off the field. Phil Blatcher, who started the season as our third-string running back, had the game of his career, rushing for a total of 247 yards, 180 in the second half. We had 488 yards of total offense, our best of the year. Our running game had 397 of that. Meanwhile our defense limited the Spartans to 37 rushing yards and shut them out in the final two quarters as we won convincingly, 36-7.

With all the drama that unfolded that afternoon, the fans' reaction was predictable, but still unbelievable. The capacity crowd didn't want to leave the stadium. Our players and coaches were mobbed on the field. Roses were everywhere, as if they had been dropped from an airplane. Darkness had fallen by the time we got the players to the locker room and settled them down. The aura and glow in the stadium that day provided a feeling most players and coaches seldom experience.

I remember tears running down my face as I talked to the players, trying to put their achievements in perspective. I was so happy for them. It was great to see a group of young men who had been kicked around and maligned come together and fight their way to the top. I told them to remember the moment and to cherish it, just as I would as their coach. Nobody gave us any Rose Bowl consideration when the season started. But we fooled them, and we were on our way to Pasadena.

In the next couple of weeks we settled in and began preparations for playing Washington, the Pac-10 champion and our Rose Bowl opponent. We couldn't begin practice until mid-December, but the coaches had scouting reports to assemble and the players were busy studying for final exams. All-star teams and other honors were being announced and the achievements of the Hawkeyes had not gone unnoticed.

For the first time ever, Iowa had two consensus all-Americans in the same season, Andre Tippett and Reggie Roby, who set a NCAA punting record with an average of 49.8 yards. Our defense led the Big Ten in most categories and was among the national leaders in several. Five players were named first-team all-Big Ten: Tippett, Mark Bortz, Mel Cole, Pat Dean and Lou King. Roby and Ron Halstrom were accorded the same honor, giving us a total of seven all-conference players. And thanks to the great job done by my players and coaches, I received Big Ten and national coach-of-the year awards.

By the time we began practice for the Rose Bowl winter had arrived in Iowa. It was bitter cold with some snow, and we tried to conduct workouts in the stadium, where the field was protected from the wind. We built a little room constructed of see-through plastic on the sideline and put a heater in it. Five or six players could squeeze in at the same time to warm up. It was so cold there were usually more players lined up to get into the plastic warm-up room than we had on the field. Then we borrowed some artificial turf from the University of Northern Iowa and laid it in the Fieldhouse, but space was inadequate and we continued to have poor practices.

We decided to leave early for the warm weather on the west coast—about two weeks before the game—and got into a logistical nightmare. Big Ten teams had to stay at the Huntington, a turn-of-the-century resort hotel in Pasadena. It was a grand old resort, but not a good place to house a football team. Coaches had little control over the players and the security was not good. Then we made the mistake of feeding the squad buffet style: some of the players gained weight and got fat and sluggish. Our practice facility was too far away, and we spent most of our time riding buses on the freeways. When we started attending all the events the Rose Bowl has before the game, bus rides on the freeways got even worse.

One of the best events is the dinner for champions hosted by the Big Ten Club of Southern California. For a long time, Bob Hope was the master of ceremonies and star of the show, held at the Paladium. I've known Bob since I was a student at Baylor, where we had a group known as the Nose Brotherhood. Bob came to the campus one time and we made him Brother Ski Nose. I also got a title: Brother Crotch Grabber, as in T-formation quarterback. Bob went along with the gag as only he could. Bob did charity work at SMU when I coached there and we built the Bob Hope Theater. At North Texas he helped us out again when we needed to raise money. So it was great to see him at the dinner for champions, where we had a good time visiting about the past.

The Rose Bowl is a first-class operation run by great people. The players are provided wonderful entertainment from the moment they hit town and they have a blast. It's a memorable experience. I've never heard anyone going to the Rose Bowl and not having a terrific time. But because of that, practice and preparation are difficult. It's very hard to keep the players' minds on the game, especially when, like ours, they have never experienced any bowl before.

We probably had more fun than any team that ever went to the Rose Bowl and our performance in the game showed it. We actually played pretty well for most of the first half, and we decided to go for a first down on fourth-and-short at midfield. We didn't make it, and Washington scored a touchdown just before halftime to go ahead 14-0, and that was pretty much the ball game. We weren't a good come-from-behind team, the tempo got away from us and we ran out of gas. We were beaten 28-0 by a very fine Washington team.

The best thing about the game was the number of Iowa fans, estimated at 35,000, who gave us great support until the game was over. They were obviously thrilled to see their Hawkeyes back in the Rose Bowl after a 23-year absence. The bad thing was my physical condition, which had been getting worse as the game neared. I was diagnosed with pneumonia and in awful shape. I was taking quite a bit of medication and running a fever, and couldn't even attend the final press conference the day before the game. At the game, I was too weak to stand up very long. A manager kept a towel folded so I could kneel on it.

Despite the outcome of the game, the Rose Bowl was a great experience for all of us. We learned a lot about dealing with diversions and demands on our time. A bowl game is supposed to be a reward for the players, and there is no question our guys had a wonderful time at the Rose Bowl. I know they did, because when I see them again after all of these years, they still talk about it.

The 1981 Iowa football team achieved more than anyone thought possible. It had wonderful chemistry and great senior leadership. I can't adequately explain how hard it is to make a perennial loser a big winner—to get a losing program to the top. It is extremely meaningful, and provides an unbelievable sense of accomplishment to the players and coaches. The '81 Hawkeyes laid the foundation for our program at Iowa. Now we had to build on it.

Chapter Eighteen

IOWA, 1982

After we unexpectedly shared the 1981 Big Ten championship and played in the Rose Bowl, the obvious question was, could we sustain success? It's not uncommon for a team to have one exceptional season, then fall back in the pack. What about the Hawkeyes? Were there more good years ahead for us, or were we one-year wonders?

After analyzing our personnel losses, most experts thought we had little chance to succeed in 1982. Another bowl game seemed to be out of the question. Although I thought we had the potential for a decent team, it was hard to refute that thinking. For one thing, we lost nine starters from the Big Ten's best defense, which played a huge role in our '81 success. That defense held seven opponents to a touchdown or less, and there was no way we could duplicate that. The only returning regulars were Mark Bortz and Bobby Stoops.

But our kicking game, with Reggie Roby and Tommy Nichol, was as solid as any team's in the country. Reggie was going into his senior season as the best punter in college football, and Tommy proved as a freshman he could deliver under pressure. Also, his field goal range improved considerably during spring practice.

What about the offense? I thought it would be a little better, even though six starters were missing. We had some good, young players at the skill positions, and I believed we would score more points and take some pressure off the defense. The biggest problem was the schedule. After opening at Nebraska, we had to play Iowa State and Arizona. We could be pretty decent and still not have a victory when we began Big Ten play.

Our biggest concern on offense was replacing quarterbacks Gordy Bohannon and Pete Gales, steady players who gave us good leadership. At this important position, a coach likes to have some experience, even if it's limited, but we had virtually none. We went into spring practice with Tom Grogan and Chuck Long as the leading candidates, and Long emerged the clear winner. He had tremendous scrimmages, completing 78 percent of his passes for nearly 1,000 yards.

I was so impressed with Chuck's performance in the spring I told the news media he was "destined for greatness," a quote they grabbed and ran with. They compared it to my prediction three years earlier when I said Dennis Mosley would be Iowa's first 1,000-yard rusher. I was right on that one, but was I going overboard this time? I didn't think so; it was not an offhanded remark.

But I couldn't blame anyone for doubting me. Chuck had been an option quarterback in high school and was not considered an exceptional college prospect. Northwestern and Northern Illinois were the only Division 1 schools we competed with in recruiting him. I personally approved all scholarship offers and after visiting at length with Chuck, I was extremely impressed. He had the intelligence and leadership qualities you see in great players. He had the size, the bearing and the presence found in great quarterbacks. He had never thrown the ball much in high school, but in the spring of 1982 he proved to me he could pass with great efficiency and accuracy. So I really didn't think I was going overboard or putting undue pressure on him when I said he was destined for greatness.

We went to Lincoln, where Nebraska was waiting to get even for its loss in Iowa City the previous season, and started the season with only one senior, tackle Brett Miller, in the offensive unit. The Cornhuskers threw a lot of different defenses at our new quarterback, and they had Chuck running for his life. We couldn't move the ball, and they were having their way with our defense.

We had possession of the football midway in the second quarter when, for no apparent reason, Chuck called time out. I didn't understand what he was doing, and when he came over to the sideline I jumped all over him. Then I noticed his color wasn't good and his expression was unusual, and before I could say another word, he threw up on my pants and shoes. I'd been a football

Here I am with my daughter and four sons. I'm the proud father of (from left) Zach, Robin, Randy, Adrian and Kelly.

My sister, Margaret (right) and I with our spouses, Shirley and Bob.

I'll be doing
more of this
in the
future.

When actor
Jackie Cooper
came through
Odessa he made
friends with an
impressionable
young teenager.

My first plane trip was to Miami with the Baylor football team. Coach Bob Woodruff is on the right, assistant coach Frank Broyles is crouching on the left and I'm wearing a Stetson.

Here's the young quarterback from Baylor.

Lt. Fry, USMC.

My first coaching job was at Odessa, replacing Cooper Robbins.

SMU Athletic Director Matty Bell gave his new 31-year-old football coach a firm handshake.

On my first SMU coaching staff were Pug Gabrel, Charlie Driver, Herman Morgan, Glenn Gossett, Ty Bain and Dudley Parker.

I got a ride off the field after my first victory at SMU.

I competed against Darrell
Royal, the greatest coach in
Texas history, for 11 years.

At SMU, we worked hard at
promoting the Mustangs.

Taking part in the announcement by Jerry Levias to attend SMU were his father Charlie, mother Leura, uncle Fred, Jerry and sister Charlena. Assistant coach Chuck Curtis was the primary recruiter.

Arthur Goldberg, then the Chief U.S. Representative to the United Nations, received an SMU Red Stallion Award in 1966. He later became a Supreme Court justice.

Founder of the now-popular Academic All-America teams was Lester Jordan, my assistant AD at SMU.

Captains of SMU's 1966 Southwest Conference champion-ship team were (left to right) Mac White, Pat Gibson, Jerry Griffin, Lynn Thornhill and John LaGrone.

When SMU played in the 1967 Cotton Bowl, I got together with all-time great Mustangs Kyle Rote and Doak Walker. The hand gesture we're displaying signifies SMU's Pony Ears.

I was privileged to know legendary Southwest Conference coaches (left to right) Ray Morrison, Dana X. Bible, Matty Bell, Homer Norton and Frank Bridges.

Bob Hope receives a special award for his strong support of the SMU Mustangs.

Chuck Hixon and Rufus Cormier show off the trophy SMU received for beating Oklahoma in the 1968 Bluebonnet Bowl.

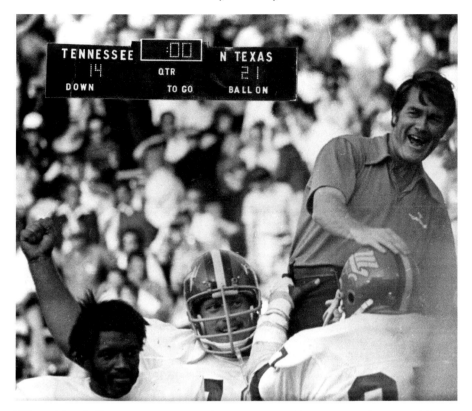

When North Texas State scored an upset at Tennessee, I got a ride off the field and Tennessee canceled the remaining game on our contract.

Texas Governor John Connelly and North Texas State booster Rex Cauble get a good laugh at my joke.

When I was introduced as Iowa's new football coach, I wore pinstripes and a serious expression.

My coaching staff at the 1982 Rose Bowl included Bill Snyder, Carl Jackson, Don Patterson, Barry Alvarez, Dan McCarney, Bernie Wyatt, Bill Brashier, Del Miller and, my eventual successor, Kirk Ferentz.

Part of the Rose Bowl fun for Hawkeyes Ron Halstrom, Mike Hufford and Paul Postler was meeting legendary jockey Bill Shoemaker.

All-America punter Reggie Roby was my first big recruit at Iowa.

Roy Carver supported the Hawkeyes with his presence and financial contributions.

After the Hawkeyes won at the Metrodome, I had fun with the Minnesota press corps by dressing like an Iowa farmer.

Before going to Kansas State and becoming the 1998 Coach of the Year, Bill Snyder was my offensive coordinator at Iowa and North Texas State.

Bill Brashier, a close friend since childhood, was my defensive coordinator for 23 years.

Dan McCarney and Barry Alvarez, on my Iowa staff through the 1980s, became head coaches at Iowa State and Wisconsin.

The Hawkeyes never lost in three appearances at the Holiday Bowl, one of my favorite post-season games.

Five of the best players I coached at Iowa were 1985 captains Hap Peterson, Chuck Long, Larry Station, Ronnie Harmon and Mike Haight. They were also the best dressed.

coach for more than 20 years and had just about seen it all, but this was a first for me.

I thought my quarterback was experiencing a severe nervous stomach, which would have been understandable. But he collected himself and said it was a combination of the heat on the artificial turf and overindulging at the pregame meal. He said he didn't want to vomit on the field so he took time out. As it turned out, his decision made me the target. After Chuck lost his meal we lost the opening game 42-7.

I decided to take some pressure off Chuck by starting Tom Grogan in our next game, Iowa State at home. But our offense struggled again; the only touchdown we scored was by Tony Wancket on a pass interception. The Cyclones got four field goals from Alex Giffords and won 19-7. That was our third straight loss to Iowa State, which fired Coach Donnie Duncan when the season ended. I used to kid Donnie about using all his ammunition against the Hawkeyes. After beating us, his teams faded. I learned from Frank Broyles that a coach should pace his team's progress. As the saying goes, you want to be a contender, not a pretender, in November when games are really important.

We had lost our first two games of the '82 season and hadn't been able to move the football. With Arizona coming up, it was time for important decisions. We moved Long back to the top of the depth chart and worked hard with him all week. We believed he was our quarterback of the future and we had to help him fulfill his potential. We had a good week of practice and were well-prepared for our night game in Tucson.

Everyone played well and we outgained the favored Wildcats by almost 200 yards. Chuck was sharp at quarterback, firing touchdown strikes to J.C. Love-Jordan and Dave Moritz. But the game was still in the balance when Tommy Nichol booted a short field goal with two minutes remaining. It allowed us to go home with a hard-earned 17-14 victory and a better feeling about the future.

I could see signs of our young offense coming around after it totaled 431 yards against a pretty strong Arizona defense. Eddie Phillips and Owen Gill gave us a good running-back tandem and Norm Granger was a very fine all-around fullback. And our defense was coming together. Also, two freshmen we had brought in that year, Larry Station and Ronnie Harmon, looked like high-impact players. Station was already seeing a lot of action at linebacker, and Harmon was working in at wide receiver.

So I wasn't too surprised when we made Northwestern a 45-7 homecoming victim. Gill ran 52 yards for a touchdown on the second play and when Long hit Moritz on a 36-yard scoring strike a few minutes later, the rout was on. Our defense held Northwestern to 54 yards rushing and sacked the quarterback seven times.

At Indiana, we ran into the red-hot passing combination of Babe Laufenberg and Duane Gunn. Laufenberg threw for 390 yards, and 156 of that total went to Gunn. The Hoosiers led 17-14 at halftime but our defense kept them out of the end zone the rest of the way. Our biggest play came in the third quarter when Long tossed a screen pass to Norm Granger, who raced 63 yards for a score. It looked like Nichol iced the game when he hit a field goal to put us up 24-20 in the fourth quarter, but our defense had to withstand two more Indiana scoring threats. Ron Hawley stopped the first by intercepting a Laufenberg pass at the two-yard line, then Devon Mitchell saved the game when he tackled Scott McNabb just short of the goal line as time expired.

We had turned our season around by winning three straight games. And two of those victories, both on the road, were decided by less than a touchdown. Those kinds of results do wonders for a team's confidence and morale. But our next test was Michigan, which was on its way to another Big Ten championship. The game was scoreless in the second quarter when we drove 80 yards, only to fumble inches from the goal line. The Wolverines, as good teams do, took advantage of that break and beat us 29-7.

Iowa hadn't beaten Minnesota in five years, so I had never seen Floyd of Rosedale, the traveling trophy that goes to the winner of this game. Hawkeye fans accounted for half the capacity crowd of 62,000 at the Metrodome, and they cheered loudly as Eddie Phillips ran for a career-high 198 yards. Our defense intercepted four passes and two—by James Erb and Nate Creer—were turned into touchdowns as Iowa won another close one on the road, 21-16.

Illinois came into Kinnick Stadium with one of the Big Ten's best teams, and we had to reach deep into my bag of exotic plays to pull this one out. We tricked the Illini with double reverses, halfback passes and a fake field goal, and everything was working. Phillips had another big game, running for 158 yards and a touchdown that was set up by his 36-yard pass to Ronnie Harmon. We nursed a one-point lead and faced a third-and-29 late in the game, when Phillips ran for 30 yards on a draw play for a critical first down. I can still see the expression on Coach Mike White's face as Eddie raced past the Illinois bench. When we finally had to punt, Nichol's pooch kick rolled dead at the Illini two-yard line to preserve a 14-13 Iowa victory.

At Purdue, uncharacteristic mistakes in the kicking game beat us. We allowed a Roby punt to be run back for a touchdown, then we fumbled a punt and a kickoff to set up two Purdue field goals. We had a sizable advantage in total yards, and we held the Boilermakers to 41 rushing yards, but we couldn't overcome our mistakes and let one get away, 16-7.

Our defense took care of Wisconsin with seven pass interceptions, a school record. James Erb swiped two; one killed a Badger scoring threat and the other set up an Iowa touchdown. Owen Gill ran for 157 yards, the best in his young career, while Chuck Long scored twice and had another fine passing day as we put ourselves in a position for a bowl bid with a 28-14 victory.

Peach Bowl representatives were standing by at Michigan State, ready to extend us an invitation if we beat the Spartans. We were coasting to victory in the fourth quarter when we threw an interception and lost a fumble that led to two quick touchdowns by the Spartans. They were threatening again when Bobby Stoops made an interception that preserved a 24-18 Iowa win.

One of the funniest things I've ever seen on a football field happened in that game. Michigan State installed light wooden goal posts—almost like balsa wood—for the final game of the season, when it was traditional for the students to tear them down after a Spartan victory (they must have expected to beat us.) Nobody mentioned it to me, so we didn't know about it. Late in the first half Ron Hawley was covering Daryl Turner on a pass that sailed out of the end zone, and Hawley ran squarely into one of the uprights. The impact knocked him flat on his back, and the goal posts started teetering.

It was like somebody hollered T-I-M-B-E-R! Everything seemed to be in slow motion as the posts wobbled back and forth for several seconds, then crashed to the ground. The crowd whooped and hollered, players doubled up laughing and they tell me the press box went up for grabs. To top it all off, Hawley and Turner exchanged high fives in the end zone. The game was stopped for several minutes while maintenance workers put the posts back together and held them up so the Spartans could try a field goal, which was successful. The whole episode is now on football videos and I still see it occasionally on TV. It was an unforgettable moment for those of us who saw it.

After a rocky start, we finished the regular season with a 7-4 record and a Peach Bowl invitation, which we accepted. Our 6-2 record in the Big Ten was good for third place, not bad for a team that had to replace 15 starters. Reggie Roby earned all-America honors again, and Mark Bortz joined him. They, along with Bobby Stoops, won first-team all-Big Ten honors. In exceeding far more than was expected of them, the '82 Hawkeyes proved that success could be sustained at Iowa.

Our Peach Bowl opponent was Tennessee, coached by my old friend Johnny Majors. The Volunteers had a good football team and were installed as a slight favorite. Our weather in Iowa was decent during December, and we got in some good practices before leaving for Atlanta.

Once there, the logistics were good. We stayed at the Marriott downtown and conducted practices at a good facility with a convenient location. The two teams got along well at all the functions we attended and Johnny and I had a good time recalling the old days and playing off one another at the microphone. At one luncheon I was especially loose and made up a story about Johnny and I being out on the town at a club that had a very unusual interior, and I asked the fellow I was dancing with if he knew the name of the place. Later Johnny pulled me aside and said, "Hayden, you just gave me a good reason to kick your butt, telling stupid stories like that." I think I stretched his sense of humor a little too far.

The Peach Bowl was well organized, and we had wonderful hosts. Ours was a man named George Crumbly, who my coaches and players began kidding, nicknaming him "Seven Minutes." Every time we asked him how long it was going to take to get from one place to another, he always replied, "About seven minutes." But George knew all the shortcuts in Atlanta, and it never took us very long to get anywhere.

I never put pressure on my teams to win bowl games, which are rewards for good seasons, but it seems to me there is more emphasis to win bowl games than there used to be, which is not good. When a coach applies pressure to win, he can easily get his players and coaching staff uptight and take away the enjoyment they're supposed to get from post-season games. I have never paid much attention to a coach's bowl record. There are some great coaches who don't have very good ones—Bo Schembechler and

Bear Bryant to name a couple—but that doesn't take away from their great achievements. It always makes me mad when someone picks on a coach's bowl record.

That doesn't mean I didn't want to win the Peach Bowl game. I believed a victory would be a great way for a young ball club to finish the year and build on the future. Tennessee was a formidable opponent, however, and I didn't want to expect too much and get my team tense going into the game, which we started slow, falling behind 7-0 after one quarter. In the next 15 minutes, however, we put on the greatest passing show in Peach Bowl history.

Chuck Long connected with Dave Moritz on a 57-yarder to start our scoring, and before the quarter ended, Chuck threw two more touchdown passes, both to Ronnie Harmon. On one, he was just trying to get rid of the ball by throwing it out of bounds, but Harmon made a spectacular leaping touchdown catch at the back of the end zone. When you're hot, you're hot, and Chuck was that, completing 14 of 17 for 231 yards by halftime, most of that in the second period.

Tennessee rallied in the second half, but we cut it off with an inspired goal line stand in the final minute to earn a well-deserved 28-22 Peach Bowl victory. James Erb led our defense with 12 tackles. Nate Creer had eight stops and blocked an extra-point attempt. Long and Moritz set Peach Bowl records for yards passing (304) and yards receiving (168). Our successful fake field goal in the third quarter was critical in deciding the outcome. It got us a first down, and we went on to score our only touchdown of the second half on a short run by Eddie Phillips.

This is one of my favorite Iowa teams because it finished with an 8-4 record when nobody thought that was possible, and it proved the Hawkeyes could put successful seasons back to back. Although very young, it developed the poise to win close games, five by a touchdown or less. It also had the good fortune to stay healthy and avoid injuries to key players.

This team sent a signal that Iowa football would have to be reckoned with in the years ahead. Many of the top players on this team would be back for another season; some had three years remaining. All statistical leaders were underclassmen; the leading tackler was Larry Station, only a freshman. The secret was out—the Hawkeyes were going to be good for awhile.

Chapter Nineteen

IOWA, 1983

There was plenty of hype about the 1983 Hawkeyes and we were ranked No. 16 in the nation on the eve of our season opener. I didn't do anything to dampen the optimism of Iowa fans. In speaking to I-Clubs around the state during the spring and summer, and I told them that barring injuries to key players, we were going to be good. We had a lot of proven talent at the skill positions—veterans like Chuck Long, Eddie Phillips, Owen Gill, Norm Granger, Dave Moritz, Ronnie Harmon and J.C. Love-Jordan. In fact, our first two offensive units had returned virtually intact.

So it was no big surprise when we went to Iowa State and hit the Cyclones with 535 yards and seven touchdowns in a 51-10 victory. Gill scored three times as we ended a three-game losing streak to the Cyclones and started a 15-game streak of our own. The biggest crowd in the history of Iowa State Stadium (54,000) turned out to see the debut of Jim Criner, who had succeeded Donnie Duncan as head coach.

I enjoy taking teams to Penn State, which has that big stadium in beautiful Happy Valley. It's a great setting for a college football game and everything about the place is first class. The Nittany Lion fans are very vocal and supportive of the home team, and they really like to get on the visitors. At least they do our players, who really got worked over before the '83 game. Our kids took exception to some of the remarks aimed at them, and gave some fiery speeches in the locker room before the game. They felt like they were being intimidated and didn't like it.

Maybe that's why they went out on the field and scored more points than any visiting team ever has at Beaver Stadium. The capacity crowd of 85,000 saw a spectacular offensive explosion that produced more than 1,000 yards and 76 points. The lead changed hands five times. We trailed in the third quarter 28-21, then scored three straight touchdowns. The first two were on short runs by Long and Granger, setting up the most exciting play of the game.

Deep in his own territory, Long threw down the sideline to Harmon, who curled back for the ball and literally pulled it away from a defender, then raced to the end zone on a play that covered 77 yards. Harmon made the spectacular play right in front of our bench, and I'll never forget it. That pretty much clinched the game, although Penn State got another touchdown to make the final score 42-34. The crowd was in an uproar the entire game until it became obvious we were going to win, then it got eerily quiet.

Not many teams beat Penn State and Ohio State back-to-back, but we did it in '83. The Hawkeyes and Buckeyes were both ranked in the Top 10 for a nationally televised game at Kinnick Stadium, and fans were clamoring for tickets to see us play our first home game of the season. Fortunately, the stadium had just been enlarged to 66,000, an addition of 6,000 seats.

Unlike the previous week at Penn State, there weren't a lot of big plays in this game, with one exception. Early in the fourth quarter, leading 13-7, we faced a third-and-six at our own 27, and did we surprise the Buckeyes on the next play! Instead of throwing a short pass trying for a first down, we went for the whole bundle. Moritz slipped behind the defense, and Long hit him in stride with a perfect pass. Moritz had average speed, but he sort of snaked his way down the field, managing to stay ahead of the Buckeyes pursuing him and scored on a 73-yard play. Ohio State got another touchdown, but we won the game, 20-14.

We were 3-0 with consecutive victories over Top 20 teams and ranked No. 3 in the nation in the coaches' poll. The team was scoring a lot of points and on its way to establishing many Iowa records, some that still stand. But some of our biggest offensive outbursts were ahead of us. Twice we scored 61 points, and once I got accused of running up the score when we scored 49.

At our homecoming against Northwestern, we went on an offensive binge that put 17 new records in the Iowa and Big Ten books. The biggest was a new conference mark of 713 total yards. Chuck Long threw for 420 yards and three touchdowns in less than three quarters, and Tom Nichol became Iowa's career scoring leader. This was during a string of games against the Wildcats when we could do nothing wrong. We'd run a simple dive play and it would go for a touchdown. The final on this one was 61-21.

Smokey Joe Salem, the Minnesota coach, told me before our final game of the season that he'd been fired and he wanted to shake my hand, because as soon as the game was over he was getting out of the stadium real quick. Eddie Phillips ran 80 yards for a touchdown on the first play and when the game was over we had three players—Phillips, Granger and Gill—with more than 100 yards rushing. Our team rushed for 517 yards, an Iowa record.

We won 61-10, and as soon as the game ended, I saw Coach Salem running toward the Minnesota locker room. He must have had a car waiting outside. I've never seen him again. Joe did a good job, but the school fired him and has since gone through four coaches. You'd think college administrators would learn that a football program is built by supporting the coach, not firing him. But they never do.

After we beat Indiana at mid-season, Sam Wyche took his Hoosiers to the middle of the field, had them kneel down and look at the scoreboard. It read Iowa 49, Indiana 3. Sam thought we'd run up the score and he told his players to remember this game when Iowa played in Bloomington the following season. Our band was waiting to come on the field for its postgame show, but Sam was mad and the band had to wait.

What led to Sam's anger was this: George Davis intercepted an Indiana pass to give us the ball deep in their territory with a minute remaining. I sent Cornelius Robertson, a third-string quarterback, into the game with a couple of simple running plays. He had aspirations to be a NFL quarterback, and when he got to the line of scrimmage I heard him check off and call a pass play. He took the snap and threw a touchdown pass to Scott Halverson. I felt terrible about the call and was mad at Robertson. In his press conference, Wyche told reporters, "That was a crummy thing to do." I agreed. I don't believe in that kind of thing, and I didn't blame Sam for being mad. But before he got a chance to get even, he left to coach in the NFL.

Accusations of running up the score are as old as college football, and because the weekly polls often reflect margins of victory, it seems to be getting worse all the time. And there are other factors. When a team gets behind by a big margin, it often crowds the line of scrimmage, because if the other team starts passing, it looks bad. Sometimes it depends on how much a coach likes (or dislikes) the guy on the other side of the field. When Joe Paterno pulled off the dogs at Indiana in 1994, it probably cost Penn State the national championship. But knowing Joe, I don't think he's sorry he did it.

I had my SMU team at Arkansas in 1968, and the Razorbacks led 35-0 at halftime. Frank Broyles, wanting to be kind to his former assistant, told his team that he would play his No. 1 unit for only one series in the second half, then go to his reserves. But we had a team that could score points in a hurry, which we did when he pulled his starters. We got momentum, and Arkansas couldn't shut us off, even when its regulars came back in the game, which ended 35-29. We very nearly wiped out the entire 35-point deficit. I got a telegram after the game from my old athletic director, Matty Bell, saying, "Congratulations! You haven't coached until you've been fired or behind by 35 points at the half." I thought it was funny then, but the firing was yet to come.

We used our '83 game at Illinois as motivation for the future. Mike White won the Big Ten championship with a great defense, which sacked Chuck Long seven times in winning 33-0. Both teams had reserves on the field late in the game, and we were threatening to score when Illinois inserted its starters to preserve the shutout. I made sure my players remembered that.

Our other regular-season loss was at Michigan. With the score tied at 13 we were moving into field goal range when Owen Gill, who had a fine game with 120 yards rushing, fumbled the ball. Michigan recovered, picked up a couple of first downs and kicked a 45-yard field goal in the final seconds to win 16-13.

Robert Smith's punt return for a touchdown was the key play in our 31-14 victory over Purdue. We won a 12-6 defensive battle at Michigan State, which blocked a punt for a touchdown in the fourth quarter to give us some anxious moments. Mike Hooks had 13 tackles and was named the Big Ten's defensive player of the week.

Our game at Wisconsin in November matched two teams battling for bowl berths, but we jumped on the Badgers early and had a surprising 27-0 lead at the half. Chuck Long threw four touchdown passes, broke six school records and hit 13 of 15 first-half passes. Eddie Phillips ran for 162 yards. Eight bowls had representatives in the press box, and they were all anxious to visit our dressing room after we won 34-14.

With a 9-2 record and ranked 10th in both wire service polls, we accepted an invitation to play Florida in the Gator Bowl. We had a disadvantage right off the bat, because Florida played one or two games in the stadium at Jacksonville every season. The Gators would have far more fans that we would at the game, and they would be playing on a familiar field. But when northern teams play at bowl games in the south and west they often run into those disadvantages. They have to accept them and do the best they can. We had a good team and our kids were anxious to play an outstanding opponent like Florida.

As it had been two years earlier, the weather in Iowa was bad that December, making practice difficult. So we went to Jacksonville early, where the weather was cold and rainy. We moved further south near Daytona, but ran into rain there, too. We had an awful time. But the weather remained consistent—it was just as bad, probably even worse, the night of the game. The temperature was at the freezing mark and at sea level, the cold air was damp and penetrating. There were 20,000 Iowa fans at the game that night, and I think every one of them has told me they've never been as cold. We had one heater on our sideline, while Florida had its whole sideline heated.

I don't know if it was because of the weather, but two explosive offensive teams wound up in a defensive struggle. Neither team's offense cracked 300 yards. Florida scored a touchdown in the first quarter and got another one when Tommy Nichol, back to punt, dropped the snap and the Gators recovered in the end zone just before halftime. Nichol kicked two field goals for us, making the final score 14-6, much lower than expected. Florida was then under NCAA investigation, and was later hit with some major penalties. About 10 players on that team went on to play in the NFL, including Wilbur Marshall, a tremendous linebacker.

But a loss at the Gator Bowl didn't diminish the accomplishments of a great season. We finished 14th in the nation and third in the Big Ten. Our nine wins equaled a school record. The '83 Hawkeyes broke 35 school records, tied four others and established a lot of new Big Ten standards, including total offense for a season and a game. The numbers put up by this team are still sprinkled all over the Iowa record book.

Larry Station earned all-America honors as a sophomore and Chuck Long was named the all-Big Ten quarterback. Four other Hawkeyes also won all-conference honors: John Alt, Paul Hufford, Dave Moritz and Mike Stoops. We had a lot of good players returning for the '84 season, and there was no question we would have another fine team. Everyone was feeling good about the Hawkeyes.

So was I, but we had just experienced another poor preparation for a bowl game and it was obvious we going to be regulars on the bowl scene for awhile. The University had made a commitment to me when I took the job five years earlier and had not kept its promise. I decided it was time to take action, which meant I'd have to stir things up and make some people mad.

Chapter Twenty

IOWA, 1984

When I was offered the Iowa job following the 1978 season, I gathered information and sought advice. One person I called was Forest Evashevski, the only coach who had any success at Iowa since World War II. He had a run of great teams in the 1950s, winning three Big Ten championships. I asked for his input.

Evy had some specific recommendations, including an indoor practice facility. He said it was needed because five or six teams from the Big Ten were invited to bowl games every year, and also because of the uncertain weather in Iowa during spring practice and late in the regular season. He said an indoor facility was necessary to keep up with the competition, because they were popping up around the Big Ten and elsewhere.

When I gave Iowa a list of requirements—things it would take for me to accept the job—an indoor facility was one of them. I got the commitment, but President Willard Boyd stayed at Iowa less than two more years, and his successor, James Freedman, was either unaware of the promise or ignored it. Money had been quietly raised for the facility, but every time I suggested we start construction, I was told the timing wasn't right because of tight funding from the legislature. It wouldn't look right to build a football facility when the Regents were rejecting other construction on campus, I was told. There was always a reason to put me off.

Shortly after the Gator Bowl, in which our preparation had been hindered by bad weather, I told the press that if the University didn't honor its commitment for an indoor facility, I was going to start listening to offers and feelers I was getting from other schools. I explained that money for the facility was already in the bank. Going public with my grievance was something I did with great deliberation and careful consideration, because I realized it would cause a stir and the administration wouldn't like it. But it was the only way I knew to get construction moving, and I meant what I said about listening to offers.

I mobilized some University supporters, who put pressure on the president. I didn't enjoy it, but I publicly crossed swords with him. Our fans rallied behind our efforts and it didn't take long for public pressure to get the facility approved. Construction was started late that year, and midway through the '85 season we were practicing indoors. Now that we have what we call "the bubble" it's hard to imagine how we got along without it. It's also been a boon to sports such as baseball, softball, field hockey and soccer. The marching band sometimes uses it. We found out how important it is to our football program when storms twice knocked it down and we had to go without it for awhile.

We started preparations for the 1984 season with knowledge that we would soon have an indoor facility, which wouldn't help us that season but gave us comfort for the future. We also got good news when the Big Ten approved a retroactive redshirt rule, and one of the players it covered was Chuck Long. He had two more seasons of competition if he chose to take them, but there was a possibility he might put his name in the next NFL draft, where he would undoubtedly be a high pick, following the '84 season. We'd have to wait and see how that played out.

We returned 20 of our top 22 defensive players including Larry Station, Paul Hufford and Mike Stoops, making us believe that this unit would be almost as good as our great defense of 1981. But graduation had wiped out our offensive line, and although we had some tremendous players such as Long, Owen Gill and Ronnie Harmon at the skill positions, we didn't expect to ring up the big numbers of the previous season. Our kicking game looked good, with Tommy Nichol back for his senior year. Our preseason ranking was No. 12.

In the opener at Iowa State, our defense forced eight turnovers, including an interception for a touchdown by Dave Strobel in a 59-21 victory. We had a lot of big plays. Long threw scoring passes of 63 yards to Robert Smith and 68 to Harmon, who had a 86-yard run for another TD. It was a good way to start the season, but we had two of our toughest games of the year immediately ahead.

We knocked off Penn State and Ohio State back-to-back in '83 and they both got even. We got a terrible pass interference call against Penn State that cost us the game. The call should have been made in our favor, not Penn State's. It was made by a substitute official who happened to be from Iowa, and I think he was determined not to be a homer. We pled our case to the other officials to no avail. Penn State subsequently scored a late touchdown, and we lost 20-17.

The only recourse a coach has in those situations is to send a complaint and videotape to the Big Ten supervisor of officials, who reviews it. But it doesn't change the call and it doesn't change the score. In this case, the supervisor confirmed that the official made a mistake, but we still lost. I don't think the official ever worked another Big Ten game.

At Ohio State, our own turnovers and penalties hurt us. So did Heisman Trophy candidate Keith Byars, who not only ran for two touchdowns but also threw a pass for one and had a reception for another. After the 45-26 loss, we had a 1-2 record and dropped out of the polls. We had work to do.

Illinois, the defending Big Ten champion with another strong team, had reason to think it could beat us before a record crowd at Kinnick Stadium. But we put Ronnie Harmon and Owen Gill in the same backfield and they combined for 306 yards rushing. Harmon scored all three of our touchdowns in a very important 21-16 victory, while linebackers Larry Station and Kevin Spitzig led the defense with 23 tackles.

Our defense really came together and didn't allow a touchdown in the next three games. Northwestern managed only 49 total yards while Harmon sparked us with his third straight 100-yard rushing effort in a 31-3 victory.

At Purdue, Robert Smith tied a school record with three touchdown catches on plays that covered 51, 31 and 38 yards and had one called back that went 72 yards. Long threw them all, and had another that went 56 yards to Scott Helverson. The 40-3 victory was Iowa's first at Purdue in 28 years.

Leon Burtnett, the Boilermakers coach, had invited John Ralston to give motivational speeches to his team prior to our game. Ralston had coached at Stanford and Denver in the NFL and was an old friend. I'd given him my fake punt play called the Bumerooski before he took Stanford to the Rose Bowl one year. He was on the Purdue sideline during the game, and I caught up with him afterwards and jokingly told him to be sure and come back and motivate the Boilermakers again next year. He has a good sense of humor, and we both laughed.

Back home, we handed Michigan a rare shutout, limiting the Wolverines to 187 total yards. Devon Mitchell intercepted two passes and returned one of them 75 yards. Our offense scored in every quarter in the 26-0 win. This was one of the few times Bo Schembechler and I faced each other that the game didn't go down to the wire.

Long set a NCAA record by completing 22 consecutive passes in a 24-20 win at Indiana, and for the second straight game, Mitchell made a late-game interception to preserve an Iowa victory. We had overcome consecutive early-season losses and entered November with a 5-1 Big Ten record. With three conference games remaining, two at home, we would win the league title and go to the Rose Bowl by winning them all. We controlled our destiny.

What happened to the Hawkeyes in November of 1984 is a perfect illustration of how injuries, especially those to key players, influence what happens to a football team. Playing Wisconsin at home, Ronnie Harmon broke his leg and Chuck Long injured his knee on consecutive plays, taking the guts right out of our offense. Our defense was brilliant, holding the Badgers without a first down on 11 straight possessions, but we couldn't muster enough offense to win and had to settle for a 10-10 tie.

The following week, again at home, our defense held Michigan State to less than 200 yards and we had a 13-minute advantage in possession time. But the Spartans got a touchdown by driving 35 yards after a poor Iowa punt, then scored again by blocking a punt. With a bad knee, Long entered the game and rallied his team to two fourth quarter touchdowns. After the second, with less than a minute left, we went for two points and got a bad call by the officials. TV replays showed Long getting the ball over the goal line, but the refs didn't see it that way and we lost a heartbreaker 17-16. An officiating mistake cost us our second game of the season.

We went to Minnesota no longer thinking Rose Bowl. We were just trying to salvage a successful season. The Gophers were 3-7, so this was their bowl game under new coach Lou Holtz. For the second week in a row, we had a big advantage in yardage and possession time, but one mistake killed us. Our injury list was getting longer and included speedy Robert Smith. Bill Happel filled in for him to return punts, and ran one back 95 yards for a touchdown. But late in the game, with Iowa leading 17-13, he mishandled a punt, and the Gophers recovered to score a cheap touchdown. They added a field goal to make the final score 23-17.

We had a tie and two losses in November when a 3-0 record with a healthier team was a possibility, if not a probability. But we didn't have time to sit around and dwell on our misfortune and feel sorry for ourselves. We had a 12th game coming up at Hawaii, which had a seven-game winning streak and was tough to beat in Honolulu. The Hawaii game had taken on new significance, because the last thing we wanted to do was go to a bowl game with three straight losses. We had accepted an invitation to the Freedom Bowl, a new post-season game in Anaheim.

We flew to Honolulu a couple of days early to let the players overcome jet lag before they had to play the game and to let them take in some of the sights and scenery. One of the reasons you schedule a game in Hawaii is to give the players an opportunity to visit a part of the world they've never seen. It was the first trip to the islands for almost everyone on our squad.

We were still pretty banged up for the game, which developed into a defensive battle. After three quarters, three field goals had been scored, only one by us. We were really hurting at running back. Not only was Harmon out for the year with a broken leg, but Owen Gill was also nursing an injury. Our running game wasn't getting much done until we inserted Rick Bayless, a walk-on who had played very little all year. He picked us up with some strong running in the fourth quarter, when we scored two touchdowns to pull out a satisfying 17-6 win.

We had a few weeks to get ourselves together and improve the health of the football team before meeting Texas in the inaugural Freedom Bowl. This game had an interesting angle. It was the first time the Hawkeyes had played a school from Texas since my coaching staff, mostly from Texas, arrived at Iowa. The coaches had a special reason for wanting to win the game, and the players were aware of it.

The executive director of the Freedom Bowl, Tom Starr, was delighted to get two high-profile teams for the bowl's first game. Tom is an Iowa native and a graduate of the University of Iowa, so it was old home week for him. We had reasonably good weather for our preparations, but the night of the game was awful, with a lot of rain.

Despite the bad weather, another big contingent of Iowa fans was in Anaheim Stadium, but for some reason our kids were uptight during pregame warmups. So when we got back to the locker room I told 'em some stories about Texans that are a little off-color. That must have loosened 'em up, because neither the rain nor the Longhorns' man-to-man pass coverage could slow us down. Chuck Long had a career night, hitting 29 of 39 passes for 461 yards and six touchdowns, all Iowa records. Two of his TD throws went to Jonathon Hayes.

Texas had a team good enough to contend for a Cotton Bowl berth that season but ran into a buzz saw against us as we released the frustrations caused by November disappointments. Coach Fred Akers told me after the game that he couldn't believe we were able to pass so successfully in the rain. We kept passing because Texas never made adjustments to slow us down, and we set a scoring record for all bowls in winning 55-17.

We overcame the November setbacks to win at least eight games for the fourth straight season and a No. 15 national ranking. It was a bittersweet ending, because I believe this team would have won the Big Ten championship had it not been for all the late-season injuries. We had the momentum and the confidence and a schedule that was in our favor. But it wasn't to be, and we had to point to the future.

Our personnel losses included Owen Gill, who set a new school career rushing record, and three members of the defense who were first-team all-Big Ten: tackles Paul Hufford and George Little and strong safety Mike Stoops. But a lot of good players were returning, especially on offense. The biggest question mark about 1985 was whether Chuck Long would be quarterbacking the Hawkeyes or a team in the NFL. He had a big decision to make, and Iowa fans were anxiously awaiting the answer.

Chapter Twenty-one

IOWA, 1985
BIG TEN CHAMPIONSHIP

It has unfortunately become commonplace for a college athlete to turn professional before completing his eligibility and earning a diploma. I say unfortunately, because in many cases, it would be wise for the athlete to stay in school, enjoy his college days and get a degree to serve him well the rest of his life. But the lure of money is so great that some athletes jump to the pros after only a year or two of college, often with disastrous results.

Each individual is different, of course. If he comes from an impoverished background, or even a modest one, the potential financial rewards for signing a professional contract must seem overwhelming. But if a youngster comes from a good economic background and is interested in completing a degree, he should finish college. If an athlete is good enough to make it in the pros as a sophomore or junior, his stock will be even higher after his senior year, but it's hard to convince 19 and 20 year olds of that.

Major League Baseball has the most intelligent rules about drafting players. If a baseball player doesn't sign a professional contract right out of high school, he can't turn pro until his 21st birthday or after his junior year of college. College football and basketball coaches have tried to get the NFL and NBA to adopt the same policy, but we're told that would violate antitrust laws. I don't understand that response. If baseball does it legally, why would football and basketball be breaking the law?

Many professional agents are a blight on the college sports scene. They will tell a kid anything to make money off his talents. There are some good agents who do what is right for the youngster, but others are parasites who will stoop to anything. They offer money and other inducements that are NCAA violations, and try to work through girlfriends or others close to the athletes. At Iowa, we strongly advise our players to thoroughly investigate an agent before signing an agreement with him.

In January of 1985, Chuck Long was making an important decision about his future. He could play another season for the Hawkeyes, or he could enter his name in the NFL draft, where he would be taken high in the first round, which would guarantee a big contract. I spent a lot of time talking to Chuck and his parents about this important decision. He was a three-year starter who had developed into a great quarterback, and we naturally wanted him back for another season, but I never try to talk a player out of turning professional. I just try my best to provide counsel and give him honest opinions.

When Chuck announced at a press conference that he had decided to remain at Iowa one more season, I joked that it was the greatest recruiting job I ever did. But in the end the decision was his, and I think he made it for the best of reasons: he was having fun and wanted to be a college student one more year. The fact that we expected to have a strong football team undoubtedly played a role in his thinking, but mainly he just wanted to stay in college awhile longer before embarking on a professional career. I wish more young men would follow his example.

Ironically, at the same time Chuck decided to delay his professional career, another Hawkeye, tight end Jonathon Hayes, announced he was leaving school a year early. But he had a valid reason. He was concerned his diabetic condition would curtail his football career and he wanted to play in the NFL for a few years. He was drafted by Kansas City, stayed healthy and remained a professional for about 10 years. Jon is the only player I've ever had who went pro before his eligibility was completed. Some coaches seem to lose a player or two almost every year.

When word circulated about Chuck Long's decision to stay at Iowa another year, expectations for the 1985 Hawkeyes, already high, zoomed even higher. Chuck was considered a strong candidate for the Heisman Trophy. He already owned 16 school records and had twice been named all-Big Ten. As I remind the press every year, teams that go into a season with a veteran quarterback have a big advantage, and we had the best returning quarterback in college football.

We also had two other seniors who were stars in their own right. Larry Station was a 1984 consensus all-America linebacker who had led our defense in tackles three straight seasons. He was also an exceptional student and an academic all-American. Ronnie Harmon had recovered from a broken leg and I didn't hesitate in calling him the best all-around running back in college football. Ronnie had done us a favor his first two seasons by playing wide receiver when we needed help at that position. He was a double threat to either run or catch the ball.

We expected to have an explosive offense and a pretty good defense, even though we had significant personnel losses in that area. But we'd led the Big Ten in total defense three of the last four years, and it was assumed Coach Bill Brashier would develop another solid unit. Our steady kicker, Tommy Nichol, had graduated, but a walkon named Rob Houghtlin had been impressive during the spring.

By the time the '85 season opened, the Football Writers had us ranked No. 3 in the nation and the Associated Press had us No. 4. We made the experts look good when we scored 163 points in our first three games in beating three overmatched opponents—Drake 58-0, Northern Illinois 48-20, and Iowa State 57-3. Long, who had taken a policy with Lloyd's of London to insure against injury, threw 10 touchdown passes to seven different receivers as our offense averaged 500 yards in the three non-conference wins.

Those three lopsided victories vaulted us all the way to the top of the wire service polls, the first time Iowa had been ranked No. 1 in 25 years. Our Big Ten opener was against Michigan State at home, and we were still mad about not being credited with the two-point conversion that would have beaten the Spartans a year earlier. Long threw 60 yards to Robert Smith and 17 to Mike Flagg to put us up 14-0. But the Spartans, behind their great running back Lorenzo White, scored 24 straight points.

Before the third period ended, Long again found Smith and Flagg on scoring strikes and we led 28-24, setting up one of the great finishes in the long history of Kinnick Stadium. Michigan State ground out 89 yards for a touchdown to go ahead 31-28 with three minutes remaining. After receiving the kickoff, we found ourselves 78 yards from the Michigan State goal line and we needed a touchdown to win. Long completed pass after critical pass until we reached the Spartan one-yard line with less than a minute remaining.

On fourth down, we called a play named "Fake 47 sucker pass" in which Long faked a handoff to Harmon, then bootlegged right with the option to run or pass. Flagg, at tight end, faked a block, then released into the end zone to catch the ball. But because the Michigan State cornerback came down so hard on the fake to Harmon, there was no defender between Long and the goal line. All he had to do was stroll into the end zone.

Chuck was still at the five-yard line when he held the ball high over his head celebrating the winning touchdown he was about to score. Or maybe he just wanted to make sure the officials didn't miss the call like they did a year earlier. The stadium exploded when everyone realized that Long, not Harmon, had the ball. Ronnie made a tremendous fake on the play, so good it badly fooled the defense. The clock showed 27 seconds remaining when Rob Houghtlin's extra point made the final score 35-31.

In an important, pressure-packed game that we had to win to stay No. 1, Long gave the capacity crowd and a national television audience a spectacular performance. He completed 30 of 39 passes for 380 yards for four touchdowns and scored the winning TD himself. His stock in the race for Heisman had risen considerably.

Before a capacity crowd at Camp Randall Stadium in Madison, Wisconsin tried its best to knock us off the top of the polls, but Houghtlin kicked three field goals to provide a 10-point cushion in a 23-13 Iowa victory. We didn't know it at the time, but he was just warming up for the following week.

Michigan was our mid-season opponent at home in a game that lived up to all the hype it received. It was a classic. Both teams were 5-0 and ranked 1-2 in the polls. Iowa's potent offense was matched against Michigan's great defense, which hadn't allowed a touchdown in its previous four games. Portable lights were brought in for the first night game at Kinnick Stadium. Even the nearby World Series between St. Louis and Kansas City couldn't detract from the buildup. A national television audience was anxious to see this one.

I had to dust off all my Texas jokes to keep our players loose for this game, and when kickoff arrived they were ready to play. We were able to move the ball against Michigan's defense, but we weren't scoring any touchdowns. At least none that counted. Long completed a pass to Scott Helverson in the end zone, but an official ruled he was out of bounds. TV replays revealed it should have been ruled a touchdown.

Michigan led 7-6 at the half, and we were still down 10-9 late in the game when the Wolverines faced a third and one at midfield. If we couldn't force a punt, we would probably lose the game. Michigan gave the ball to its fine tailback, Jamie Morris, and Larry Station made the defensive play of the game, slicing through to slam Morris for a two-yard loss. Station made the play on his own; it wasn't a stunt. He just anticipated what they were going to do and stopped it.

After fielding Michigan's punt, we were 82 yards from the goal line and had one last chance to win the game. Long did a masterful job of using his passing game to conserve time. It took 16 plays to reach the Michigan 12-yard line where, with two seconds on the clock, we called timeout. Houghtlin had already kicked three field goals for all of our scoring. Now we were going to ask him to kick one more.

I joked around on the sideline trying to keep him loose, but I really didn't need to. Rob wasn't tense, he was amazingly calm. When our field goal unit lined up on the field, Michigan called timeout. Rob came over to the sideline laughing and said, "Can you believe it, Coach? They're trying to ice me, but it's not gonna work."

Our field goal unit lined up for a second time, and again Michigan called timeout. This time Rob came to the sideline with a serious look on his face, which bothered me. I thought perhaps the stress was getting to him, but I was wrong. He said, "You know, Coach, my grandfather died not long ago, and I'm going to kick this one for him." Then he walked back on the field and kicked the game-winning field goal as time expired. The scoreboard glowed against the night sky: Iowa 12, Michigan 10.

This game, with its dramatic ending, stands out as No. 1 in my coaching career. It had a huge pregame buildup, and the result had a great impact in the national polls, the Big Ten race, and the Rose Bowl picture. It was one of the few times the game exceeded the hype. The victory was special because it came against a traditional power like Michigan and its great coach, Bo Schembechler. It was the third time in five years that a late field goal determined the outcome of our game.

It would have been extremely difficult for us to accept a loss, because we really dominated the game. We had a huge advantage in total yards (422-182), first downs (26-9) and possession minutes (38-22). Those statistics make it look like we won by a couple of touchdowns. But in this game the stats were misleading, because Michigan managed to keep us out of the end zone and we had to kick a field goal on the final play to win.

When Houghtlin's field goal split the uprights, our fans spilled our of the stands to celebrate. Security estimated that 30,000 were on the field, and it was a little scary because nobody could move. Our own players celebrated by jumping on Houghtlin and his holder, Mark Vlasic, and seven were hurt in the pileup. Vlasic, the No. 2 quarterback, suffered the worst injury and missed a couple of games. Some fans were hurt tearing down the goal posts. Now we have collapsible posts to prevent that.

After Chuck Long tied his own school record by throwing six touchdown passes in a 49-10 win at Northwestern, we were No. 1 in the nation for the fifth straight week, and we went to Ohio State with new decals on our helmets. The decals displayed the letters ANF, which stood for America Needs Farmers. Our country was in the middle of a farm crisis, and Iowa is a great agricultural state. I thought the Iowa football team should do something to call attention to the farmers' economic problems. Our marketing director, Jim White, came up with idea for the ANF decals. The Farm Bureau gave me an honorary membership, which rattled some of my friends at the agricultural school in Ames. We wore the decals for several seasons, and because we played so many games on television, they drew the attention of fans all over the country.

We also wore something else at Ohio State: a big bull's-eye on our back. It was no surprise that we met a fired up bunch of Buckeyes, but a crowd of 90,000 and a driving rain gave us even bigger problems. The crowd noise made it impossible for Long to call an audible, which was a big part of our offense, and the referee wouldn't enforce the crowd noise rule. Coach Earl Bruce had been telling Ohio State fans all week to make more noise, as if there isn't enough already in the big horseshoe stadium. Another problem was the driving rain, which hurt our passing game. It all added up to a 22-13 defeat, which dropped us to No. 6 in the polls.

We went home and played Illinois, which was also in the Rose Bowl hunt. The Fighting Illini, with another strong defense, were coming off a 3-3 tie with Michigan. Bobby Stoops, a former player who was then a graduate assistant, had broken down a lot of Illinois film to study tendencies. When he saw them line up in a formation early in the game he hollered, "Reverse! Reverse!" over the press box phones. I heard him and yelled the same thing to our defense. Sure enough, Illinois ran a reverse and we threw David Williams, a speedy wide receiver, for a big loss. He fumbled, Hap Peterson recovered, and David Hudson scored a quick Iowa touchdown.

That ignited our offense, which exploded for five touchdowns in the first 15 minutes! It's hard to get the football five times in one quarter; to score on every possession against a very good defense is almost unbelievable. By the time the half ended Long had thrown four touchdown passes, Hudson had scored again and Ronnie Harmon ran 49 yards for another TD. We had a 49-0 lead and Illinois hadn't crossed the 50-yard line.

The final score was 59-0, and as I look back on that game, I'm not sure how we did it. I mean, Illinois had an excellent defense that had just held Michigan without a touchdown. Coach Mike White did a good job of rebuilding his team's confidence and saving the season after that loss. Illinois went on to finish third in the Big Ten and win the Peach Bowl. It just shows what can happen in college football from game to game, week to week. Sometimes things are impossible to explain, and our 59-point victory over Illinois in 1985 is one of them.

The two best quarterbacks in the Big Ten—Chuck Long and Jim Everett—went head to head in our game at Purdue. Both had big days, each throwing for more than 250 yards, but a kicker again decided the outcome. The score was tied at 24-24 when Long engineered a drive that stalled at the Purdue eight-yard line. With a 1:07 remaining in the game, Houghtlin kicked a field goal that pulled out a 27-24 Iowa victory.

The first time I saw Rob Houghtlin was early that spring when he was working out with some walkon kickers in Kinnick Stadium. I was observing from up in the stands, and he stood out from the rest. He really grabbed my attention. He had great concentration and was very sound in his mechanics. I told one of our coaches I'd like to talk to him, and I really liked his personality. He was obviously intelligent and quietly confident without being cocky. I recall telling our coaches that we had a kicker with the qualities of Chuck Long. My first impression of Rob was accurate. In less than a full season and he had already made two game-winning pressure-packed field goals.

Going into the final weekend of the regular season, the Rose Bowl berth was still in the balance. Michigan and Illinois were both in the picture, but we had the inside track. A victory over Minnesota at home would give us an outright Big Ten championship and the trip to Pasadena that goes with it.

There was no dramatic ending in this game. Our players did a workmanlike job putting away a good Gopher team, building a 17-3 halftime lead and winning 31-9. Four different players scored our touchdowns and our defense was solid. It was a team victory all the way.

The 1985 Hawkeyes did something that is very difficult in sports: they lived up to great expectations. They were favored to win the Big Ten and they did. They were ranked No. 3 going into the season and No. 2 afterwards. The players who were expected to perform at a high level did so. It's one thing to slip up on people as we did in 1981. It's also a great accomplishment when you start with a bull's-eye on your back and still win the race.

Individual honors began rolling in, and Chuck Long and Larry Station were named consensus all-Americans, Station for the second time. He also had the distinction of leading us in tackles for the fourth straight season and was again named academic all-America. Ronnie Harmon made several all-America teams and became the only player to ever lead the Hawkeyes in both rushing and receiving.

Long was showered with recognition. He became the first Hawkeye in 27 years to be named the Big Ten's Most Valuable Player. At Philadelphia, he was presented the Maxwell Trophy, which goes to the nation's top athlete. At Ft. Worth, he was given the Davey O'Brien Award, which goes to college football's best quarterback. The O'Brien award is named for TCU's great quarterback, and it was especially meaningful to me, because I knew him when I was coaching in the Southwest Conference and he was with the FBI.

Perhaps Chuck's greatest achievement is noted in the Big Ten Record Book. He is the only player in the 105-year history of the conference who has ever passed for 10,000 career yards. Considering all the great quarterbacks who have played in the Big Ten during that time, Chuck has reason to be enormously proud of that record.

The all-Big Ten team included eight Hawkeyes, the most ever honored. Defensive tackle Jeff Drost, offensive tackle Mike Haight, strong safety Jay Norvell and noseguard Hap Peterson made the team in addition to Long, Station, Harmon and Houghtlin. A coach likes to see his players rewarded for their performance, and they were all very deserving of the recognition.

The Heisman Trophy is the last individual award announced and Chuck Long was one of the leading candidates to win in 1985. Surveys by the news media indicated that Chuck and running back Bo Jackson of Auburn were getting the most support from voters around the country. Those two, along with running back Lorenzo White of Michigan State, were the three finalists invited to New York for the announcement in mid-December. Hawkeye fans everywhere were pulling for Chuck, hoping he would win the same prestigious trophy Nile Kinnick had in 1939.

About 200 people gathered at the New York Athletic Club, which sponsors the award, for the announcement to be aired by NBC-TV. The chairman of the Heisman committee that year was an Iowa graduate who had been to a couple of our games that season and was privately hoping Chuck would win. When the time came for him to go to the microphone to make the announcement, he made it a point not to look my way, and I knew before he opened the envelope that Chuck was not the winner. Bo Jackson won the closest Heisman vote in history.

Football teaches us to deal with disappointments, and Chuck's not winning was a major disappointment to Hawkeye players, coaches and fans. I think Chuck would have won if he hadn't had such strong competition within his own league. Lorenzo White and quarterback Jim Everett of Purdue both got support from midwest voters while Jackson had the south to himself. I felt Chuck's performance made him worthy of winning football's top individual award, but Jackson was a great football player and nobody could quarrel with his selection. Ironically, when I coached in the Japan Bowl a month later, two of my players were Long and Jackson, along with three other Hawkeyes: Station, Harmon and Happel.

We turned our attention to UCLA, our Rose Bowl opponent, and we had an indoor facility in which to practice. The Bubble, as we call it, contains a full-size football field with an artificial surface and a high enough ceiling to conduct a full-scale scrimmage. It's functional but not frivolous. After preparing for our last four bowl games outdoors, we fully appreciated our new indoor facility.

When we got to Los Angeles, both our practice facility and hotel were an improvement over 1981. Our preparations were good and our players were focused, and I felt good going into the game.

But first-half fumbles just killed us, and every time I looked at the scoreboard, we were down one or two touchdowns.

UCLA got 300 yards out of its running game, and we later found out why. They detected from looking at our films that one of our linemen put his left hand down when he was going to slant left, and his right hand down when he was going to slant right. They based their game plan on that discovery. Their running backs cut back against our pursuit with great success.

Our offense moved the ball well enough. Long set some Rose Bowl passing records, hitting 29 of 37 for 319 yards, and Harmon some receiving records with 11 catches for 102 yards. But we got behind early and never could catch up. We gave up far too many yards and points and lost the game 45-28.

Harmon took a lot of heat because he lost four fumbles, all in the first half. That was uncharacteristic of him; I think he fumbled once during the regular season. The game film reveals that every fumble he lost was caused by a UCLA defender making a hard hit. They just knocked the ball loose. They did a great job of tackling. UCLA made bad things happen to Iowa; Iowa didn't self-destruct. Ronnie Harmon had a tremendous football career with the Hawkeyes, and I hated to see it end that way. He enjoyed a long, successful career in the NFL, and I always enjoy seeing him when he comes by to visit.

The 1985 Iowa football team is one of the best in school history. It is certainly the best team in my 20 years as head coach. It won a school record 10 games and set 44 Iowa records and seven Big Ten records. It was a team with a lot of pride and heart, as well as a lot of talent. It was also a team with a lot of seniors, leaving us with a lot of holes to fill in the coming season.

Chapter Twenty-two

IOWA, 1986

The era of Chuck Long, Larry Station and Ronnie Harmon was unprecedented at Iowa. It produced 35 victories, four bowl appearances and a Big Ten championship. It was a period when the Hawkeyes became regulars in the national polls, rising as high as No. 1 and finishing in the Top 10. But the era was over, and it was time to move on. There is a certain amount of rebuilding every year in college football. In 1986, we had some major construction work to do at Iowa.

We had 11 starters to replace, and the experts weren't sure what to make of us. Previews of the Hawkeyes were mixed. The coaches' poll had us 18th going into the season, but we were unranked by the writers. In the Big Ten, we were viewed as a middle-of the pack team. With the loss of so many stars—players who had been fixtures at their positions—it was hard to get high on the Hawkeyes.

Long had been a four-year starter at quarterback and four candidates were competing to replace him. Mark Vlasic, who had been patiently waiting in the wings for three years, won the job of leading an untested offense into the season opener. We only had five returning offensive starters and had been pretty much wiped out at the skill positions. The new quarterback wasn't surrounded by a lot of veterans.

The non-conference schedule wasn't too demanding, however, giving our offense some time to grow. But we surprised even ourselves in rolling up big scores against Iowa State (43-7), Northern Illinois (57-3) and Texas-El Paso (69-7). With so many new players, both our running game and passing game were functioning surprisingly well. We threw for more than 300 yards against Iowa State and ran for well over 300 against the other two opponents. The Northern Illinois coach was Jerry Pettibone, who had been my freshman coach at SMU. Our defense knocked his top two wishbone quarterbacks out of the game, and I felt sorry about that.

We owned three lopsided victories going into the Big Ten opener at Michigan State, but we weren't sure how good we were. Playing the Spartans on the road was a tough test, and we had an even bigger problem. Vlasic couldn't play after hurting his shoulder in the Texas-El Paso game, leaving us no choice but to go with an untested, inexperienced quarterback. Everyone expected that choice to be Dan McGwire, a 6-8 freshman with a powerful arm. In the spring game, he had thrown a 75-yard pass that had our fans buzzing all summer.

But Bill Snyder, my offensive coordinator and quarterback coach, decided at the last minute to go with Tom Poholsky, a sophomore with a little more maturity and limited experience. It was a good decision. Poholsky threw for 240 yards and two touchdowns, one a 50-yarder to Jim Mauro, as we opened the Big Ten campaign with a 24-21 victory. A field goal by Rob Houghtlin in the fourth quarter was the margin of victory.

The game was televised by CBS, and the announcers were really surprised when McGwire didn't start. Brent Musburger said he was shocked, and it always amuses me to shock the media. There was an interesting baseball angle to this story, too. Poholsky's father, Tom, had been a major league pitcher, and McGwire's brother, Mark, was just emerging as a home run hitter for the Oakland Athletics. But nobody at that time was predicting that our quarterback's brother would someday hit 70 home runs in a season.

Richard Bass, who was filling in for injured David Hudson at fullback, scored a touchdown on a 12-yard draw play at Michigan State, and he followed that with a 100-yard rushing game the next week in a 17-6 win over Wisconsin. Richard was a sophomore that season, and I nicknamed him my "Rolling Ball of Butcher Knives" because of his running style.

Bass was a marginal high school student who had a hard time getting admitted at Iowa. Because of his poor academic background, there was a question whether he could make it in college. But when he got into a good academic environment, he became smarter and smarter, just like a lot of youngsters do when they get the opportunity. It's amazing what happens to a young man when those around him show faith in his ability. By the time Richard received his degree at Iowa, he was a good college student. He went on to earn a doctorate in education, and today is a high school administrator. The success of players like Richard Bass has been a big factor in keeping me motivated as a coach.

At Michigan, Bass scored the first touchdown of the game, then learned how to deal with adversity. Vlasic's 15-yard touchdown pass to Robert Smith in the fourth quarter made the score 17-17. We got the ball back and were moving in for the winning field goal when a defender knocked the ball loose from Bass and the Wolverines recovered. Michigan, not Iowa, won on a late field goal 20-17.

For the fourth time in six years, a field goal decided a game between teams coached by Bo Schembechler and me. Iowa and Michigan had each won twice. Over the years I developed great respect for Bo. Before I came to Iowa I didn't even know how to spell his name, but I knew he was one of the best coaches in the game, and I learned that firsthand when our teams started playing every season.

I always had fun with Bo during pregame warmups. One year I had guards snapping to the punters, trying to keep my players loose. Bo noticed all the wild snaps and cracked, "Why don't you let those guys snap during the game?" I replied, "Bo, we don't plan on punting during the game." He threw his hands up in the air and walked away. I ran after him to get some of that sugarless gum he chewed, then told him I'd heard he was keeping his managers busy papering the pink walls in his locker. He said, "I know what you're trying to do, by God, and you're not putting my ball club to sleep with that stuff."

I also liked to kid Bo about the headset he wore on the sideline. I told him I was scared to death he was going to choke himself with the cord someday. We always had a good time when our teams played, and the games often turned into a chess match. I have great admiration for Bo as a man and a coach, and I miss competing with him. The Big Ten lost a great coach when he retired.

We finished the regular season by winning three of our remaining five games, beating Northwestern 27-20, Purdue 42-14 and Minnesota 30-27. The losses were to Ohio State 31-10 and Illinois 20-16. Injuries plagued us all season; we had a different lineup every game. Quarterback was a good example, with Vlasic's shoulder injury allowing him to start only six games. He and Poholsky each won four times as the starting quarterback.

At Minnesota, Vlasic didn't play until the second half, then rallied us to a 30-27 victory that had some wild moments. Peter Marciano returned a punt 89 yards for our first score, then Vlasic went to work throwing the ball, completing 16 of 21 passes for 199 yards and a touchdown. After the Gophers kicked a 49-yard field goal to make the score 27-27 with a minute remaining, we moved the ball far enough to allow Houghtlin to try from 52 yards as time expired. He missed, but Minnesota was penalized 15 yards for having 12 men on the field, giving him another chance from 37 yards. I remember reminding him he hadn't missed two kicks in a row since becoming a Hawkeye. He got the message and split the uprights on his second chance and we won, 30-27.

Vinny Vinson was at the game representing the Holiday Bowl, and after the game he stood on top a training table and invited us to the postseason game in San Diego. Vinny was a Texas A&M graduate, and I told him that was the nicest thing an Aggie had ever done. Before meeting the press, I put on some bib overalls and a straw hat. The Minnesota press was always making jokes about Iowa farmers, and I wanted them to know I was proud to be one.

The Holiday Bowl is an extremely well-run event, and the fact that it is in a beautiful city with an ideal climate makes it all the better. This was our sixth straight bowl game, so our players were bowl savvy. They really enjoyed their time at the Holiday Bowl. Our biggest concern about the game was the opponent, San Diego State, which played all its home games in Jack Murphy Stadium, site of the Holiday Bowl. The Aztecs were champions of the Western Athletic Conference and loaded with seniors. For the second year in a row, we were playing a bowl opponent on its home field. It was also our first game of the year on natural grass. All of our 11 regular-season games had been played on an artificial surface.

The Holiday Bowl is known to for its exciting, high-scoring games, and we didn't tarnish that reputation. We were down 35-21 in the fourth quarter when Vlasic threw a 29-yard touchdown pass to Marv Cook. We followed that with the most important play of the night, a two-point conversion pass, Vlasic to Mike Flagg, on a fake extra-point kick. The play caught San Diego State flat-footed; Flagg was wide open in the end zone.

Moments later, after Vlasic threw to Flagg for a touchdown, Houghtlin's extra point put us up 36-35. San Diego State kicked a field goal to go ahead 38-36 with less than a minute left, then made the mistake of kicking the ball deep to Kevin Harmon, who made a great 48-yard runback. We ran a special play with Rick Bayless for good yardage and Houghtlin had another chance to be a hero. He kicked a 41-yard field goal as time ran out, giving Iowa a thrilling 39-38 victory.

The 1986 Iowa team exceeded all my expectations, and I don't think I was alone. After losing so many all-Americans and starters from a Big Ten championship team, I doubt that anyone anticipated the '86 Hawkeyes would finish with nine victories, third place in the Big Ten and 19th in the nation. Two of our three losses were decided by a total of seven points. Two were to Big Ten co-champs Michigan and Ohio State.

Rick Bayless, who came to us as a walkon, became Iowa's third 1,000-yard rusher, following in the footsteps of Dennis Mosley and Ronnie Harmon. Offensive tackle Dave Croston won All-America honors. Defensive linemen Jeff Drost and Dave Haight, and offensive guard Bob Kratch were all-Big Ten, along with Bayless. Despite losing all those offensive stars of the previous season, Iowa led the Big Ten in scoring.

Considering the lack of expectations and the injuries they had to overcome, the '86 Hawkeyes gave me one of my most satisfying seasons in coaching. By beating San Diego State in the Holiday Bowl, they also gave me my 150th career victory.

Chapter Twenty-three

IOWA, 1987

Every season is a new challenge for a college football coach. Rosters turn over each year and there are personnel decisions to be made. Sometimes you're lucky and there aren't too many changes. Other times they are significant, which was the case in 1987 when we had to replace half the starting lineup.

Graduation hit our defense harder than our offense, and I told the fans and news media prior to the season that we would have to outscore our opponents to win early games. Our non-conference schedule, which included Tennessee and Arizona, was tougher than in recent years. We had a 12-game schedule and played only five times at home all season. It was going to be a real challenge for a team in transition.

Offensively, our biggest uncertainty was at the important quarterback position. Tom Poholsky had started some games in '86, but Dan McGwire and Chuck Hartlieb both had strong performances in the spring and deserved an opportunity to prove themselves. We decided to use all three in the opening game against Tennessee at the Kickoff Classic played in Giants Stadium at East Rutherford, N.J.

McGwire started and threw a 75-yard incomplete pass on the second play. We knew the fans wanted to see his powerful arm so we decided to get that out of the way. Dan's presence in the

New York area drew attention because his brother Mark was hitting a lot of home runs for the Oakland Athletics and was playing at Yankee Stadium across the Hudson River the same day.

We decided before the game to change quarterbacks at specific intervals, and in the second quarter, as we approached the goal line, it was Hartlieb's turn to play. I called offensive coordinator Bill Snyder in the press box and asked him if we should allow Poholsky to finish the drive. He said the quarterbacks had been told specifically when they would play and it was Hartlieb's turn.

So Chuck entered the game as we threatened to score. On a fourth-down option play from the one-yard line, his pitchout was intercepted by a big lineman named Darrin Miller, who lumbered the length of the field for a touchdown. The play amounted to a 14-point swing. That experience would have badly rattled most inexperienced quarterbacks, but on our next possession, Chuck took his team down the field for a touchdown.

We lost the game, 23-22, when Tennessee kicked a field goal with three seconds remaining, but we had reasons to be encouraged. Our defense, led by Joe Schuster, Dwight Sistrunk and Dave Haight, held Tennessee to one touchdown. Our offense generated 375 yards, and Rob Houghtlin demonstrated his usual field goal accuracy, kicking three.

Rob kicked three more field goals at Arizona and Richard Bass scored the winning touchdown as we came from behind in the fourth quarter for a 15-14 victory. After Bass scored, our defense forced a punt, and the offense sustained a long drive to kill the clock. It was a big win on the road.

We scored decisive victories over Iowa State, 48-9, and Kansas State, 38-13. Kevin Harmon ran for more than 100 yards in each win, and Houghtlin booted a 55-yard field goal at Iowa State, the longest of his career. J.J. Puk led us in tackles in both games.

Between losses to Michigan State and Michigan, we used a 19-minute possession time advantage at Wisconsin to win, 31-10. Hartlieb, by now established as the No. 1 quarterback, threw touchdown passes to Quinn Early and Marv Cook. Kerry Burt made two interceptions, as the defense limited the Badgers to 58 passing yards.

By midseason, our offense, featuring the passing game, was making lots of big plays and scoring a lot of points. We never lost another game. Against Purdue we ran 88 plays, then a record number for my Iowa teams, for 520 yards in a 38-14 victory. Hartlieb had touchdown strikes of 38, 55 and 46 yards, Quinn Early caught

11 passes for 142 yards and Greg Brown intercepted two passes.

Indiana had us down, 21-20 in the fourth quarter, but a touchdown by David Hudson and Houghtlin's third field goal lifted us to a 29-21 victory. Dave Haight's 18 tackles and Dwight Sistrunk's two interceptions sparked our defense.

Dyche Stadium in Evanston was the scene of some of our biggest offensive explosions in the 1980s, and the '87 Hawkeyes produced their share of fireworks in beating Northwestern there 52-24. We broke or tied 19 Iowa, Big Ten and NCAA records that day behind Hartlieb, who threw seven touchdown passes, and Early, who caught four of them, one for 95 yards. Northwestern kept playing the run, so we kept passing. After throwing his seventh TD pass in the third quarter, Hartlieb came over to the bench and said, "Coach, let someone else play. I've had enough." Although we won by a big margin, we twice trailed by 10 points in the first half.

The scene was set for our visit to Ohio State and one of the most memorable touchdowns in Iowa history. The Hawkeyes hadn't won in the big horseshoe stadium in 28 years, and when the Buckeyes took a 27-22 lead with 2:45 remaining, 29 years seemed a good bet. But Kevin Harmon returned the kickoff 35 yards, and Hartlieb completed five passes to give us some hope. Then a sack and a penalty put us in a seemingly impossible position—fourth and 23 at the Ohio State 28, with only seconds remaining.

It seemed likely the Buckeyes would be in a prevent defense, dropping everyone deep, so we improvised on what we call a trail route. Marv Cook altered his route by running deep, then hooking back. On a perfectly executed pass from Hartlieb, Marv caught the ball at the nine-yard line and literally dragged two defenders into the end zone. With three seconds remaining, we had scored an improbable, if not impossible, winning touchdown. As the final score of 29-27 sunk in, 90,000 Buckeye fans fell silent.

There were a lot of big plays in the game. Harmon had a 50-yard touchdown run. Houghtlin kicked three field goals for the fourth time that season. Our defense stopped a two-point conversion attempt after Ohio State's final touchdown. But the play that is carved into the memory of Iowa fans is the winning touchdown pass from Hartlieb to Cook. It was the ninth time in the game the two roommates hooked up for a completion as Chuck became the first Iowa quarterback to pass for more than 300 yards four times in one season. Marv's receptions were good for 159 of our 333 passing yards that day.

For the first time in my coaching career, the first visitor to our locker room was the president of the other school. Ed Jennings came by to shake hands and offer congratulations. Ed had hired me at Iowa nine years earlier when he was the University's vice president. He and Bump Elliott had flown down to Dallas to offer the job. In fact, he did me a favor the night before I was introduced at a press conference in Iowa City. The heat went out in my motel room and he and his wife brought me an electric blanket to stay warm.

As he left the locker room, President Jennings quietly told me, "Earl Bruce is in trouble." So I wasn't surprised when Ohio State announced two days later it had fired Bruce as its football coach. Bruce made that look like a dumb decision when he took his Buckeyes to Ann Arbor and beat Michigan later that week. Apparently Bruce never hit it off with Ohio State's big contributors, who were always sniping at him. It's too bad, because he was a good coach with a good record. Having personally experienced the same thing, I have great empathy for a coach who loses his job when administrators cave into pressure from contributors. Contributors are important to college athletic programs, but when they are allowed to call the shots, the schools are in trouble.

Minnesota came into Kinnick Stadium for our traditional season-ending game looking for a seventh victory and a bowl bid. We already had seven wins and an eighth would put us up a little higher in the bowl structure. It was an important game for both schools. Chuck Hartlieb continued to have a hot hand, completing 14 consecutive passes in the first half, two for touchdowns. The Gophers led 6-3 before we hit them with three TDs in the second period and we went on to a 34-20 victory. Hartlieb passed for more than 300 yards for the fourth time in five games. Our defense, led by Brad Quast's 13 tackles, limited Minnesota's nationally ranked rushing attack to 79 yards.

We had such a good time at the Holiday Bowl the previous year, we accepted another invitation to play in San Diego. This time our opponent was Wyoming, coached by Paul Roach. He had been a successful coach of the Cowboys before becoming the school's athletic director, and when the football team fell on hard times he was brought back to coach. He'd obviously done a great job in rebuilding the program; Wyoming came into our game as the WAC champion with a 10-2 record.

I was pleasantly surprised to run into some old friends from West Texas before the game—Kenny Jastrow from Midland and his wife, Elaine. My daughter Robin's middle name is Elaine, after Elaine Jastrow. Kenny was a star basketball player at the University of Denver and went on to play with the Phillips 66ers when they had the best amateur team in the world. Gerald Tucker, another boyhood pal, also played for the 66ers. Gerald had a great voice and used to sing the national anthem before Midland baseball games that George Bush and I attended together.

The football job at Southern California was open while we were in San Diego preparing for the Holiday Bowl, and USC officials wanted to talk to me about the position. USC has a great football tradition, and my coaches thought it was something we should investigate, so I agreed to meet with Athletic Director Mike McGee in San Clemente. That meeting and some follow up discussions produced an attractive offer, but my coaches ultimately decided they preferred life in rural Iowa to metropolitan Los Angeles. When word got out that USC was talking to me, I was surprised at the negative reaction by the Iowa news media. I thought it was a credit to the Iowa program that USC was interested in the Iowa coach, but some reporters made me out to be a turncoat. That reaction still puzzles me, and it put a damper on the bowl trip.

Our game with Wyoming was typical for the Holiday Bowl—plenty of excitement and down to the wire—and we won it with our special teams. We were in real trouble in the fourth quarter, trailing 19-7. Our only touchdown was on a blocked punt that Jay Hess ran into the end zone. In the final period, Anthony Wright intercepted a Cowboy pass and returned it 33 yards for a touchdown. Then David Hudson scored on a short run to give us a 20-19 lead, our first of the game. Wyoming had time to move the ball into field goal range, but Merton Hanks blocked the kick with 46 seconds remaining, and we had our second straight one-point victory at the Holiday Bowl. It was a good football game with a thrilling finish, and I know the Cowboys were disappointed with the outcome. They wanted badly to beat a Big Ten team, and they very nearly did.

Just as my Iowa teams of 1982 and 1986, this ball club had a better record (10-3) and Big Ten finish (second) than predicted. This team had a great capacity to come from behind, six times overcoming deficits to win games. Fortitude, character and perseverance—those are words that come to mind when recalling the '87

Hawkeyes.

Chuck Hartlieb, who started the season as our No. 3 quarterback, led the Big Ten in passing and made the all-conference team, as did Marv Cook, Quinn Early, Rob Houghtlin, Kerry Burt and Dave Haight. Hartlieb and Cook also earned academic all-Big Ten honors.

Houghtlin finished a brilliant career by kicking 21 field goals as a senior, an Iowa season record. He also holds the school scoring records for a season (105 points) and a career (290). His kicks provided the winning margin nine times in his three-year career. Many of those came in the final minute, some in the final seconds. He never missed a kick that cost us a victory. In fact, he never missed many kicks. The first time I saw him on the practice field I thought he might be something special. I was right.

The '87 Hawkeyes contributed to two notable achievements: Iowa owned the best pass efficiency rating in the nation over the past five seasons and ranked third in total offense during that period. But perhaps the greatest accomplishment was breaking through the "Big Two—Little Eight" attitude that had gripped the Big Ten for so many years. In the last seven seasons, Iowa owned 62 victories, more than any other Big Ten team. Even more than Michigan and Ohio State.

Chapter Twenty-four

IOWA, 1988

How many times have you seen a football game end in a tie? Probably not often. Even before the NCAA adopted a rule to eliminate ties a few years ago, tie games were uncommon. But for me, one was too many. Most coaches don't like ties, and I am one of them. Nobody—the fans, the players or the coaches— ever came away from a tie feeling good. I was one of the leaders whenever our national organization suggested a tie-breaking rule, but it took years before one was finally adopted. I'm not sure we adopted the best rule, but at least it determines a winner and a loser.

I've coached 420 football games in 37 seasons, and only 10 games resulted in a tie. That averages out to roughly one tie every fourth season, which isn't many. Although I never liked tie games, I was able to tolerate them. At least I thought I could until the 1988 season, when the Hawkeyes played three tie games in a seven-week period, pushing frustration to a new level.

The '88 Iowa team lost only one Big Ten game, but because of three ties, it finished third. Two of the ties were with teams ahead of us in the standings, Michigan and Michigan State. The other was with Ohio State. With a tie-breaking rule, we could have won the championship. Or we might have finished with three more losses. But at least we would have had the opportunity to be the Big Ten's Rose Bowl representative.

Three outstanding seniors led us into Iowa's 100th year of football. Quarterback Chuck Hartlieb, tight end Marv Cook and noseguard Dave Haight were ending great careers and getting preseason all-America recognition. Mainly because of their presence, we were considered a Big Ten contender. Other veterans such as offensive tackle Bob Kratch, fullback David Hudson, linebacker Brad Quast and defensive end Joe Mott supported the notion that we would have a strong football team.

Our first game was at Hawaii, which should be a great place to start a campaign, but our season got off on the wrong foot. We had a 21-14 lead after three quarters but lost the game, 27-24. In the final minute, Hartlieb threw what looked like a winning touchdown pass to Travis Watkins, but the play was nullified by a holding call. Hawaii used the same officials every game. They were members of the school's PE department, and we went out there knowing that, but they made some particularly brutal calls that night. Tony Stewart, our sophomore running back who was getting his first start, had 147 yards rushing in 19 carries.

Our defense picked off five Kansas State passes in a 45-10 victory at Manhattan. Brad Quast ran one back 94 yards, tying a school record, and Brian Wise had an 81-yard runback for another touchdown. We came close to a NCAA record with 224 yards on interception returns.

We continued playing Big Eight opponents, with two more at home. Against Colorado, we had a 21-17 lead when a fumble by Hartlieb killed a scoring opportunity that would have probably clinched a win. The Buffaloes capitalized by driving 85 yards in the final minutes to hand us a 24-21 defeat, our second three-point loss in three weeks. Against Iowa State, Tork Hooks intercepted a pass at the goal line with 16 seconds remaining to preserve our 10-3 victory. Stewart rushed for 194 yards but scored the only touchdown of the game on a pass from Hartlieb. Our defense was led by Quast, who had a hand in 20 tackles.

In a steady rain at Michigan State, we played our first tie. Each team had a field goal and a touchdown pass—ours was a halfback pass from Stewart to Jon Filloon—and the game ended in a 10-10 draw. Both teams missed long field goals in the final minute. After Michigan State failed on a 44-yard attempt, Hartlieb passed to Watkins for 38 yards, giving Jeff Skillett an opportunity from 51 yards. His kick got mixed reviews from the officials. One called it good, one called it wide, and the final call stood. It didn't make us feel any better when film taken by our end zone camera indicated that the official who called the kick good was right.

Skillett's three field goals gave us a 9-3 halftime lead over Wisconsin, then Hartlieb got hot and completed 16 of 19 passes for 225 yards to sustain three long touchdown drives in the second half. Our defense punctuated the 31-6 homecoming victory with 11 tackles for minus yardage.

Our shotgun formation took Michigan by surprise, and we jumped to a 17-3 lead. After the Wolverines closed to 17-10, both teams blew scoring opportunities by losing fumbles at the goal line. After we missed a scoring chance when Stewart lost the handle, Michigan drove 99 yards to tie the game. The Wolverines were moving in for the winning score when they dropped the ball at our one and Melvin Foster recovered with a minute remaining. After the game ended in a 17-17 tie (there's that word again) two angry coaches met at midfield, but Bo Schembechler was the maddest because his team had fumbled most recently. "What a waste of time," he grumbled. The tie was the only blemish on Michigan's Big Ten record that season and it won the championship.

We got a season-high 266 yards rushing at Purdue while holding the home team to a season-low 184 total yards. Mike Saunders had a 72-yard touchdown run and Tony Stewart rushed for 140 yards in our 31-7 victory.

Despite Chuck Hartlieb's record-setting passing performance —44 of 60 for 558 yards—we couldn't overcome a 32-point deficit at Indiana and lost 45-34. For awhile it looked like we were going to get a great comeback victory, especially when Brad Quast intercepted a pass and ran it back to the one, but we got a penalty and never did score. We wasted two other scoring chances inside the 20. Hartlieb's passing statistics are still school records, as are Nick Bell's 13 receptions.

A 35-10 victory over Northwestern preceded our final home game and third tie of the season. We had to settle for a 24-24 draw with Ohio State despite a big statistical advantage that included 360 passing yards by Hartlieb. We tied the game in the final minute when Skillett kicked a 40-yard field goal. Then we tried an onside kick that caught Ohio State by surprise and nearly worked. If we had recovered the ball, I would have tried another field goal. I thought our chances of winning the game that way were better than the conventional strategy of going for the touchdown on fourth and long. Some of the fans and news media thought I was settling for a tie, but that was the last thing I was trying to do.

Three ties in one season may seem like a record, but they are actually one short of the national mark. In the Big Ten, we tied the record for ties. Ohio State, Wisconsin and Northwestern have all suffered through seasons with three ties. Northwestern endured it twice.

Tony Stewart went over 1,000 rushing yards for the season against the Buckeyes, becoming the first Hawkeye sophomore to reach that total, but in injury kept him out of the season-ending game at Minnesota. So freshman Mike Saunders stepped in and ran for 123 yards and three touchdowns in a 31-22 victory. We controlled the game and the ball with a 15-minute advantage in possession time.

One of our good Iowa fans made a tie for each of our tie games and gave them to me when the regular season ended. Each tie displayed the opponent and score of the game. They were very nice ties, and I really appreciated the thoughtfulness, but I did not take them with me when we left for Atlanta to play North Carolina State in the Peach Bowl. I didn't want anything to remind me of those three tie games.

This was our second trip to the Peach Bowl, and we were hopeful we could end the season by winning two straight games, which we hadn't done all year. Both teams had similar records, and the game was viewed as a toss up. North Carolina State even had one tie. Hard to believe that the field on which we played is now used for a parking lot. Fulton County Stadium was demolished when Turner Field was constructed next door.

We received the opening kickoff, which Chet Davis fumbled at the three-yard line, giving North Carolina State a quick touchdown. That set the tone for the game, which included 14 turnovers, seven by each team. Ours came early and we got behind 28-3, forcing us to rely far too much on the passing game. Hartlieb did the best he could, throwing for 428 yards. Deven Harberts caught two touchdown passes and Marv Cook had 122 yards receiving, but we came up on the short end of a 28-23 score.

Thus ended one of the most frustrating and peculiar seasons of my coaching career. Besides the three ties, we could have also won all four games we lost. Whereas the 1987 Hawkeyes had six come-from-behind victories, this team, with many of the same players, had none. But it still managed to finish third in the Big Ten with the very unusual record of 4-1-3.

We won six games, but none on consecutive Saturdays. Injuries prevented us from developing any real continuity. Only six players—Greg Divis, Dave Haight, Merton Hanks, Chuck Hartlieb, Jeff Koeppel and Joe Mott—started every game. The offensive line, with 10 different lineups, and the defensive backfield, with seven, were hit hardest by injuries.

Marv Cook became the sixth consensus all-American in my first 10 years at Iowa. Dave Haight also received first-team all-America recognition. Chuck Hartlieb earned all-Big Ten quarterback honors for the second straight season, made the academic all-America team and was named the Honda Scholar Athlete of the Year. All-Big Ten honors also went to Deven Harberts, Bob Kratch, Joe Mott and Brad Quast. Six of the seven honored players were seniors, leaving us with heavy personnel losses and a lot of work to do for the following season. The '89 Hawkeyes would definitely have a new look.

Chapter Twenty-five

IOWA, 1989

The 1980s were golden years for Hawkeye sports. It was a decade in which Iowa football teams became regulars at bowl games, basketball teams were annual participants in NCAA tournaments, and the wrestlers won every Big Ten championship and most NCAA titles. Other sports such as gymnastics, swimming and baseball were also enjoying success.

Football entered the final year of that decade with a team in transition. Graduation had cut severely into our starting lineup, and most of our key players were gone. We had a lot of positions to fill, including the important quarterback spot. Also missing was Bill Snyder, my offensive coordinator since I arrived at Iowa 10 years earlier. He went to Kansas State as head coach, and Carl Jackson, a long-time member of my staff, replaced him as offensive coordinator. Uncertainties about our personnel were significant, and some experts suggested Iowa might finish in the Big Ten's second division for the first time since I arrived.

So there was little reason to be very optimistic about the 1989 Hawkeyes. There was even less when we were blindsided by two huge distractions. One came from within the University. In fact, it came from the very top. The other came from an unexpected source and involved two of our former players.

Sports agents Norby Walters and Lloyd Bloom had been indicted by a federal grand jury for conspiracy to commit fraud and were on trial in Chicago. They had signed several college football players to contracts in the players' final year of eligibility and given them money, a NCAA violation. The contracts were postdated to a time when the players' college careers were over, and prosecutors argued they were false documents.

Bloom had been an established agent in the entertainment world who was just getting into sports. The players he signed were from schools in the midwest, including Michigan, Purdue, Notre Dame and Iowa. Ronnie Harmon and Devon Mitchell, who played their final year at Iowa in 1985, were two of the players the agents had signed. In exchange for testimony, the players were unindicted co-conspirators.

The trial was conducted during the winter of 1989, and received a lot of attention from the news media. Defense attorneys for Walters and Bloom tried taking blame off their clients by putting the universities on trial. They claimed the schools, not the agents, exploited the players. Players transcripts were introduced as testimony; Harmon's and Mitchell's were printed in Iowa newspapers. They had taken courses in art and physical education and we were accused of putting them in those courses to keep them eligible. They were legitimate courses with unusual names. One had something to do with water coloring. I told some of our administrators, including the president, that my coaches didn't create the courses, the University did. If the courses were embarrassing to the University, they should have been removed from the curriculum.

The trial seemed to go on forever and was played up big by the press. Walters and Bloom were convicted, but the verdict was overturned. Bloom was later gunned down in his own home in a murder some thought was mob-connected. The entire experience had a profound affect on Ronnie Harmon. It really impacted his life and put him in a shell. It was too bad, because he's a great young man as well as a tremendous athlete. He's probably as good as any football player we've had at Iowa. Although his transcript looked suspect to some people, he is only one semester short of graduation, and I hope he comes back to get his degree some day.

My opinion of sports agents was expressed earlier in this book, so I won't go into that again. But I will emphasize that we regularly remind our players about the dangers in dealing with agents. Harmon and Mitchell must have done business with Walters and Bloom sometime between the end of the regular season and the Rose bowl, but none of my coaches were aware of it.

The whole episode put my staff in a defensive posture. It wore us down and affected morale. Every time we appeared in public we were asked about it. There were a lot of wisecracks. It demanded our time and attention when we should have been devoting our energy to recruiting and preparing for spring practice. It had a negative effect on Iowa football and what happened next just exacerbated our problems.

Do presidents or football coaches at major universities stay in their jobs the longest? Most people would answer "presidents" to that question; football coaching is not known for job security. But I had been coaching at Iowa less than 10 years when I met my third president. Willard Boyd hired me in 1978 and left for the Field Museum in Chicago in 1981. He was succeeded by James Freedman, who was president in the seven years we won 62 games and two Big Ten championships. Hunter Rawlings took over in 1988 when Freedman accepted the presidency at Dartmouth.

Rawlings played basketball and baseball at Havorford College, and at 43 years old, he still enjoyed athletic participation. He liked to come out to the football practice field and throw passes to our wide receivers. He got involved with the baseball team, pitching in intra-squad games. At 6-8, he was an imposing figure on the basketball and tennis courts. A gregarious man who enjoyed a good time, he was well-liked by the athletes and coaches.

As a former vice-president at Colorado, Rawlings was well aware that a successful football program could be a great asset to a university. When he traveled with us on road trips during the '88 season, he always came by the locker room after the games to shake hands with the players and coaches. He told an Iowa reporter that his president at Colorado once advised him, "Two things can bring down a president faster than anything. One is the football team. The other is the hospital." He was fortunate that both were in excellent condition when he arrived at Iowa.

Rawlings had been president for less than a year when he dropped his bombshell on Hawkeye coaches in all sports. He suggested to a *Des Moines Register* reporter that he was going to ask the NCAA to declare freshmen ineligible, and if he couldn't get the legislation passed, he would withhold Iowa freshmen from varsity competition. The first part we could have lived with; the second part was a killer. There was no way that Iowa could compete in the Big Ten with its own set of rules regarding freshmen eligibility. It would have been suicide; our recruiting would have been dead.

The president made his comments without consulting his coaches or administrators. Athletic Director Bump Elliott was dumbfounded. Rawlings might have been reacting to the Walters-Bloom trial in Chicago that involved two of our players, but if he thought that trial had anything to do with freshmen eligibility, he was wrong. That's why he should have consulted with his athletic director and his coaches before he shot from the hip and damaged his own athletic program.

Rawlings' comments drew attention from the national media, which he seemed to enjoy. One day he showed up without notice at one of my press conferences and reaffirmed his plans to make freshmen ineligible. After he finished talking to the reporters, he turned to me and asked, "What do you think, coach?" To which I responded, "I'd like to redshirt my president." He might have thought I was kidding, but I was dead serious.

The president never retracted his statement about making freshmen ineligible at Iowa, even after we gave him data that showed all athletes, including freshmen, do better academic work when they are in season. It didn't take long for his comments to be used against us as negative recruiting. Schools we compete with in and out of our league were laughing about it. To them it was funny. They couldn't believe what our own president was doing to us, and they were taking advantage of it. The morale of all Hawkeye coaches was very poor; some thought Rawlings' next step would be to eliminate athletic scholarships. It was a time of gloom and doom in the Iowa athletic department.

I don't think Rawlings intentionally set out to hurt his own athletic department. He was sincere and honest in his beliefs, in my opinion, but he made a huge mistake in not consulting his athletic director before speaking out. Then he compounded that by not softening his position. It would have been suicide for Iowa to withhold freshmen from competition when other schools weren't doing the same thing. Most freshmen think they're ready to compete; they won't go to a school where they would be required to sit out a year.

How much did this hurt the Iowa program, and for how long? It's impossible to make an absolute statement about that, but there is no question it caused considerable damage and had a lingering effect. There still may be recruiters out there who show high school kids clippings that say the Iowa president isn't going to let freshmen participate. That wouldn't surprise me. There is no doubt in my mind that Rawlings' comments severely hurt our football program, but I have never used that as an excuse. As my granddaddy liked to say, "Never lean on a broken crutch." We had to move on and do the best we could. But in the back of our minds there was always the question: What was the president going to do next?

The 1989 football season was like the first half of the year, a downer. Nothing much went right for us; we lost five times at home, beating only Tulsa at Kinnick Stadium. We did win four road games, but for the first time in nine years we failed to have a winning season and play in a bowl.

The redeeming thing about the season was that most of the players were underclassmen who would be back for two or three more years. We weren't happy with our 5-6 record, but the young players were getting valuable experience, and I could see improvement as the season progressed.

Our biggest concern was filling the quarterback spot, where Chuck Hartlieb had set school records and been all-Big Ten quarterback the past two seasons. We settled on Matt Rodgers, and he really made progress, becoming only the second sophomore in Iowa history to pass for more than 2,000 yards in a season.

A lady called me on my radio show and took exception with the way I treated Matt in a TV game at Ohio State. He wasn't seeing open receivers and I jerked him by the face mask to get his attention. I explained to the lady that I was telling Matt, "You're a better quarterback than that!" Matt had great potential, and I had to convince him of that. It's sometimes hard for a coach to get a player's attention. Matt's father Jimmy, who was then coaching the Boston Celtics, knew exactly what I was doing—trying to help his son become a better quarterback, and in the next two seasons he was.

We took some lumps during the season, but we also had our moments. Nick Bell rushed for 217 yards and three touchdowns in Iowa's seventh straight win at Wisconsin. Rodgers threw three touchdown passes in his first start at Iowa State and completed 20 of 24 for 256 yards at Northwestern. We got our first shutout in 51 games at Purdue (24-0), holding the Boilermakers to a minus 73 yards rushing, an Iowa record. Jim Johnson had four of our nine quarter-back sacks.

Probably the best thing about the season was that for the first time in 18 years, Kinnick Stadium had a grass playing field. Artificial turf was removed during the spring and replaced with natural grass. I pushed hard for the change because I believe grass is a better playing surface and causes fewer injuries. Artificial turf was the rage in the early 1970s; now most schools have gone back to a natural surface.

A clever columnist suggested that a grass field was the reason we slipped to a losing season in 1989, but that wasn't it. And as I said earlier, I wouldn't use the president's comments or the Chicago trial as an excuse. Youth and inexperience played the biggest role in our season, but our players would be a little older and we would be considerably better in another year.

Chapter Twenty-six

Iowa, 1990
Big Ten Championship

Our 1989 football team had fallen into the Big Ten's second division for the first time in my 11 years at Iowa, finishing sixth, and many experts thought the 1990 Hawkeyes were headed to a similar fate. I didn't necessarily agree with that, but I didn't put up a big fuss because we had a very difficult schedule as well as three new assistant coaches who needed to learn our personnel and our system.

But we had some good players returning, including the quarterback and a 1,000-yard running back. Matt Rodgers and Tony Stewart gave us two proven performers at important positions and we had another fine running back emerging in Nick Bell. Most of our defense returned, led by tackle Jim Johnson, linebacker Melvin Foster and cornerback Merton Hanks. We had veteran kickers, and overall I liked the looks of this football team even though we only had 13 seniors on the roster.

The schedule, however, was perhaps the most difficult in my time at Iowa. We had to play at Miami, the defending national champion, and our toughest Big Ten games were all on the road: at Michigan, Michigan State and Ohio State. All three teams were considered title contenders. Road tests like those keep your optimism in check.

Two coaches who had been with me for 11 years, Dan McCarney and Bernie Wyatt, left to join another former assistant,

Barry Alvarez, the new head coach at Wisconsin. Kirk Ferentz, who had been on my staff for nine seasons, went to Maine as the head coach. My new assistants were John O'Hara, Ted Gill and Milan Vooletich.

Kinnick Stadium had a new look for our opening game with Cincinnati. An additional 2,600 seats had been installed during the off-season to increase the capacity to more than 70,000. We set a school record with nine rushing touchdowns, five by quarterbacks Matt Rodgers (3) and Jim Hartlieb (2). But the defense had an even more impressive performance, limiting the Bearcats to four first downs and 69 total yards in a 63-10 victory.

Nick Bell and Tony Stewart both ran for more than 100 yards as we beat Iowa State 45-35. The largest crowd ever to see a game in the state, 70,389, saw us race away to a 38-14 lead and waltz home with our eighth straight victory over the Cyclones. Moses Santos and Eddie Polly led our defense with 14 tackles each.

By the time we flew to Miami for a night game we felt like we had a pretty decent team. The Hurricanes had the top college football program in the country, and my coaches were interested to see how our players would react to Miami's exceptional team speed and the Orange Bowl environment. We got a favorable answer. We played them close for three quarters, trailing only 24-21. Then they got two quick touchdowns off our mistakes. First they scored when Doug Buch fumbled a punt, then they stripped the ball out of Stewart's hands and returned it 75 yards. The final score was 48-21, but the 27-point margin didn't reflect the way we played, and we were a fairly confident football team as we opened the Big Ten.

We started the conference season on the right note by winning at Michigan State 12-7, keeping me unbeaten in six visits to Spartan Stadium. Jeff Skillett kicked two field goals and Rodgers threw a touchdown pass to Bell to complete our scoring. The Spartans had a 10-minute advantage in possession time, but our defense cut off every scoring threat except their TD in the fourth quarter. Melvin Foster had a hand in 20 tackles and was named the *Sports Illustrated* defensive player of the week.

Three of my former staff members came to Kinnick Stadium as Wisconsin coaches for the first time and saw their team take a 10-3 lead before we scored the last 27 points and won the game 30-10. Nick Bell (146 yards) and Tony Stewart (124) both had big games and so did our special teams. Jason Olejniczak turned a pass interception into a touchdown, and Merton Hanks blocked a punt for a safety. Our defense limited Wisconsin to one first down and 37 total yards in the second half.

Back in Michigan for the second time in three weeks, we had one of my most satisfying victories, coming from behind to beat the eighth-ranked Wolverines, who seldom lose at home before their 105,000 fans. We won despite missing a golden opportunity to score just before halftime. We were at the goal line with no time outs remaining when Michael Titley got knocked out of the game. With only a few seconds remaining, we sent in his replacement, Matt Whitaker, with a play. As Whitaker ran on the field, Titley's head cleared on the sideline and he decided to put himself back in the game. This confused everyone, especially quarterback Matt Rodgers, who spread his palms and looked at me as if to say, "What now, coach?" Amid the confusion, the clock expired, and we never got off another play, ending the half behind, 14-7.

We were still behind 23-17 late in the game with the ball deep in our territory. We drove 85 yards in nine plays, never facing a third down. The key play was a 12-yard pass from Rodgers to Stewart, who caught the ball with one hand, pinning it against his ankle. Rodgers had to thread the ball between two linebackers to get it to Stewart, and that set up Paul Kujawa's short touchdown run. Skillett's extra point gave us our first lead of the game, 24-23. Only a minute remained, and our defense insured the victory when Moses Santos threw Michigan quarterback Elvis Grbac for a big loss and John Derby intercepted Grbac's pass on the next play.

Michigan had a first-year coach, Gary Moeller, who made a decision in the third quarter that was a key to the outcome. He tried to trick us with a two-point conversion that failed, which left the door open for us to win the game on Skillet's extra point. Bo Schembechler had just retired as Michigan's coach and was watching the game from the press box. He never told me what he thought of Moeller's strategy. It was the first time in 22 years that Michigan had lost a homecoming game, and the first time the Hawkeyes had won at both Michigan and Michigan State in the same season.

That prompted our players to dance the Hokey Pokey in the locker room, a tradition we had following really big wins. It's something we started doing shortly after I became the coach at Iowa. It just happened—I can't even recall the first time we did it. But the players liked it, and the Hokey Pokey carried over from team to team. It not only caught on with the players, it also caught on with the fans, who gave me advice on how to dance the Hokey Pokey.

They sent me sheet music and recordings. It's one of those silly traditions that got to be a lot of fun for everyone.

We were out front in the Big Ten race and there was concern we might look past Northwestern, sandwiched between games with Michigan and Illinois. But we put the Wildcats away with a 29-point explosion in the second quarter and coasted to a 56-14 victory. Bell and Stewart combined for 258 of our 371 rushing yards as we played our third straight game without a turnover.

We were moving up in the polls after being unranked to start the season. But we hadn't yet cracked the Top 10, and Illinois was No. 5 in the nation and favored to beat us in our big match at Champaign. The game was played on the first Saturday of November and received a huge buildup. ABC was televising the contest to a national audience with my old friend Keith Jackson at the microphone. I always enjoy seeing Keith; he's a great friend of college football and really understands the game.

The Illinois media tried to distract me going into the game. An Illinois basketball player named Deon Thomas was the center of a recruitment controversy that involved Iowa assistant coach Bruce Pearl. Thomas had been ruled ineligible by the NCAA, and the Illinois basketball people were really sore about it, with much of their anger directed at Iowa.

The week of the game, some Illinois reporters asked me if I wasn't concerned about playing at Champaign because of the controversy, and I responded by saying we weren't going to Illinois to play basketball. But the *Champaign News Gazette* must not have believed me, because the morning of the game the paper ran a headline on page one that blared: BAD BLOOD BOILS OVER! That was ridiculous, because Illinois coach John Mackovic and I got along fine and there weren't bad feelings between our teams.

If the paper was trying to help the home team win, it didn't work, because we had 28 points on the board before Illinois had its second first down. Then after Illinois scored a touchdown, we lined up for a field goal but caught 'em by surprise when Hartlieb threw a pass to Whitaker in the end zone. That bit of trickery gave us a 35-7 lead, and we withstood an aerial blitz in the second half to win 54-28. When the game ended, our players ran down to the section of the stadium where a few thousand Iowa fans lucky enough to have tickets for the game were located. The Hawkeye players and fans had an extemporaneous celebration that was a special moment, although the 70,000 Illinois fans probably didn't appreciate it.

For this game, we put in some running plays off the spread formation because of the way Illinois keyed its defense, which led the Big Ten and ranked third nationally. Several of their defenders, such as Moe Gardner, Mel Agee and Darrick Brownlow went on to the NFL. We bounced the ball outside with Nick Bell, which really confused them early. Bell and Stewart both had more than 100 yards rushing, the fourth time that season they did it in the same game. The offensive changes we made for this game worked to perfection. We couldn't have asked for more than 540 total yards and 54 points. Those are big numbers against anybody, and Illinois was one of the best defensive teams in college football that season.

For the first time since 1958, Iowa had won its first five Big Ten games, but the streak ended when Ohio State scored touchdowns on the last play of each half to hand us a gut-wrenching 27-26 loss at Kinnick Stadium. The first half ended as an Ohio State pass bounced off Merton Hanks' shoulder pads into the hands of a Buckeye receiver to complete a 48-yard touchdown play. On the final play of the game, Greg Frey threw a short TD pass that beat us. I used to kid Frey that we were probably related but that he spelled his name wrong. He broke our hearts on a day when we had a big advantage in total yardage and possession time and forced Ohio State to punt 10 times. We jumped out to an early lead and kept it until the last play of the game.

Quarterbacks stole the show in our final home game. Purdue's Eric Hunter set Kinnick Stadium records for pass attempts (60) and completions (32) that still stand, but Matt Rodgers was much more efficient—he threw four touchdown passes. Our defense, led by Melvin Foster and Brian Wise, held the Boilermakers to minus rushing yardage for the second straight season and kept them out of the end zone until late in a game we won, 38-9.

The Rose Bowl berth hung in the balance in the final week of the season. We could win it outright with a victory at Minnesota, and an estimated 30,000 Iowa fans were in attendance to witness another noisy, high scoring, exciting game at the Metrodome. After we got off to a 10-7 lead, Minnesota scored 17 straight points, getting one touchdown by recovering a blocked punt in the end zone. We never overcame that mistake and lost, 31-24. Something happened in this game I never saw before. Iowa fans made so much noise that the officials stopped play twice in the third quarter to quiet them. The home quarterback couldn't call signals because the visiting fans were making too much noise! That was a first for me, and I couldn't have been prouder of our fans.

For the first time in the 95-year football history of Big Ten, there was a four-way tie at the top. We were there, along with Michigan, Michigan State and Illinois, but we had beaten all three to earn the Rose Bowl berth. We had, in fact, beaten them all on their home fields. Ohio State was in position to win the championship but lost at home to Michigan. The Buckeyes finished with a 5-2-1 Big Ten record, the rest of us were 6-2.

Back in Pasadena for the third time in 10 years, our opponent was Washington, the Pac-10 champion. The fifth-ranked Huskies had an outstanding team and were a solid Rose Bowl favorite. On game day, we nearly didn't get on the field in time for the opening kickoff. I asked D. Wayne Lucas, the famous horse trainer and a good friend, to speak to our players before the game. I thought he might loosen them up with some funny race track stories. He gave a good motivational speech that went on quite a while. When he finished we rushed to the field to avoid a delay-of-game penalty, which would have been an embarrassing way to start the Rose Bowl.

In that game, Washington capitalized on our mistakes, scoring its first two touchdowns on a blocked punt and a pass interception and had us down 33-7 at halftime. I decided to run every exotic we had in the second half, and most of them worked. Tight end Michael Titley passed to wide receiver Jon Filloon for 53 yards and wide receiver Danan Hughes threw to Nick Bell for 66 yards. A successful on-side kick helped us score two quick touchdowns without Washington running a play. It was the highest-scoring game in Rose Bowl history, but we were on the short end, 46-34. Jim Murray wrote in his *Los Angeles Times* column, "Iowa didn't lose, it just ran out of time." He was right about that.

The 1990 Hawkeyes rose from the Big Ten's second division to the top in one season, the first time a team had done that 24 years. They had unusual balance, so good they led the Big Ten in both total offense and total defense. They played before nearly one million fans, more than any Iowa team before or since. In their 12 games, the average crowd was more than 75,000.

When you have a good season the honors roll in, as they did in 1990. Nick Bell was named the Big Ten's Most Valuable Player by the *Chicago Tribune*. Conference coaches selected Bell and Matt Rodgers as the Big Ten offensive players of the year. All-Big Ten recognition went to seven Hawkeyes: Bell, Rodgers, Jim Johnson, Melvin Foster, Merton Hanks, Michael Titley and Matt Ruhland. I was honored as the Big Ten coach of the year.

Nick Bell became Iowa's fifth 1,000-yard rusher. He was a special talent who had both size and speed. He was so big, other schools wanted him as a tight end out of high school, but we ensured him a shot at running back and he made good at the position. Nick had dyslexia, but he overcame that handicap. He was very bright and eager to learn, and I really enjoyed coaching him.

Tony Stewart, the other half of our running back tandem, established a school record for career rushing yards. This was the final year for Bell and Stewart, as it was for five other all-Big Ten Hawkeyes. We didn't have a lot of seniors on this team, but the ones we had played a big role in our successful season. They ended their careers the way every player hopes to—winning a Big Ten championship and playing in the Rose Bowl.

Chapter Twenty-seven

IOWA, 1991

Maybe the two most important people in a football coach's life are his wife and his athletic director. In January of 1991, I lost my athletic director when Bump Elliott retired after serving Iowa for 20 years in that position. The announcement that he was going to retire at age 65 surprised a lot of people, but it didn't surprise me. I had talked him out of leaving two years earlier—begged him to stay would be more accurate. Then, after we won the '91 Rose Bowl berth, he told me he would announce his retirement after the game. There was nothing I could say to change his mind this time.

I admit selfish interests for wanting Bump to stay. He was a football man who understood the complexities of my job. He played the game and coached the game, both with great success and distinction. He did it all and he understands what it takes to win and, more importantly, how hard it is to win. I was losing a wonderful boss, and the University was losing a great athletic director.

Bump had the reputation of being a coach's athletic director, and rightly so. He had a simple philosophy he preached to his staff: Let's do everything we can within the rules to help our coaches win. Bump worked as hard as he could to help every one of his coaches do their best, and he demanded the same thing from those around him. The coaches knew that and they appreciated it.

When I was offered the job to coach the Hawkeyes in 1978, the only person at Iowa I'd ever heard of was Bump Elliott. He had a national reputation as being a fair and honest man, and I found out that the person is even better than the image. He has a great knack of working with people and helping them succeed. He also has a pretty good temper, although the public never saw that side of him. He could really get mad and blow off steam, but he could also harness his anger and he never carried a grudge.

Bump became athletic director during a turbulent period in Iowa sports, and it took him awhile to build a successful program. But once he did, the Hawkeyes really rolled. During the decade of the '80s, Bump directed one of the best college sports programs in the country. He built a model other schools tried to follow. Bump is a special friend with a wonderful family, and although I hated to lose him as a boss, I wished him the very best in retirement.

Before we started the '91 football season we had a new athletic director, Bob Bowlsby. Bob is an Iowa boy, having grown up in Waterloo. He got an advanced degree from Iowa and came to us after serving as the athletic director at Northern Iowa. I was happy to see us settle on someone who knows the lay of the land as Bump's replacement. Bob's a very bright, hard working administrator, and I expect him to have a long and successful career as an athletic director.

Our 1991 football team wasn't going to sneak up on anyone the way we did a year earlier. Although some very good players from the Rose Bowl team were gone, our losses were more quality than quantity. Returning players included 14 starters, both kickers and most of the No. 2 unit from the Rose Bowl depth chart. And as I have said before, when you have a proven quarterback, as we did in all-Big Ten Matt Rodgers, the old coach has reason to smile.

We had to replace two exceptional running backs, Nick Bell and Tony Stewart, and we decided to move Mike Saunders into that position. A versatile senior who had been a wide receiver most of his career, he was an intelligent and gifted athlete. We had good receivers, led by Danan Hughes. Center Mike Devlin and guard Rob Baxley were our best returning linemen. Defensively, our leaders were end LeRoy Smith, linebacker John Derby and tackle Ron Geater. Our schedule was favorable and we thought that barring crippling injuries, we could be a Big Ten contender again.

Preseason rankings had us No. 18, and we looked like a Top 20 team in rolling to a 41-3 halftime lead in our opener with Hawaii. Brian Wise got us going by blocking a punt that Phil Bradley ran into the end zone for a quick touchdown. We introduced a new running back tandem of Mike Saunders and Marvin Lampkin, who combined for 135 yards on 20 carries. Fullback Lew Montgomery scored three touchdowns. Our defense and special teams, led by Rod Davis' 13 tackles, added spice to the 53-10 win with five quarterback sacks, two interceptions and two blocked punts.

When the wind blows at Cyclone stadium it makes things tough for the offense. So after we jumped out to a 17-0 first quarter lead on a very windy day at Iowa State, we buttoned it up and coasted to a 29-10 victory. Matt Rodgers threw a 46-yard scoring pass to Danan Hughes on our first possession. Our defense, led by Leroy Smith's 12 tackles, held Iowa State to 168 total yards.

We were ranked in the Top Ten after two wins, and we made the pollsters look good with a 58-7 cruise past Northern Illinois. Reserves played much of the game, and three quarterbacks—Matt Rodgers, Jim Hartlieb and Paul Burmeister—threw for 367 yards and four touchdowns.

The Big Ten opener at home featured two Top Ten teams, No. 7 Michigan and No. 9 Iowa. It was a one-point game at halftime—the Wolverines led 19-18—but they scored the next 26 points and won 43-24. We never found an answer for their running game, which accumulated 371 yards and was led by freshman Jesse Johnson, a third-string tailback who got 168 of that total.

I'd liked to have played Michigan a little later in the year. Our defense got better and better and finished the season ranked No. 1 in the Big Ten, as Bill Brashier and his staff did a marvelous job. But Michigan was too much for us to handle the day we played, and we suffered our only loss of the year. We took a lesson from that defeat, however, and our defense gave up a total of six points in the second halves of the next four games.

Wisconsin's offense couldn't score on our defense, but the Badgers owned a 6-3 lead in the final minute on the strength of Troy Vincent's 65-yard interception return for a touchdown. On fourth down with 44 seconds left, Rodgers and Saunders connected on a 14-yard scoring pass to give us a 10-6 victory. A crowd of 75,000, Wisconsin's largest in five seasons, saw us control the ball for more than 40 minutes and hold the Badgers to four first downs and 82 yards, the best defensive performance in Division I that year. John Derby was our defensive leader with 10 solo tackles.

We trailed Illinois 21-17 at halftime, but our defense held the visitors to a minus seven yards in the second half, and we won the game, 24-21, moving us to No. 8 in the CNN/USA Today coaches poll. Matt Rodgers was named the Big Ten's offensive player of the week after scoring the winning touchdown late in the game and completing 24 of 32 passes for 281 yards and two TDs. Our defense, led by Mike Wells, John Derby, Ron Geater and Leroy Smith, sacked the Illinois quarterback five times.

We again faced a halftime deficit at Purdue, this time 15-7, but our offense had a big second half in our 31-21 victory. Mike Saunders scored twice and rushed for 151 yards on 22 carries. Purdue managed only 58 total yards after intermission, thanks mostly to Ron Geater, who had four quarterback sacks, knocked down two passes and recovered a fumble. For that great performance, he was named the *Sports Illustrated* defensive player of the week.

I doubt that a team ever went into a game on a more depressing note than we did at Ohio State. The afternoon before the game a graduate student went on a shooting spree on the Iowa campus, killing five faculty members and paralyzing another student before taking his own life. When we heard the news in Columbus, our immediate concern was for the wife of assistant coach John O'Hara, who worked in the building where most of the shootings occurred. Thankfully, Saundra was not involved.

Everyone in our traveling party was stunned by this awful event. How could this happen on our peaceful campus? After the decision was made to play the game and we had a chance to collect our thoughts, we decided to strip our helmets of the stripes and decals. We played the game with plain black helmets and black armbands on our white jerseys. It was the most fitting way we could think of to pay tribute to those who had died in a senseless act.

A record Ohio Stadium crowd of 95,357 fans and a national television audience witnessed a good football game between two nationally ranked teams. The biggest play decided the outcome, and we put it in just for this game. In looking at Ohio State video, we noted that their defensive ends rushed when the opponents' tight end blocked. So we designed a play that put a man in motion, taking their cornerback to the other side, and having our tight end fake a block and go out for a pass. When we ran it late in the first half Alan Cross was so wide open it shocked everyone in the sta-

Iowa Governor Terry Brandstad and UI President
James Freedman offered congratulations after Iowa
beat Texas at the 1984 Freedom Bowl.

Chuck Hartlieb was a two-time all-Big Ten quarterback.

Marv Cook, a consensus All-America tight end in 1988, is now a strong supporter of Hawkeye sports programs.

All-Big Ten Matt Rodgers quarterbacked Iowa to the 1991 Rose Bowl.

Hayden Fry

Bump Elliott enjoyed presenting me with the 1990 Big Ten championship trophy.

Legendary NFL coach George Allen was a frequent visitor to our practices for the 1991 Rose Bowl.

I appreciated this recognition for
my 100th victory at Iowa, achieved against
Minnesota on a snow-covered field at Kinnick Stadium in 1991.

Iowa's 1982 Rose Bowl team enjoyed its 15-year reunion in 1997.

One of my good buddies is Ohio State Coach John Cooper.

When we played Michigan, Bo Schembechler and I laughed before, but not during, the games.

As long as my good friend Joe Paterno stayed active at Penn State, there was always one coach older than I.

I got a good laugh out of a joke by Texas Tech Coach Spike Dykes at the 1996 Alamo Bowl.

At the 1982 Rose Bowl, our opponent was Pac-10 champion Washington, coached by Don James.

Eddie Robinson, the legendary coach at Grambling, holds a Master's degree from Iowa.

Tennessee AD Doug Dickey and Bob Neyland Jr. presented me with the 1996 Neyland Award, named in honor of the legendary Volunteer coach.

Shirley and I had a good time getting together with Texas buddy Tom Landry, long-time coach of the Dallas Cowboys.

Bo Jackson, who nosed out Chuck Long for the 1985 Heisman Trophy, was on my team at the '86 Japan Bowl.

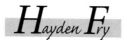

Keith Jackson, one of my favorite TV announcers, and I retired at the same time.

Jay Randolph was the voice of the SMU Mustangs when I was their coach.

The way Jim Zabel is smiling, I must have picked up the tab. "The Z" hosted my TV and radio shows for 20 years at Iowa.

Bob Brooks, the dean of Iowa sportscasters, called Hawkeye games for more than 50 years.

The Roy Firestone Show is always good for a laugh.

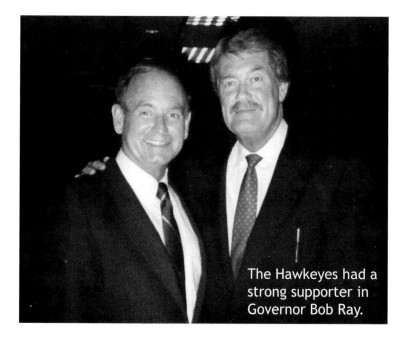

The Hawkeyes had a strong supporter in Governor Bob Ray.

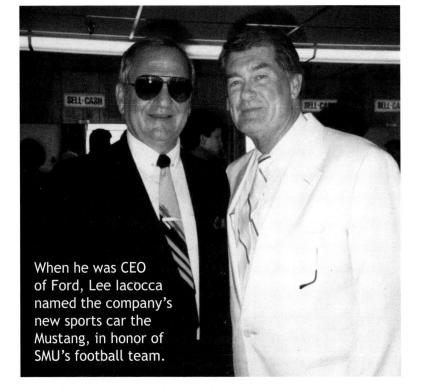

When he was CEO
of Ford, Lee Iacocca
named the company's
new sports car the
Mustang, in honor of
SMU's football team.

George Foerstner, founder of Amana Refrigeration, is a
close friend and long-time supporter of the Hawkeyes.

The popular Amana VIP golf tournament held at Finkbine drew celebrities like President Jerry Ford and Joe Garagiola.

Ernest Borgnine and I and our wives enjoyed an Amana VIP party.

Baseball great Stan Musial gave me some tips on hitting a curve ball.

My namesake, Hayden Fox, alias Craig T. Nelson, is the legendary coach at Minnesota State.

Texas friend Robert Strauss is the former U.S. Ambassador to Russia and chairman of the Democratic Party.

Inviting me to his house party, George "Goober" Lindsey said, "We don't have a swimming pool, but I'll turn the hose on you."

When the Big Ten made a TV deal with TBS, I was in the company of (left to right) Bob Wussler of TBS, OSU athletic director Rick Bay, OSU football coach Earle Bruce, Big Ten commissioner Wayne Duke, and TBS founder Ted Turner.

When Doug Flutie (right) won the Davey O'Brien Award, Lamar Hunt and I were there to congratulate him.

George Bush, an old friend from the oil fields of West Texas, dropped by for a visit while successfully campaigning for president.

Four of my best players in the '90s were:

Sedrick Shaw ▪ Tim Dwight ▪ Tavian Banks ▪ Jared DeVries

Kirk Ferentz has my full support as Iowa's new football coach.

dium, even our coaches who drew up the play. Matt Rodgers read the defense perfectly and lofted a short pass to Cross, who had good speed and clear sailing to the end zone. The play covered 61 yards.

Ohio State blocked our extra point and ran it to the other end zone for two points, but that didn't change the momentum. We had a 13-9 halftime lead, and Jeff Skillett tacked on a third quarter field goal to make the final score 16-9. The seven-point margin was much closer than the statistics. We had twice as much yardage as Ohio State, 443-221, plus a 14-minute advantage in possession time. Our defense pitched a second half shutout for the third time in four weeks, and Leroy Smith was named the Big Ten defensive player of the week after making five quarterback sacks, an Iowa record.

Indiana arrived at Kinnick Stadium for an important game in the Big Ten race. The Hoosiers and Iowa were both 4-1 in the conference, tied for second place behind Michigan. With Matt Rodgers sidelined by injury, this was expected to be a close game, but it turned one-sided when Mike Saunders scored three touchdowns in the first quarter. Mike scored again in the second half, tying the school record of four TDs in one game. We coasted to a 38-21 victory, and Mike was named the Big Ten offensive player of the week. Our defense intercepted four passes, and Leroy Smith had three quarterback sacks, giving him a school record 20 for the season.

At Northwestern, Jim Hartlieb started at quarterback for the second straight week and played a solid game. The score was tied 10-10 at halftime, but our defense got another second-half shutout in a 24-10 victory. John Derby led the defense with 16 tackles, including 10 solos.

An overnight blizzard left a more than a foot of snow on Kinnick Stadium for our last game of the regular season with Minnesota. Facilities Manager Del Gehrke and his crew did a super job of making the field ready for play, and more than 30,000 hardy fans managed to conquer the elements and make it to the game. Both teams had spent Friday night in Cedar Rapids motels, and both had a dickens of a time making it to the stadium. I made our players do their pregame exercises in the locker room because I didn't want them getting cold and wet before the game started. The wind chill was below zero when we kicked off.

Considering the elements, the game was very well played. With Matt Rodgers back in action, we gained almost 400 yards on the icy field. Matt threw two of his three touchdown passes to Danan Hughes, who made a snow angel in the end zone after each catch to punctuate our 23-8 victory. The toughest thing about playing in the snow is the kicking game, and ours was pretty good that day. Jeff Skillett even kicked a field goal. And if you have a good defense, you have a good chance to win in that kind of weather, and ours was the best in the Big Ten. The victory was our 10th of the season, tying a school record, and my 100th as Iowa's coach.

As the season ended, we were in serious negotiations with the Cotton Bowl, where my old friend Jim Brock was executive director. The "Hoss" as we called him, had been my assistant athletic director at SMU years 20 years earlier. We thought we had a deal, but the Cotton dropped us at the last minute and invited Florida State to play Texas A&M. With a No. 5 national ranking and a second-place Big Ten finish, we were in danger of getting shut out of the bowl picture. At the last minute, the Holiday Bowl extended us an invitation to play Brigham Young, which we happily accepted. We had a great experience in the San Diego twice previously, and although the Holiday's payoff is not as much as the January 1 bowls, it offers some things they do not, ideal weather being the most notable.

Not many head coaches are over 60 years old, but two were in the 1991 Holiday Bowl. LaVell Edwards and I are about the same age, and we enjoyed each other's company at the social events. At one of the luncheons, we were asked to explain why neither of us wears a headset on the sideline when most coaches do. "I'm concentrating," he said. "I'm coaching," I said. The audience thought that was funny but I don't think LaVell did.

The game matched the Heisman Trophy winner, BYU quarterback Ty Detmer, against the Big Ten's best defense. We were really concerned about Detmer, but Bill Brashier and his defensive coaches put in some schemes that slowed him down. Both of our previous games in the Holiday Bowl had been decided by one point, and this one was even closer—it ended in a tie. We scored the first 13 points and BYU got the last 13. The Cougars were in a position to win the game, but instead of playing it safe and kicking a field goal, Detmer threw a pass that Carlos James intercepted at the goal line with 16 seconds remaining. It was the last pass Detmer threw in his brilliant college career.

Both teams had problems with their kicking game. BYU missed two field goals and we missed one. Both teams missed an extra point. Maybe that's why BYU went for a touchdown rather than a field goal to win the game. Our best pass rusher, Leroy Smith, didn't play after getting hurt in the first quarter, and we missed him against a team that led the nation in passing. Teddy Jo Faley, with 13 solo tackles, had the game of his Hawkeye career. Mike Saunders scored both of our touchdowns and became the sixth Hawkeye to rush for more than 1,000 yards in a season.

Although this team didn't win a championship, it was certainly one of my best at Iowa. It won 10 games to equal a school record, and its only loss was to Big Ten champion Michigan early in the season. It won seven straight Big Ten games, which Iowa hadn't done since the early 1920s. It was unbeaten on the road, and it ended the season ranked No. 10 in both national polls.

Leroy Smith won consensus all-America honors and was named the Big Ten's defensive player of the year. Matt Rodgers gave us the all-Big Ten quarterback for the seventh time in nine years. Other Hawkeyes receiving all-Big Ten honors were Mike Saunders, Mike Devlin, Rob Baxley, Danan Hughes, Ron Geater and John Derby. They and their teammates performed so well, I was named the Big Ten coach of the year for the second straight season.

Chapter Twenty-eight

IOWA, 1992

Adversity is part of football. It goes with the game. Usually it has a negative effect, but the results can also be positive. Adversity sometimes brings a team closer together and makes it mentally stronger. One thing is for sure: if you coach or play football, you better learn how to deal with injuries, penalties, fumbles and other things that adversely affect your team.

But death is more than adversity. It is a tragedy, especially when it strikes down a man in his prime, as it did John O'Hara. John was my offensive line coach when he died suddenly, shortly before spring practice in 1992. Hawkeye coaches and fans were ending our annual Caribbean cruise and John and his wife Saundra were attending a performance in the ship's theater. He told her how much he enjoyed the musical number they had just seen, then she heard him exhale deeply. When she looked at him he had his chin on his chest and his eyes closed. He was pronounced dead by the ship's doctor shortly afterward.

John was a robust 47-year-old who worked out regularly and appeared to be in excellent health. We had played golf the day he died, walking a course in Mexico. He liked his new set of clubs and joked that he was at the top of his game. He was pleased with his round that day—I think he shot 80—and he seemed to be feeling great. There was no way anyone could have imagined he would be dead before the day ended. John's sudden death stunned his immediate family and the Hawkeye family, and it took a long time for many of us to recover.

I had known John for years, going back to the days when he coached at Midland, Texas, near my hometown of Odessa. He had been the offensive coordinator at Baylor and the head coach at Southwest Texas State and had the potential to become an outstanding Division I head coach. He was only with us for two years at Iowa as the offensive line coach, but he had a tremendous impact on the program in that short time. He was a real gentleman, a great coach and an even better recruiter. The players respected him and loved him. He is memorialized on a plaque in our dressing room.

John is the only assistant coach I ever had who died suddenly, but I lost a player in each of my first two years at Southern Methodist. Both collapsed and died on the field on first day of practice after passing physical exams. They apparently had undetected heart conditions. Both times we were in light workouts, wearing shorts. The deaths of both players shocked everyone, especially their teammates, but youngsters have amazing resilience, as they did in these tragedies. One of the players who died was linebacker Mike Kelsey, who was voted captain as a sophomore, an unusual honor. A "Fighting Heart Award" was established in his name.

Shortly before John O'Hara died, we had another significant coaching change when Carl Jackson left us to join the San Francisco 49ers staff. Carl had been with me since my days at North Texas. He coached offensive backs, then became my offensive coordinator when Bill Snyder became head coach at Kansas State. Carl did a great coaching and recruiting job for me and was difficult to replace.

We had to make adjustments on the coaching staff and at the same time deal with the emotional aspect of O'Hara's death, which the players took very hard. Don Patterson, who came to Iowa with me from North Texas, became the offensive coordinator. Frank Verducci took over the offensive line after serving as recruiting coordinator. Carl Hargrave became the new man on the staff, coaching the tight ends.

The new alignment of coaches settled in to prepare for the '92 season, which presented two big obstacles. The first was the schedule, which included Miami and Colorado, the past two national champions, and a good North Carolina State team. Seven of our 12 opponents had played in bowl games the previous season.

We also had major personnel losses to deal with, having lost six all-Big Ten players. They included quarterback Matt Rodgers and defensive end Leroy Smith, a consensus all-American.

Despite the coaching changes, the schedule and the personnel losses, we were ranked No. 16 in the preseason, which illustrates how silly those polls can be. We were coming off two exceptional seasons and the voters, without investigating, just assumed we were headed in that direction again. If it were only that easy!

We played North Carolina State even for three quarters in the Kickoff Classic, but the Wolfpack scored 10 points in the final period to win the season opener 24-14. Their exceptional speed finally did us in. Quarterback Jim Hartlieb, whose brother Chuck was all-Big Ten 1987 and 1988, threw two touchdown passes to Danan Hughes.

Against No. 1 ranked Miami at home, we again played a solid first three quarters, but the Hurricane scored two late touchdowns in a 24-7 victory. Our defense held Miami's running game to less than 100 yards, but Gino Torretta set a Kinnick Stadium record by passing for 422 yards. Jason Olejniczak led our defense with 15 tackles.

After our 10th straight win over Iowa State, this time with a score of 21-7, we played Colorado and Michigan, both Top 10 teams. We lost at Colorado, 28-12, when the Buffaloes sacked Hartlieb nine times and scored two late touchdowns to break open a close game. At Michigan, Hartlieb became the first Iowa quarterback since his brother Chuck to pass for 300 yards, but the Wolverines got off to a 31-0 lead and beat us 52-28.

Hartlieb and Anthony Dean were the heroes in our last-minute win over Wisconsin. They connected on a touchdown pass, then did it again for the two-point conversion that we needed in a 23-22 victory. Dean was playing in place of the injured Danan Hughes, our leading receiver. Hartlieb threw for 297 yards and two scores and was named the Big Ten's offensive player of the week. Maurea Crain had 13 tackles.

Our second straight Big Ten victory, a 24-14 win at Illinois, came with a heavy price. Hartlieb, who was really coming on at quarterback, was lost for the season when he suffered a shoulder separation while attempting to recover a fumble. Matt Hilliard had a big game with 12 tackles, a pass interception and a fumble recovery.

Losses to Purdue and Ohio State followed before we settled on Paul Burmeister at quarterback. Our defense, which had been struggling, gave us a big lift in a 14-0 win at Indiana, holding the Hoosiers to 106 total yards. Carlos James was named the Big Ten defensive player of the week after intercepting two passes and blocking a punt.

I'd never seen an onside kick returned for a touchdown until Ernest Crank did it in our 56-14 win over Northwestern. Burmeister's passes accounted for 283 of our 500 total yards. Alan Cross had nine receptions for 137 yards and two touchdowns.

We had a Copper Bowl bid waiting if we could win at Minnesota, but the Gophers scored 18 points in the fourth quarter to beat us 28-13. This was a game of blocked kicks. We blocked three extra points, and the Gophers blocked a punt, turning it into a score. Danan Hughes caught five passes to tie Ronnie Harmon for the Iowa record of 146 career receptions.

Although this team won only five games, I was proud of the way it was able to deal with the tragedy of a coach's death, a demanding non-conference schedule and adversity caused by injuries. We lost four of our first five games—to North Carolina State, Miami, Colorado and Michigan—but bounced back to win four Big Ten games and finish in the first division. Five of our losses were to Top 20 teams.

The injury to Jim Hartlieb, just when he was becoming a fine quarterback, was painful to both him and the team. It robbed him of what would have been a fine senior season, and it disrupted our offensive continuity. I know from experience that when a team has quarterback problems, it affects the win-loss record. Danan Hughes, one of the best wide receivers I've ever had, was slowed by injuries as a senior but still set Iowa career records with 21 touchdown catches and 2,216 yards receiving. Injuries also cut into our defensive unit.

We had some fine players on this team, and five of them were named all-Big Ten: tight end Alan Cross, offensive tackle Scott Davis, center Mike Devlin, cornerback Carlos James and defensive tackle Mike Wells. In other years, under different circumstances, their contributions would have probably meant a few more victories and a bowl games for the Hawkeyes.

Chapter Twenty-nine

IOWA, 1993 AND 1994

Losing streaks severely test a football team. When you only play 11 games and lose several of those in a row, the fans get down on the team, and the team can get down on itself. Losing steaks, like any adversity, tests a team's character and mental toughness. If a team can fight through a string of consecutive losses, it is often a stronger and better team. That, however, is very difficult to do; it is one of the great challenges of being a football player as well as a football coach.

In both 1993 and 1994, we went more than a month without winning, losing five straight games both seasons. Yet both teams survived those negative streaks and won half their games. One even went to a bowl game. Both seasons were difficult and rewarding at the same time—difficult because of the losing streaks, rewarding because of the way our players snapped back.

In 1993, we only returned four players who had started every game the previous season, and all of them played defense—ends Larry Blue and John Hartlieb and backs Jason Olejniczak and Scott Plate. Graduation had wiped out our offense. Wide receiver Harold Jasper, with eight starts in '92, was our most experienced player.

Despite our offensive inexperience, we scored enough points to win our first two games, both by narrow margins. In the opener with Tulsa, we needed a two-point conversion to pull out a 26-25 win in the final minute. After Ryan Terry scored to complete a 96-yard drive, Paul Burmeister passed to Scott Slutzker for the winning two-points. The real hero of this game, however, was Todd Romano, who tied a school record with four field goals, one from 53 yards, a new Iowa mark.

We scored the first three touchdowns and Iowa State scored the last three in our 31-28 victory at Ames. The Cyclones recovered their onside kick in the final minute, but Maurea Crain forced a fumble that Mike Dailey recovered to seal our win. Ryan Terry and freshman Sedrick Shaw rushed for 189 yards as we controlled the game with a 12-minute advantage in possession time.

For the first time in 40 years, the Big Ten had more than 10 teams competing for its football championship. Penn State, the new member, was our first conference opponent. The Nittany Lions really exposed our inexperienced offensive line and had Paul Burmeister running for his life. They sacked him nine times and intercepted him three times in shutting us out 31-0.

Penn State's admission to the Big Ten was met with a fair amount of resistance and resentment around the league. Big Ten presidents made the decision without consulting with anyone, and that didn't go over well with some administrators and coaches, but they didn't include me. I was as surprised as anyone when it was announced the Big Ten had expanded, but I was happy to hear the 11th member was Penn State, which not only brought the conference additional prestige, it also brought Eastern exposure. And Joe Paterno is a longtime friend with one of the great programs in college football.

Now I would like to see the Big Ten expand one more time and bring in a 12th member. An odd number of teams creates scheduling problems for a conference. An additional member with two six-team divisions for football makes sense to me. The divisional winners could have a championship game at an indoor stadium, and we have three in the Big Ten area. The financial revenue and media exposure would be a real bonanza to the conference. There is talk that Notre Dame will be that 12th member, and Missouri has been mentioned. Either school would be a great addition and a fine geographical fit, especially for Iowa.

In its first year of football competition in the Big Ten, Penn State started us on a five-game losing streak. We lost to Michigan, Indiana, Illinois and Michigan State before righting the ship. We kept reminding our players that we were losing to the league's best teams—they all wound up with winning records in conference play. Getting beat week after week takes its toll, both physically and mentally. But to the credit of our players, they hung in there and bounced back to win their last four games.

In beating Purdue, we scored on our first four possessions to get back on the winning track, 26-17. Paul Burmeister passed for a career-high 290 yards. Harold Jasper accounted for 129 of that on six catches. Mike Wells and Larry Blue each had two quarterback sacks, and Mike Dailey had 10 tackles and an interception.

Northern Illinois had the nation's leading rusher in LeShon Johnson. We kept him in check for a quarter, then he showed us why he was No. 1. His Kinnick Stadium rushing record of 306 yards included a touchdown run of 81 yards. But we responded with our own running game, led by Sedrick Shaw and Ryan Terry, who combined for 252 yards. I believe it is the only game I ever coached where both teams rushed for more than 300 yards. But we also had a strong passing game and won 54-20.

Iowa's 20th straight win over Northwestern moved our record to 5-5. Our defense keyed the 23-19 victory at Evanston, holding the Wildcats to two field goals until late in the game. Larry Blue had two of our five quarterback sacks while Mike Dailey, Parker Wildeman and Matt Hilliard combined for 34 tackles.

A 21-3 victory over Minnesota allowed me to become the 13th Division 1 coach in history to win 200 games. The Gophers tied a Kinnick Stadium record with 60 passes, but our defense prevented them from scoring a touchdown. Hilliard had two of our five pass interceptions, plus 11 tackles. Cliff King scored two touchdowns.

By finishing the season with four straight wins, we moved our record to 6-5 and qualified for a bowl game. The Alamo Bowl was a new postseason game in San Antonio and we were invited to play California. Iowa fans, recognized for the great support of their football team, get the credit for this bowl bid. The Alamo people knew our fan support was superior to our football team that year.

Although Iowa had played in 10 bowl games in the past 12 years, we hadn't traveled to Texas for a postseason game. So the Alamo Bowl provided a homecoming for my two coordinators, Bill Brashier and Don Patterson, and me. All three of us are native Texans. Our roster also included 11 players from Texas. We'd liked to have taken a better team to San Antonio to play California, which beat us, 37-3. We knew going into the game we were probably overmatched. Cal had a very good team that was contending for the Pac-10 title until injuries took a toll, but the Bears were healthy for the Alamo Bowl. When you get a bowl invitation, you better take it. A lot of teams sit at home over the holidays wishing they were playing in a bowl game.

There was no quarterback on our 1994 roster who had ever completed a pass in college, the first time I ever entered a season with such a lack of experience at the most important position on the team. But we did have some good players at the other skill positions, most notably Sedrick Shaw, who set a freshman rushing record the previous season, plus exciting rookies Tim Dwight and Tavian Banks. Veteran offensive linemen included Matt Purdy, Casey Wiegmann, Ross Verba and Scott Slutzker. With eight returning starters, we thought we could move the ball, even with an inexperienced quarterback.

Defense was another matter, however. All-Big Ten tackle Mike Wells had graduated, and only four starters returned. Of those, tackle Chris Webb was the lone player who had started every game in '93. Our kicking game was a plus, with both Nick Gallery and Todd Romano returning. Overall, this was one of my youngest Iowa teams, with only seven seniors starting the first game of the 1994 season.

Ryan Driscoll got the nod at quarterback as we opened the season by beating Central Michigan 52-21 and Iowa State 37-9, both at home. Our offense totaled nearly 1,000 yards in the two games, and Shaw twice ran for more than 100 yards. Against Iowa State, Kerry Cooks returned a fumble 51 yards for a touchdown and Bobby Diaco had 15 tackles. Driscoll and freshman Matt Sherman both played well at quarterback.

The next two weeks we traveled east and then west, losing at Penn State and at Oregon by big margins. Joe Paterno had a powerful Penn State team that finished the season 12-0, won the Big Ten title and probably should have been named the national champion. It finished No. 2 in the rankings because Joe pulled his starters in some games that he could have won by big margins. Joe is a real gentleman who would never humiliate an opponent and should have received credit for that. Instead, his team got knocked down in the polls.

Those two defeats put us into another five-game tailspin that included losses to Michigan, Indiana and Illinois. The 27-20 setback to the Hoosiers also cost us quarterback Ryan Driscoll, who was lost for the season with a broken collar bone. Matt Sherman was already on the injured list, leaving us literally and figuratively hurting. Could our luck get any worse? The answer was yes. Two more quarterbacks, Mike Duprey and Corby Smith, were knocked out of the game at Illinois, leaving us with only one healthy player at that position, Jefferson Bates.

Our running game broke loose against Michigan State for 369 yards and produced a 19-14 victory. Sedrick Shaw and Kent Kahl both topped 100 yards as we put together scoring drives of 87 and 80 yards. Kahl scored both touchdowns, and Brion Hurley kicked two field goals to provide the winning margin.

Purdue had us down, 13-0, but we rallied for three fourth-quarter touchdowns to go up 21-13. The Boilermakers scored a touchdown and a two-point conversion—both controversial officiating calls—and the game ended in a 21-21 tie. We scored twice on a draw play we installed just for this game. Shaw scored the first on a 39-yard run and Tavian Banks the second from 38 yards. Matt Sherman, playing his first game in five weeks, came off the bench in the fourth quarter to spark the offense.

With Sherman at quarterback, we buried Northwestern with 600 yards and seven touchdowns in a 49-13 victory at home. Sherman threw for 331 yards, and Harold Jasper had six catches, one for a touchdown. Bo Porter scored on a blocked punt return and also had an interception and 10 tackles. Ryan Terry scored on a 71-yard run and Demo Odems scored on a 51-yard pass from Sherman.

Our games with Minnesota at the Metrodome usually produce lots of exciting plays and this one was no exception. The two teams combined for nearly 1,000 yards of total offense, but it was our special teams that made the difference in a 49-42 victory in which the lead changed hands five times. Demo Odems and Bo Porter scored touchdowns when our coverage teams forced Gopher fumbles on a punt and a kickoff. Sedrick Shaw scored twice, one on a 46-yard pass from Sherman, and we surprised Minnesota when Sherman caught a touchdown pass from Tim Dwight on a fake reverse.

The outlook for the future was bright after overcoming another five-game losing streak to finish the season at .500. We had scored 119 points in the final nine quarters of the season, and a lot of that offensive talent returned. In fact, many of the skill position players were freshmen and sophomores. Sedrick Shaw was the first Iowa sophomore to rush for 1,000 yards. Freshman Matt Sherman had completed 75 percent of his passes for nearly 600 yards in the final two games.

We had a new football complex that housed our locker rooms, training rooms and weight-training facility. It was part of a $6.5 million fund-raising project that also included renovating the Recreation Building. The "Hawkeye Horizons" campaign had been a success and produced some badly needed facilities, not only for football, but for other sports as well. We were excited about the future and the coming season.

Chapter Thirty

Iowa, 1995

Momentum is important in football, and we had it going into the 1995 season. We had survived another five-game losing streak and won our last two games the previous year. We scored 98 points in those two victories and had most of our offensive players returning.

We were excited about our special teams, which scored four touchdowns in '94 and had a lot of key players returning. Scoring touchdowns on punt returns, blocked punts and kick coverage really excites the players and puts a charge into a team. Special teams play a big role, especially in close games, and we felt good about ours.

Our chief concern was defense, which wasn't strong against the rush in '94 and gave up too many points. If a defense can't stop the run, it's in trouble, and we needed to get stronger. But we had some promising freshmen in tackle Jared DeVries and linebacker Vernon Rollins, plus some fine juniors like end Bill Ennis-Inge and backs Tommy Knight and Damien Robinson who gave us encouragement.

When our 48-minute spring game produced 12 touchdowns and 1,000 yards, the suspicions about our offense were confirmed: We were going to be explosive. We were solid at quarterback with Matt Sherman and Ryan Driscoll, and running backs Sedrick Shaw and Tavian Banks and wingback Tim Dwight were going to be a handful for any defense to contain.

A new member of our coaching staff was familiar to Hawkeye fans. Chuck Long, a three-time all-Big Ten quarterback and a consensus all-America 10 years earlier, had wrapped up his NFL career and joined our staff as coach of the defensive backs. Some thought it strange that I was putting a quarterback with no coaching experience in charge of our secondary, but I believed Chuck had great potential as a coach. As a quarterback, he had been studying defenses the past 15 years, and I was convinced he could coach defensive backs.

Northern Iowa was on our schedule for the first time in 81 years and provided a season-opening test that we passed, 34-13. Tim Dwight scored two touchdowns, and Plez Atkins ran an interception back for another score as we built a 28-3 halftime lead. Sedrick Shaw topped 100 yards rushing for an offense that had a good mix of run and pass. I liked the idea of playing UNI, because it kept the gate receipts in the state, but because UNI is not a Division 1 member of the NCAA, a win over the Panthers doesn't count toward the six victories needed to qualify for a bowl game. There is a risk involved in scheduling teams that are not in Division 1.

The new coach at Iowa State was Dan McCarney, who was a member of my original Hawkeye staff and was with me for 11 years. So our trip to Ames had an interesting angle that was worked over pretty good by the news media. Dan is a bright and energetic coach who was taking on a tough job with the Cyclones, and I wished him the best. His team gave us a good game for awhile and trailed only 12-10 at halftime, but we scored 15 points in the second half and won 27-10. Sedrick Shaw had a career-high 178 yards rushing as our offense gained more than 450 yards for the second straight week. Linebackers Bobby Diaco and Vernon Rollins had 21 tackles, and Ed Gibson returned a fumble 67 yards to set up a score.

The win at Iowa State produced an oddity. We scored four touchdowns but failed to make a conversion. That's embarrassing. We had also struggled on extra points in the opener with UNI, so when we played New Mexico State, we trotted out a freshman walk-on the fans hadn't heard of. Some of his own teammates didn't know him; he wasn't even in the program. But when the game was over, Zach Bromert had kicked eight extra points and a field goal. Then he had to deal with a mob of reporters who didn't know how to spell his name, but they quickly found out because he was our kicker for conversions and short field goals the next four seasons.

Stories like Bromert's are wonderful. They're a big reason I stayed in coaching all those years. Zach is a little guy who had modest success as a high school player in Florida. He has family connections in Iowa and showed up on our campus wanting to try out for the team. He's one of the many players who have walked on and become successful in our program. A surprising number of walk-ons have become starters—even made all-Big Ten. They're proof that recruiting is an inexact science and they give our coaches reason to take a hard look at youngsters who have some ability plus great desire to play for the Hawkeyes.

Our offense exploded for more than 600 yards in the 59-21 victory over New Mexico State. Matt Sherman threw three touchdown passes, two to Tim Dwight. Tavian Banks and Sedrick Shaw both ran for more than 100 yards as we finished the non-conference schedule with our fifth straight victory over two seasons.

The Big Ten season opened at Michigan State, where Nick Saban was the new coach succeeding George Perles, who had won a couple of conference championships. Sedrick Shaw rushed 42 times for 250 yards, totals that ranked first and second in the Iowa record book, in our 21-7 victory. Shaw topped 100 yards rushing for the fourth straight game. Plez Atkins intercepted two passes, Vernon Rollins had a fumble recovery and seven tackles, and Brion Hurley booted a 50-yard field goal. My teams always played well in Spartan Stadium against good Michigan State teams. In eight games there, we lost only once.

Tom Knight broke open a close game with Indiana by returning an interception 60 yards for a touchdown with four minutes remaining. His big play boosted us to our fifth straight victory and a 22-13 win. Tim Dwight electrified the Kinnick Stadium crowd by scoring on a 56-yard reverse for our first TD. The Hoosiers contained our offense by keeping it off the field and had a 14-minute advantage in possession time. Bobby Diaco had a hand in 24 tackles. Vernon Rollins and Damien Robinson were each involved in 17 stops. Nick Gallery, developing into the Big Ten's best punter, averaged 45 yards on nine kicks.

For the first time in 10 seasons we had won our first five games and Penn State, the defending Big Ten champion, came into Kinnick Stadium to check out our unbeaten Hawkeyes. Joe Paterno had another powerful ball club that was probably still mad because it hadn't been awarded the national championship the previous season after going 12-0. Matt Sherman had a big game, throwing for

374 yards and two touchdowns, and when Sedrick Shaw scored on a 19-yard run early in the fourth quarter, we had overcome a 10-point deficit to take a 27-24 lead. But Penn State countered with two TD passes, both to all-American Bobby Engram, and won an exciting and entertaining game, 41-27.

That disappointing defeat started us on another losing streak. At Ohio State we scored 35 consecutive points, but the immensely talented Buckeyes scored the first 56. Although we lost the game, 56-35, we have the distinction of being the only visiting team to score five straight touchdowns at Ohio Stadium. Illinois, which had our number in those years, beat us for the third time in a row, 26-7. That took us to Northwestern, which had emerged as the Cinderella team in the Big Ten.

Iowa had beaten the Wildcats 21 straight times—16 since I became coach—and many of the games had been routs. But the longer you keep a winning streak alive, the harder it is to sustain, and ours had gone on for a long time. Gary Barnett was the fourth Northwestern coach I'd faced, and he had built a solid program. The Wildcats had two big reasons for wanting to beat us. They were aiming for their first Big Ten championship in 60 years, and they wanted to end their losing streak to Iowa. And to their credit, they did, beating us 31-20 and going on to win the Big Ten title.

Everything was going right for Northwestern in 1995, and our game was typical. We had a sizeable advantage in total yards (303-188) and possession minutes (35-25), but still we lost. As Bill Brashier, my longtime defensive coordinator, observed, "I remember games with Northwestern when we had less statistical advantage and won by two or three touchdowns." But that was then and this was now. The Wildcats were playing sound football, and the bounces were going their way. The bounce that sealed their victory against us was Sherman's pass that caromed off the shoulder pad of Derek Price and into the hands of a Wildcat defender, who had a clear path to the end zone for an easy touchdown.

We were really up against it when we traveled to Madison for a game with a good Wisconsin team. After starting the season with five wins, we were sitting on four straight defeats and in danger of dropping out of the bowl picture. I reminded our players that three of those losses were to three ranked teams—the best teams in the Big Ten—and that we had the ability to bounce back and win our last two games. The players proved me right.

Before 79,000 noisy fans at Camp Randall Stadium that included a lot of Iowa supporters, we jumped on the Badgers for a 21-0 lead and won the pivotal game, 33-20. Sedrick Shaw, who had become Iowa's career rushing leader with 135 yards the week before, ran over and through the Badgers for 214 yards to set a school single-season record. He scored three touchdowns, and Brion Hurley kicked another 50-yard field goal. Our defense swiped four Wisconsin passes, two by Damien Robinson, and held the Badgers to 27 yards rushing.

A Sun Bowl berth awaited if we could beat Minnesota at home, and our players responded with a tremendous all-around game. Our defense held the Gophers to 217 yards and no touchdowns, and our offense scored in every quarter in a 45-3 victory. Matt Sherman was especially sharp, hitting 17 of 21 passes for 240 yards and two touchdowns to Tim Dwight. Senior Damani Shakoor, who had seen very little action at running back, scored the first two touchdowns of his career and ran for 91 yards. His contributions were important, because Sedrick Shaw was slowed by an injury, and Tavian Banks couldn't play at all. Plez Atkins and Jared DeVries sparked the defense with two interceptions and 10 tackles.

For the first time, Iowa was playing in the Sun Bowl, and we went to El Paso with momentum and confidence even though we were decided underdogs. Our opponent was a very good Washington team, co-champion of the Pac-10. After finishing on top the Pac-10, the Huskies expected to get a Cotton bowl berth and weren't too happy about getting passed over for the Jan. 1 game in Dallas.

Sun Bowl officials were delighted with the Iowa-Washington match, especially executive director Tom Starr, a native of Newton and an Iowa graduate. He had a game that matched a couple of exciting offenses that were expected to produce a lot of scoring. Ticket sales were good. We were playing in our second bowl in Texas in two years, and just as we had at the Alamo Bowl in San Antonio, we were facing a strong team from the Pac-10. We hadn't given California much of a contest in that game, and we had 16 Texans on our roster who wanted to prove the Hawkeyes had a much better ball club on this visit.

We had good weather and practices in El Paso, and our players enjoyed the West Texas environment and their visits to Mexico. Nobody gave a middle-of-the-pack Big Ten team a chance to beat the Pac-10 co-champ, and I didn't disagree publicly. I just kept quiet, although I felt we could pull an upset if we played like we had in our recent games. In a poll of sports writers covering the game, only one, Greg Smith of the Associated Press, picked Iowa to win. Everyone else picked Washington, some by a big margin of victory. I made sure my players read that stuff, and I hoped the Washington players were, too.

Game day was sunny and cool, and before a near-capacity crowd and CBS-TV cameras, the Hawkeyes scored in less than two minutes when Sedrick Shaw bolted 58 yards for a touchdown. That big play set the tone as we ran away to leads of 21-0 at the half and 38-6 in the fourth quarter. Our running game, behind Shaw's 135 yards and Tavian Banks' 122, allowed us to control the ball and build an 11-minute advantage in possession time. Defensively, we stymied the potent Washington attack with four quarterback sacks and three fumble recoveries. The final score of 38-18 was shocking to CBS-TV analyst Terry Donohue, the former UCLA coach, who said he didn't think any team could dominate Washington the way we did.

A sensational kicking performance by Brion Hurley was a big factor in our win. He booted field goals from 50, 49 and 47 yards to earn honors as special teams player of the game. In all my years of coaching, I never saw a more impressive performance by a field goal kicker. A couple of his kicks would have been good from 60 yards. Shaw and Jared DeVries were the named the game's offensive and defensive most valuable players.

We had entered the season with momentum and were going out the same way. We survived a losing streak to convincingly win our last three games and finish with an 8-4 record. We soundly beat an outstanding Washington team in the biggest upset of the bowl season. It was a great way to end the year, but I had to deal with a major change on my coaching staff.

Bill Brashier, my defensive coordinator for 23 years, announced his retirement. Bill had been on my original staff at North Texas and came with me to Iowa. More than that, he is one of my very best friends. We've been buddies since our childhood days in Eastland, Texas. As my defensive coordinator, he allowed me to focus on the offense and my administrative duties as a head coach. Bill told me how we were going to defense an opponent, then did it, always very well. His defenses were often at the top of the Big Ten in several statistical categories.

I wished my old friend the best in retirement and thought briefly about going with him. Ending my coaching career with an outstanding season like we had just experienced was tempting, but I had promised some of my players like Tim Dwight and Tavian Banks that I would be their coach throughout their Iowa careers, and they had two seasons remaining. So I turned aside thoughts of retirement and focused on the future, which looked good for the Hawkeyes.

Chapter Thirty-one

IOWA, 1996

When an offensive lineman is doing his job, he's like a good official—he's almost invisible. But when running plays go nowhere or the quarterback gets sacked, the offensive lineman gets noticed. Unlike players at other positions, an offensive lineman has no statistics to provide a measuring stick for his performance. He gets no quarterback sacks, no pass receptions, no touchdowns. Because offensive linemen live in a world of anonymity, fans tend to underestimate their importance, but every coach knows his team can't run the ball and protect the passer without a good offensive line.

In 1996, we returned seven offensive starters from a unit that averaged more than 400 yards and 30 points a game. They included all the backs and wide receivers—the guys who get the headlines —but we had to replace four starters in the offensive line. Scott Slutzker, Casey Wiegmann and Matt Purdy had received all-Big Ten recognition, and Aaron Kooiker had started every game. They were a big reason we had a potent offense. Now they were gone, and that concerned me.

But it was hard to keep a lid on optimism with players like Sedrick Shaw, Tavian Banks, Tim Dwight and Matt Sherman back on offense, and seven starters returning on defense. Bill Ennis-Inge, Jared DeVries, Vernon Rollins, Tommy Knight, Damien Robinson and Plez Atkins were big-play makers for Bob Elliott, my new defensive coordinator. And there was no question our special teams were going to be good with all the kickers back, including Nick Gallery, the all-Big Ten punter. We appeared to have all the elements for another good team except an experienced offensive line, but nobody wanted to hear about that.

Arizona, with its "Desert Swarm" defense, was our first opponent at Kinnick Stadium. It was a grueling, physical test for an opener, and it wasn't very pretty. Neither team's offense could get going and defense provided the big plays. Our defense forced three turnovers that resulted in Iowa touchdowns. Rollins recovered a fumble in the end zone for the first one, then Ennis-Inge separated the Arizona quarterback from the ball, and Sherman tossed a short touchdown pass to Damon Gibson. In a span of 30 seconds, we scored twice! Knight's interception set up Shaw's short TD run for the winning points in a 21-20 victory. It was a satisfying way to open the season, and Rollins was named the Big Ten defensive player of the week.

After being held in check by Arizona, our offense unloaded for 536 yards against Iowa State. Tavian Banks received Big Ten offensive player of the week honors for his 182 yards rushing and three touchdowns, one on an 89-yard run that opened the scoring. Brion Hurley kicked a field goal from 54-yards, his fourth of more than 50 yards, and Gibson caught another TD pass in our 38-13 victory.

We scored on our first possession at Tulsa and led at halftime 17-13, but in the second half the home team scored two touchdowns and kept us out of the end zone in recording a 27-20 upset. Although we missed a couple of scoring opportunities, we didn't play badly. Tulsa played a great football game and showed us a much better passing game than we anticipated. Sometimes you have to give the other team credit for an outstanding performance, and that was the case in this game.

If there was a pivotal moment in the season it was in the Michigan State game when we faced a third-and-22 deep in our own territory. A strong wind and poor field position had prevented us from getting anything going offensively and we were already behind 17-0. We called a pass play named X-TD we thought would work against the defense the Spartans were using and it did, with Matt Sherman throwing to Demo Odems for 54 yards. We went on to score a touchdown and get our offense untracked.

But it was an uphill battle, and we were still behind, 30-23, when we scored the tying and winning touchdowns without Michigan State running a play. We discovered on the Spartans' films that two of their players had trouble catching kickoffs, so we took advantage of the wind and bright sun and booted the ball to them. We recovered two fumbles using that strategy, and wrapped two touchdowns around one of them. Coaches look at opponents' films for hours and hours, and when they detect something that decides a game as this did, it is very rewarding.

There were a lot of stars in the 37-30 win over the Spartans. Chris Knipper caught two touchdown passes from Matt Sherman, and Brion Hurley kicked another long field goal, this one from 51 yards. Tim Dwight had two long punt returns, Tommy Knight's interception set up a touchdown, and Vernon Rollins had 10 tackles. It was an impressive comeback by the Hawkeyes and built confidence for the rest of the Big Ten schedule.

For the second year in a row, Tommy Knight stole an Indiana pass and ran it back for a touchdown. His big play covered 60 yards and was critical in a 31-10 victory we had trouble nailing down. Turnovers in Indiana territory stalled us in the first half, and the Hoosiers scored their only touchdown on a blocked punt. Tavian Banks had three TD runs, and Matt Hughes was named the Big Ten's defensive player of the week with 10 tackles, including two quarterback sacks.

The two oldest coaches in Division 1 matched wits and teams on a dreary, rainy day at Penn State. Joe Paterno and I were nearing 70 years old, and both of us had been coaching more than 40 years. We were getting the "When are you going to retire?" question and our age was used by schools recruiting against us. We got some laughs about that on the field before the game. We always enjoyed exchanging stories and competing against each other.

Two big plays by Tim Dwight got us touchdowns in the first half. First he scored on an 83-yard punt return, then his 60-yard catch-and-run set up another TD. But we were trailing 20-14 in the fourth quarter when we surprised Penn State with a halfback pass —Rob Thein hitting Demo Odems on a critical third-down play. Tavian Banks scored the touchdown that gave us a 21-20 win over a Top Ten team that seldom loses on its home field. Banks was playing for Sedrick Shaw, who was sidelined with bruised ribs, and ran for 116 yards and two TDs. Damien Robinson, Matt Hughes and

Kerry Cooks were the standouts for a defense that held Penn State to 73 yards and no points in the second half.

When Joe Paterno and I met at midfield after the game, his hair was matted down by the rain and we were both soaked through. He looked at me through his black-rimmed glasses and said, "What are two old farts like us doing out here on a day like this?" We laughed and hugged and wished each other luck. Iowa and Penn State weren't scheduled to play again until 1999, but neither of us suggested that this might be the last time we would face each other across the field.

Three turnovers and a blocked punt set up four scores for Ohio State, but after falling into a 31-6 halftime hole, we rallied to make a game of it. Tim Dwight scored on an 86-yard punt return and a 19-yard reverse. He had another long runback on a day when he broke Nile Kinnick's record for punt return yardage in a season, but our rally fell short and we suffered our first Big Ten defeat 38-26.

Our defense played a major roll in a 31-21 victory at Illinois. Jared DeVries' pressure on the quarterback set up Vernon Rollins' interception for a touchdown, and Brett Chambers' diving interception set up another score. Both big plays broke open a close game in the fourth quarter and gave us a 31-21 victory. Sedrick Shaw, healthy for the first time in several weeks, had his best game of the year with 159 yards rushing and scored our first touchdown.

In our next two games, both at home, our defense flip-flopped. First, Darnell Autry punished us for 240 yards and four touchdowns as Northwestern won for the first time in 25 years at Kinnick Stadium, 40-13. Wisconsin came in the following week with the Big Ten's leading rusher, Ron Dayne, who our defense held to 62 yards in a 31-0 shutout.

Those two games illustrate how much the physical status of a team affects its performance. We were in much better health for the Badgers than the Wildcats and it showed in the results. Wisconsin had a powerful offense that averaged more than 30 points a game. The Badgers won five of their last six games, scoring 210 points in their victories.

Bill Ennis-Inge was a one-man wrecking crew against Wisconsin, sacking the quarterback four times, forcing two fumbles that led to Iowa touchdowns, and recovering a fumble. The Badgers, averaging 222 yards rushing, were held to only 26 by our defense. Sedrick Shaw celebrated his birthday by tying Ronnie

Harmon's school record of 32 career touchdowns. He scored three times on runs of 33, 29 and 8 yards.

My hat goes off to Iowa fans, who never cease to amaze me. After our win at Penn State, some of our followers who had made that long trip unfurled a big banner that said, "Happy Hawkeye Valley" and displayed it on a hillside near Beaver Stadium. For our final game of the season at Minnesota, we had about as many fans in the Metrodome crowd of 55,000 as did the Gophers.

As usual, Iowa fans created a lot of noise, especially when we broke a 17-17 tie in the third quarter and ran off 24 straight points. A 64-yard run by Michael Burger and Matt Sherman's 53-yard bomb to Tim Dwight broke open what had been a close game, and we went on to win 43-24. Sedrick Shaw became the eighth Big Ten player to rush for 1,000 yards three times and the eighth to rush for 4,000 career yards. He also became Iowa's all-time touchdown leader by scoring twice.

Iowa's fifth straight Big Ten victory on the road gave us a 6-2 conference record, and our only losses were to co-champions Ohio State and Northwestern. We had won eight games for the fourth time in the '90s, ranked in the Top 20 and were headed back to Texas to make our second appearance in the Alamo Bowl. Our opponent was a good Texas Tech team that featured Byron Hanspard, who had just received the Doak Walker Award that goes to the best running back in college football. Although the Red Raiders were installed as a slight favorite, I felt good about our chances—much better than I did three years earlier when we played California in the same bowl. We had a better football team this time.

The Texas Tech coach was Spike Dykes, an old friend. He had once coached at Eastland, Texas, where I was born, and was an assistant at Texas when my SMU and North Texas teams played the Longhorns. He has a great sense of humor, and we had a good time cutting up at the various bowl functions that preceded the game.

Practices and preparations were going well when tragic news came down from Iowa two nights before the game. Linebacker Mark Mitchell's mother, traveling to San Antonio with Mark's family, had died in an automobile accident south of Des Moines. It was the worst kind of news, and Mark naturally took it very hard. So did many of his teammates, who were regular visitors to his Iowa City home and knew his mother well. Mark went home immediately to be with his family, and the rest of us tried our best to focus on the game with Texas Tech, but it was difficult.

As the nation's best running back, Byron Hanspard received more publicity than his teammates, but we were more concerned about containing quarterback Zebbie Lethridge. He was a great scrambler capable of making big plays, so we assigned one man to contain him, regardless of the defense we were in. We were determined not to let him beat us. As far as Hanspard was concerned, we had played against seven of the top running backs in the country and held five to less than 100 yards.

We felt we had a good chance of containing Hanspard, and we were right. Our defense did a magnificent job in limiting him to 64 yards and keeping Lethridge under control at the same time. When the unexpectedly one-sided game was over, Texas Tech had only 206 total yards and we had a 27-0 shutout, our second in three games. We had a lot of defensive standouts, especially Jared DeVries, who was voted the defensive MVP of a bowl game for the second straight year, and linebackers Vernon Rollins and Matt Hughes, who combined for 19 tackles.

Sedrick Shaw, who grew up in nearby Austin and had a lot of friends and family in the Alamodome, finished his career with another brilliant performance. After setting up our first touchdown with a long run, he broke three tackles in scoring our second TD. He rushed for 100 yards for the 19th time in his career and was named the offensive MVP. Spike Dykes told me after the game, "I thought we had the best running back in the country, but I was wrong. You do."

John O'Hara recruited Sedrick out of Austin, the home of the University of Texas. Sedrick's family trusted John, which opened the door for me. Getting both Sedrick and Demo Odems out of LBJ High School in Austin was a real recruiting coup for us. Both were highly recruited and became outstanding college players.

Sedrick's mother is as strong a woman as I've ever been around, and I really came to admire her. She wanted to know everything about the University of Iowa and the other schools recruiting her son, and I mean everything. I wish more mothers were like her. She wanted what was best for her son and we had to convince her that Iowa was the best school for Sedrick, but it wasn't easy.

Sedrick is strong and mentally tough, just like his mother. He only missed one game in four years, that one at Penn State when he had badly bruised ribs. He could take punishment and dish it out. He liked to run inside as much as outside, through people or around them. You never knew what he was going to do when he got the ball. He had great moves and spins, which is what made him such an exciting player.

Because Sedrick kept to himself, not a lot of people got to know him. He wasn't much for socializing and dating. Football and academics were what interested him, and they took up most of his time. Like Ronnie Harmon, he didn't enjoy talking to the press, which might have made him seem aloof. But he isn't that at all, he is just a private person.

Only eight Iowa running backs have rushed for 1,000 yards in a season. I coached every one of them, and all were exceptional players. But Sedrick Shaw is the only one who ran for 1,000 yards more than once. He did it three times, joining the company of only six other players in Big Ten history. Of all the records he holds at Iowa, I think that is the most impressive. He is not only a gifted athlete, he is also tough and durable and competitive, and he left some records at Iowa that will be very hard for other players to match.

Postseason honors included all-America recognition for Tim Dwight and Jared DeVries. Shaw, Damien Robinson, Ross Verba and Gallery made all-Big Ten, Gallery for the second year in a row.

Remember my preseason concerns about the offensive line? They were genuine, and we were lucky, because we settled on a line that stayed virtually intact throughout the season. Ross Verba, Matt Reischl, Bill Reardon and Jeremy McKinney started every game. Derek Rose and Chris Knipper started all but one. We were fortunate we had few injuries.

In fact the entire team stayed healthy, with 17 players starting every game of the season. On offense, besides the linemen already mentioned, Matt Sherman, Michael Burger, Tim Dwight and Demo Odems answered the bell every week. On defense, Damien Robinson, Kerry Cooks, Tom Knight, Plez Atkins, Vernon Rollins, Matt Hughes, Aaron Klein, Jared DeVries and Brett Chambers started 12 times. Bill Ennis-Inge only missed one game, Jon LaFleur two.

When you have good players and they stay healthy, chances for a successful season skyrocket. In 1996, we kept getting better because we stayed healthy. We wouldn't be as fortunate the next two seasons.

Chapter Thirty-two

IOWA, 1997

After winning 17 games the previous two seasons and with a lot of key players returning from those teams, expectations were high for the 1997 Hawkeyes. Quarterback Matt Sherman had started 26 straight games, more than any player on our roster, and he had some outstanding talent to distribute the ball to. Tavian Banks was our leading scorer in '96, Tim Dwight our leading receiver.

Our defense was headed by Jared DeVries, who was developing into one of the best tackles in college football, along with linebackers Matt Hughes and Vernon Rollins. One concern was the kicking game. Nick Gallery, a two-time all-Big Ten punter, and long-range field goal kicker Brion Hurley had graduated.

The Big Ten schedule maker hadn't done us any favors, putting us on the road to play Ohio State and Michigan on back-to-back Saturdays, and Northwestern and Wisconsin later. All were bowl teams the previous season and all expected to be good again. Our streak of five straight Big Ten victories on the road would be sorely tested.

But it was impossible to not be optimistic about the season. We had a lot of good players who had experienced success the last two years and were dedicated to being even better in 1997. Injuries to key players were about the only thing that could stop us.

When we scored 221 points in winning the first four games, the national polls put in the Top Ten. Tavian Banks was sensational in victories over Northern Iowa (66-0), Tulsa (54-16), Iowa State (63-20) and Illinois (38-10). He scored a total of 13 touchdowns, with three TD runs of more than 60 yards.

Tavian became my first player to top 300 yards rushing when he set a school record of 314 against Tulsa. He's hard to describe when he's at his best, as he was in this stretch of games. I have never seen a runner with his vision, and his great acceleration allows him to just run away from defenders. His fluid, seemingly effortless running style makes him appear to be loafing, which of course he is not.

Tim Dwight put on a show at Iowa State, catching eight passes for 187 yards. He and Matt Sherman hooked up three times for touchdowns, earning Dwight honors as the Big Ten offensive player of the week. Our defense had eight quarterback sacks and Kerry Cooks ran an interception back 30 yards for a TD.

The first serious injury of the season was sustained against the Cyclones when torn knee ligaments knocked Vernon Rollins out for the season. The injury was a real blow to Vernon, as well as the team. He was developing into a great linebacker, and losing him noticeably weakened our defense. But the way our offense was mowing down opponents during this stretch, his loss wasn't considered as serious as it turned out to be.

Our first two games in October were at Ohio State and at Michigan, and both were loaded. The Buckeyes were the defending Big Ten champions, hopeful of winning the national title after finishing second behind Florida in '96. Andy Katzenmoyer, their great linebacker, had a career game against us with 11 tackles, a pass interception and a key block on a touchdown that sealed a 23-7 OSU victory. Another big factor was Ohio State's kicking game, which didn't allow Tim Dwight a single runback.

We didn't know it at the time, of course, but we went to Michigan to face a team that would go undefeated and be crowned national champion by the Associated Press. Tavian Banks had sprained an ankle, and although he never missed any games because of the injury, he couldn't make the cuts and moves we saw the first month of the season. Michigan was surprised when we moved Tavian to fullback and ran a quick trap that sprung him for 53 yards and a touchdown. He didn't have to make any quick cuts, he just bolted up the middle, right past the linebackers, who were caught by surprise.

We took a 21-7 lead when Tim Dwight scored on a 61-yard punt return as the first half expired. Michigan coaches were second-guessed for kicking the ball to Dwight, but they were kicking out of their end zone and couldn't get too cute. Their coaches took what they considered to be their best chance, and Timmy burned 'em.

Although we didn't know it at the time, Matt Sherman broke a bone in his throwing hand in the third quarter. He played the rest of the game, but the injury sidelined him for the remainder of the regular season. Zach Bromert kicked a field goal to put us up 24-21 after Michigan had tied the game, but the Wolverines scored another touchdown to win, 28-24. Jared DeVries was named the Big Ten defensive player of the week for his three quarterback sacks and 11-tackle performance.

We went from a quarterback who had started 32 consecutive games to one who had virtually no experience. Randy Reiners, a multi-talented, hard-nosed sophomore, was thrust into the starter's role and he acquitted himself well against Indiana, throwing for two touchdowns and scoring one himself. We scored on a variety of big plays, including a 64-yard pass from Tim Dwight to Damon Gibson, Dwight's 92-yard punt return, and pass interception returns by Matt Bowen (70 yards) and J.P. Lange (60 yards).

Indiana had one of four new coaches in the Big Ten, Cam Cameron, who was a Hoosier quarterback in the early 1980s. It speeds up the aging process when you face a coach who once played against you, but you also have a special feeling for him. Cam is a bright young man with a promising coaching career, and I wish him the best.

Purdue's new coach, Joe Tiller, brought his passing game to Kinnick Stadium and had us down by 10 points twice in the first half. Sparked by Rob Thein, we came to life with three touchdowns in the third quarter and went on to a 35-17 victory. Thein scored three TDs, one on a 51-yard screen pass, and was named the offensive player of the week in the Big Ten, a rare honor for a non-starter. Tim Dwight pushed his career punt return yardage past 1,000, making him the only player in Iowa history to reach that total in three categories. Pass receiving and kickoff returns are the other two.

Injuries continued to eat away at our key players. Just as Randy Reiners was becoming a good Big Ten quarterback, he hurt his knee on the last play of the Purdue game, and we had to start a third-string quarterback at Wisconsin. Dwight had a groin pull and Banks was still nursing a bad ankle. They weren't practicing. Neither were our defensive tackles, Jared DeVries and Jon LaFleur, who were both hurt.

With all of them ailing, and with Zach Brommert missing field goals because of a fatigued kicking leg, we really struggled and lost close games we ordinarily would have won at Wisconsin (13-10) and Northwestern (15-14). We played hard and sometimes we played well, but we also made critical mistakes and couldn't make the plays to put us over the top. Despite the fact our defense held the Badgers to only 225 yards, they beat us for the first time in 21 years. We out-gained the Wildcats by a big margin, but they beat us on a safety that was the result of our bad snap on a punt.

Our seniors rallied their teammates for a big effort in our traditional season-ending game with Minnesota at home. Tim Dwight made a couple of dazzling plays despite a sore groin and our defense recorded its third shutout of the season in a 31-0 victory. Dwight set a Big Ten record with his fifth career punt return for a touchdown and established another conference mark for punt return yardage in a career. Our defense forced five Minnesota turnovers, with Jeff Kramer getting two, as Floyd of Rosedale stayed in Iowa City for the fifth straight year.

We received a Sun Bowl berth, our sixth bowl game of the '90s and our 14th in the last 17 seasons. But we still had a lot of crippled players when we played Arizona State at El Paso. The Sun Devils had won five of their last six games in the tough Pac-10 and were on a roll when we played them. We were never able to get our offense untracked in a 17-7 loss. Jason Baker averaged 49 yards on eight punts, one of them a Sun Bowl record-76 yards, and was named the special teams player of the game.

I'd sum up 1997 as a season of bad luck, because we had a heck of a football team, one that could have been in contention for the Big Ten championship if things had gone our way. As I've said before, great seasons happen when good teams have good health and a little luck. We didn't have good health or much luck, and won seven games in a year we might have won 10.

Three of our losses were by one, three and four points. Narrow defeats like those really hurt and raise questions. What if Matt Sherman hadn't broken his hand at Michigan? Would Michigan have won the national championship if its fine quarterback, Brian Griese, had been knocked out for the season?

What if Tavian Banks hadn't played on a sore ankle the last eight games? I believe he was on his way to a 2,000-yard season. He got to 1,000 yards on his 125th carry, faster than any player in NCAA history. When he was healthy, Tavian was the most exciting running back I ever had at Iowa. He did some things that defied description, and he left school with 10 records, including yards rushing in a season and touchdowns in a career.

How much did the loss of a great young linebacker like Vernon Rollins in the third game of the year weaken our defense? Could he have made the difference in one of those close losses? What if we had kicked a couple of short-range field goals at Wisconsin and Northwestern? Forget about Matt Sherman—what if Randy Reiners had been healthy for those games?

You get the drift. It's not hard to imagine a couple of more wins if things had gone our way. Like they say out in West Texas, "The sun don't shine on the same dog's rump every day." It wasn't shining on the Hawkeyes' rump in 1997.

This team had a lot of great accomplishments. It broke or tied 30 individual and team school records. It led the nation in punt returns and ranked high in other national stats. It ranked third or better in 14 Big Ten statistical categories.

Banks was named the offensive player of the year, and DeVries the defensive player of the year in the Big Ten. They received all-America recognition along with Dwight. All three plus Mike Goff were named first-team all-conference.

I never coached a player I enjoyed more than Tim Dwight. He was so full of energy and inspiration that he made everyone around him better and made the game a lot more fun. Just like Jerry Levias, who I coached at SMU, Dwight brought electricity to the game. Whenever he touched the ball, something good almost always happened. Both Dwight and Levias were real game breakers, the kind of players who drove opposing coaches crazy trying to figure out how to contain them.

Timmy wanted to play every down, both offense and defense, but a player can't do that at the Big Ten level, and he finally realized that. We had Dwight and Banks together for four years, and Sedrick Shaw for three of those. We only had one football and we had to pass it around. I thought offensive coordinator Don Patterson and his coaches did a marvelous job of doing that, because all three players left Iowa with a lot of records. They were all great team players.

Banks was especially patient because he had to sit behind Shaw for three years. Tavian's an unselfish player and waited his turn. A lot of selfish players would have packed their bags and gone to another school. But Tavian persevered as a Hawkeye, had a great career and is proud of his Iowa degree.

The seniors of 1997 have much to be proud of. Their accomplishments are all over the Iowa record book and they provided Hawkeye fans with tremendous thrills and excitement. They won two bowl games by big margins against very good opponents, and they had 24 victories in their final three seasons. Theirs was one of the really good periods in Iowa football history.

Chapter Thirty-three

CHANGES IN THE GAME

When I was playing high school football more than 50 years ago, my coach at Odessa, Joe Coleman, took me to Cleveland to hear Paul Brown speak at a clinic. Brown, the founder and legendary coach of the Cleveland Browns, said some things at that clinic I carried with me throughout my playing and coaching career. One of his points of emphasis was that you stand a much greater chance of having a pass intercepted by throwing it down the middle of the field than toward the sideline. That's because there are more defenders in the middle of the field. That was true in the 1940s and it's still true today.

Although football techniques have changed considerably over the years, the fundamentals have not. Paul Brown had sound fundamentals for his passing game that apply today. For instance, we had two passes picked off in our big game at Michigan in 1997. Both were intercepted in the middle of the field.

Football is still a game of blocking and tackling, but the players use different techniques today. Defenders used to tackle a ball carrier by taking him to the ground any way they could—just wrestle him down. Now they're taught to keep their head in front and maintain a target area. Blocking has changed, because the rules have changed. A blocker can do much more with his hands and arms in today's game, so his techniques have changed.

Rules change every year. Nearly all changes are made to protect the players; they're aimed at reducing injuries. Others are intended to improve the game, to speed it up and make it more fan-friendly. The rulebook used when I played at Baylor was much different than the one used in college football today. It was pretty simple in those days: One platoon football with players going both ways. Few plays sent in from the sideline, no facemasks. But we had four downs to gain 10 yards, and touchdowns counted six points. Not everything has changed.

One thing that never changes: defenses are always trying to catch up with offenses. When they do, offenses make changes to gain the advantage. The option play revolutionized offenses years ago, and it took a long time for defenses to catch up. When defenses figured out how to stop the option by loading up, the offenses spread out and emphasized the passing game. The defense had to protect the entire width of the field.

As the offense changes, the defense adjusts, making football a constantly changing game, which is why I love it. It's like a game of chess; you're always trying to outsmart your opponent. That's why an experienced, intelligent quarterback is such an asset. He can take his team to the line of scrimmage and call a play based on the defense he sees, eliminating bad plays and sometimes making big plays.

When I came to Iowa in 1979, the Hawkeyes were still using the Wing-T offense popularized by Forest Evashevski back in the 1950s. They were lining up with two tight ends and a wingback close to the formation. Defenses were really loading up on that with an eight-man front. The defense had adjusted to the offense. When Evashevski was running the Wing-T so effectively 40 years ago, he wasn't seeing that defense.

Defensive pursuit has changed dramatically over the years. Defenders now take a more intelligent angle when pursuing a ball carrier. Previously, everyone just chased him; now the defense schemes to get everyone in the proper angle of pursuit. It's much harder for a running back to have a big game today than it was for great players like Doak Walker and O.J. Simpson. Defenses are designed to prevent the big play and to make a team drive the field using 12-15 plays, and that's hard to do. The offense often stops itself by making a mistake.

Over my coaching career, I've seen players get bigger, faster and stronger. It's been gradual, and some of it is the result of normal human development.Weight training and proper diet have also played significant roles. I never saw a set of weights when I played college football, and now everyone has them. Nebraska and LSU popularized weight training, and now all schools have strength programs with qualified people to run them. Good weight training reduces injuries and maintains muscle balance and is an important part of a winning program.

Off-season programs are important in conditioning and teaching, and allow a player to improve his strength and increase his weight. Arkansas had the first one I was associated with. Frank Broyles got it from a high school in New Iberia, Louisiana that had won a state championship.We made it fun and interesting for the players, getting them to compete against one another. Off-season work has been refined and improved through the years. Players like it because they get bigger and stronger.

How about steroids and drugs? How much have they had to do with football players getting bigger and stronger? My personal experience tells me not much. In fact, I think the stories about steroids and drugs are overblown. Only two of my players ever tested positive, and that's with more than 100 players being tested throughout a school year and nine times during a season. I'm proud of the job we did in educating our players about drugs.

At every place I have coached, there have been two sets of rules—the universities' and my own—and mine have always been tougher regarding drugs. My rule is real simple: Son, if you want to do drugs that's fine, you just can't do them as a member of my team. Which is most important to a player, drugs or football? He can't have both—not on my team. I never had many rules, but those I had were strictly enforced, especially the one regarding drugs.

Maybe I scared off the drug users in the recruiting process, because that's when I started hammering home the point that I wouldn't tolerate it. To reinforce my position, I made sure the parents got the message, too.That might have scared off some recruits, but I'd rather do that than have problems later. It's all part of discipline, like being well-groomed and well-mannered. It's part of a good behavior program and being a team member.

Athletes play a small role in drug abuse on a college campus, yet they are the ones singled out. Should they be tested while members of the marching band and the debate team are not? If athletes are tested, shouldn't administrators, faculty and coaches be tested, too? Why are athletes singled out? I've never gotten good answers to these questions and I have never been for drug testing of athletes. That doesn't mean I'd change the way I'd deal with it as a coach. It means I think the athletes are being held to higher standards, and that's not fair.

It's been interesting to watch the evolution of special teams, which didn't get much attention years ago. Your punter often played another position and sometimes he was your star player; Nile Kinnick being a good example. Your offense stayed on the field to cover punts and they often weren't the best players for doing that. For fielding punts and kickoffs, you just tried to get someone who could catch the ball. Of course with one-platoon football you didn't have much choice, but even when free substitution came along not much attention was paid to what we now call special teams. General Neyland at Tennessee was one of the first to put emphasis on the kicking and receiving teams and Johnny Majors was one of the earliest specialists. For some time now, coaches have delegated the responsibility for special teams to someone on the staff because those teams play an important role in the outcome of a game.

Scouting has changed dramatically. Years ago getting information on your opponent was like going through the CIA, FBI or Secret Service. At SMU, we once caught a guy dressed up like a cleanup man with a bag and spear, walking around our practice field. He was taking notes on what we were doing. Another time we caught a guy on top of a hotel who was filming our scrimmage; a bellboy tipped us off. One opponent wired our dressing room to eavesdrop on what we were saying. Funny but true, that was scouting in the old days. Anything to get a leg up on your opponent. Now we exchange videotape of all our games to get information on the team we're about to play. We don't get as many laughs, but scouting reports have improved greatly.

Football players get much better medical attention than they once did. Many advances have been made in medicine, of course, but we have much bigger medical staffs today—more trainers, doctors, specialists. There are so many, I've suggested we redshirt some of them. At Iowa, we're fortunate to have a great medical center located right across the street from Kinnick Stadium, and that hospital gives our players the best possible care.

There have been unbelievable changes in the area of academics in the past 15 years or so. At Iowa we have a student services office with a good-sized staff to give our players academic counseling and tutoring, if needed. Graduation rates have been put under a microscope and receive much greater scrutiny. That's been embarrassing for some schools, but at others, like Iowa, it illustrates that the graduation rate for athletes is better than it is for general student body.

I don't agree with all NCAA rules, but the one that limits players to 20 hours of football per week is a good one. The rule is great for the players, but it makes a coach refine and condense his teaching. You're not with your players very long, so you better communicate precisely with them while you have their attention.

Coaches take their jobs more seriously than they used to. There used to be time for gin rummy and domino games, but not anymore. Coaches who have a low golf handicap probably aren't spending enough time in the office. Years ago, a coach on the west coast had a sand trap installed on his practice field so he could hit wedge shots while his players were doing wind sprints.

Old timers will tell you that coaches today don't have as much fun as they used to, and there may be some truth in that. The game and the pressures that go with it have gotten bigger, no doubt about that. Perhaps that's taken some fun out of the game. I know one thing: there aren't as many characters in the game today as there were when I started out in the business.

In those days, I attended lots of coaching clinics, kept my ears open and took lots of notes. Oklahoma had a clinic that included both football and basketball, and one evening I found myself having dinner with John Wooden of UCLA, Adolph Rupp of Kentucky and Henry Iba of Oklahoma State. They were already legendary basketball coaches and provided me with one of the most entertaining and interesting evenings I ever spent. I still have the table cloth they used to draw up plays. They tossed around a lot of ideas that a young football coach at the table later applied to his game.

Football coaching staffs have grown as squads have gotten bigger, and they are about the right size now. The NCAA limit is nine assistant coaches; 20 years ago at North Texas I had five. Recruiting requires a lot of time and impacts every coach on the staff, both in and out of season. It's not uncommon for coaches to work 15-18 hour days during the fall. I don't know of anyone who works harder than football coaches.

Money is more important in today's game because football is asked to financially support more than it ever did. At schools like Iowa, football supplements just about all the sports—men's and women's—except men's basketball. If football is having an off year and gate receipts and television revenue are down, other sports get pinched financially. That puts tremendous pressure on football coaches to win. Football shouldn't be expected to play the role of the rich uncle, but that's the way it is. Is it any wonder football is overemphasized at some schools?

Football is leaned on heavily as a marketing tool. Most major schools now have marketing and licensing programs that generate much-needed income. The Hawkshop brings in a lot of money at Iowa, selling football-related paraphernalia. Signage in Kinnick Stadium is a relative new income device. Luxury boxes, which rent for a lot of money, are common at most big college stadiums. Football has deep pockets, but there is a bottom down there somewhere.

Major college football needs a playoff, in my opinion. It's the only sport in any NCAA division that doesn't produce a true national championship. That's because of the traditional bowl setup, which allows 18 teams to finish the season with a victory and make their fans feel good during the winter. I'm for trying a two-week, four-team playoff, which would increase the interest in college football tremendously. It would also produce millions of dollars, and that might be the carrot that eventually brings on a playoff.

As we approach another century, football remains a great game. It is still the ultimate team sport because it involves more players than any other. Yes, it has changed a lot since I started playing more than 50 years ago, and it continues to change. But the fundamentals are the same after all these years. It remains a pretty basic game. The team that knocks the other one off the line of scrimmage generally wins.

Chapter Thirty-four

Iowa Fans and Other Observations

I've had a love affair with Hawkeye fans for 20 years and they are the biggest reason I stayed at Iowa all that time. Whenever someone came around with another job opportunity—and there were some good ones—Iowa fans were always the biggest factor in my decision to stay. They are absolutely the greatest people in the world. They love their Hawkeyes and support their program. They fill the stadium on Saturday and they put their money where their mouth is with financial contributions.

The fans haven't always agreed with everything we've done as coaches, but that's OK. We're not above criticism and at times we deserve it. But Iowa fans are fair and reasonable. For every negative letter or comment I've received, there have been 100 positive ones. That's a pretty good ratio.

The I-Clubs have been a source of real joy to me. The huge turnouts at every stop on the spring circuit, and the devotion given to the Hawkeyes is truly amazing. I really enjoy the question-and-answer segment of the programs. Sometimes the questions are serious and sometimes they're funny, but the main thing is they come from loyal supporters of the Hawkeyes, the people who really matter.

I don't know of another support group like our I-Club. We have them all over the state and all around the country, and they're vital to the success of Iowa athletics. I-Club officers and board members are tireless workers who put in countless hours to help the Hawkeye program. My only complaint about the I-Club outings is the food, which is always good and I eat too much of it. I gain about 15 pounds every spring and spend the summer trying to take it off.

My radio call-in program offers the opportunity to talk to the fans every week, and I enjoy that. It's a good way for a coach to stay connected with the people who support his program and answer their questions. Because WHO radio in Des Moines has such a strong signal, I've gotten calls from all over the country. Several years ago one came in from a trucker in Colorado, and the conversation went like this:

Caller: I happened to be listening to your station and heard the name Hayden Fry.

Host Jim Zabel: That's right, Hayden's on the line with us.

Caller: I'm from Odessa, Texas and played high school football with a fella named Hayden Fry. Could this be the same person?

Zabel: Indeed it is. Go ahead and talk to him.

Caller: Hayden! This is Henry Johnson. How in the world have you been?

Me: Great! How are things with you?

Caller: They're going OK. I'm out here in Colorado driving through a snowstorm. Been driving for the same trucking company since we left high school. How about you, Hayden—what are you doing now?

Zabel thought the question was hilarious, and we still joke about the call. I think it came after we lost a close game, and I needed a good laugh.

Iowa fans love their football team and they like to talk to the coach. Shortly after I got to Iowa, my wife and I were having dinner in a public restaurant and I kept getting interrupted by fans who wanted to visit and get my autograph. After this went on awhile, Shirley could see I was getting irritated because I couldn't eat my dinner.

She leaned across the table and said, "I can see you have a problem, Coach, but you'd have a bigger problem if they left you along and ignored you." She drove home the point and I tried to be more patient after that, even if I had to eat a cold dinner.

It's hard to win at Iowa; we have no natural recruiting base because of our state's small population. But our fans make recruiting easier because of the great support they give the football team. Kids are aware of that, and they like to play where there is strong fan interest and the stadium is usually full. Iowa fans are a great asset, and I have always appreciated that fact.

The cost of operating a major college athletic program has gone up astronomically over the years. If you buy football tickers you're aware of how prices have increased, and the additional revenue doesn't necessarily go toward operating the football program. Every time an athletic department needs money for anything it leans on the football team to produce more income.

That is where I think football players are being cheated, and it is why I think they should be paid. Players are providing much more revenue for their schools than they did 40 or 50 years ago, yet they receive the same thing they did then—room, board, books and tuition.

Players producing television and bowl revenue for their schools should share in the wealth. In real life, if you produce a profit you get paid accordingly. Why shouldn't athletes participating on teams that make money get some of it? Let's pay the players before someone organizes them and we have a revolution.

League commissioners, the head of the NCAA, athletic directors and coaches are getting hundreds of thousands of dollars a year in compensation for their work. Their income has gone up dramatically as revenue has increased. Some are paid over a million dollars a year. Yet the players are still getting the same compensation of room, board, books and tuition. That's not right!

The NCAA Manual is so thick and full of rules it's kind of comical. A rule was recently added that allows athletes to earn up to $2,000 during the school year. The rule is full of potential problems and is basically unenforceable. Which athletes in which sports —men's and women's—get the best jobs? And what is reasonable pay for these jobs? I know of a school where players working as valets get $100 tips for parking cars. We don't have job opportunities like that in Iowa City. The people who voted in favor of this rule weren't around 40 years ago when something similar was tried, cheating went out of control and the rule was rescinded.

Throw out the new rule and simply add $2,000 to a scholarship. Players at schools like Iowa deserve it. They've earned it. The people running college sports should realize that the game will go on without administrators and coaches. Try playing it without the players.

If football has changed in the last 50 years, and it has, the news media has changed even more. In my early years of coaching, the press was simply referred to as "the writers," and we had some great ones. I'm not sure why Texas produced so many outstanding sports writers, but it was probably because most of them played the game. I've always thought a football reporter has an advantage if he participated in the sport and understands how hard it is to play. Many today have not had that experience.

When *Sports Illustrated* started publishing more than 40 years ago, it got its best writers out of Texas. Dan Jenkins, Bud Shrake and Tex Maule were products of the Longhorn State and helped make the magazine an instant success. They were some of the colorful Texas sports writers in my early years of coaching. Others were Blackie Sherrod, Harold Ratliff and Louis Cox in Dallas; Bill Van Fleet in Ft. Worth; Dave Campbell in Waco; Jack Gallagher and Mickey Herschowitz in Houston; Dub King in Fort Worth; and Spec Gammon in Odessa. They are legendary writers and some are still active.

Iowa has had its share of top sports writers, too. Some who covered my Hawkeye teams for many years were Maury White and Buck Turnbull in Des Moines; Gus Schrader in Cedar Rapids; Al Grady in Iowa City; Russ Smith in Waterloo; and Bob Brown in Fort Dodge. They are retired now, but some good young writers are coming along to keep Iowa fans informed about their favorite team.

No school in the country had better radio coverage than Iowa during my years as coach. Bob Brooks, Jim Zabel, Frosty Mitchell and Ron Gonder called all the Hawkeye games, home and away, and they each had a loyal audience. Now there is a new and exclusive voice of the Hawkeyes that belongs to Gary Dolphin, who has a solid background in Iowa athletics and does an excellent job.

When television came along to give us the 6 o'clock news and the 10 o'clock news the competition for stories increased. TV also gave us live coverage of sporting events, and the way those events were reported in the press began to change. The race to be first sometimes created inaccurate and unfair stories, and the relationship between the coach and the news media was damaged. Instead of dealing with writers holding notepads, a coach was confronted by a battery of microphones and video cameras. Pack journalism was born.

Then evolved the 24-hour TV sports channels, the radio sports talk shows and computer technology that gives newspapers a place where fans give anonymous opinions. There's some good in all this, but the days when a coach knew all the names of the reporters covering his team, plus the names of their wives and children, are gone forever. And that's too bad.

There was a time when sports writers accepted gifts and money from professional teams, putting themselves in a compromising position. A writer once asked me to financially help him though a divorce. When I reacted with surprise, he told me the local pro team was giving writers expensive gifts and their wives fur coats. He said it was common practice. I refused to get involved in buying favors, but I guess pro teams did it for years. I believe they operate more ethically today.

The popular notion is that Watergate changed the way journalists cover—or uncover—stories and that carried over to sports. Get out the knives and daggers and dig up some dirt. Above all, don't be for the team you're covering. Don't be a homer. I've never seen anything wrong with a reporter rooting for the team he follows. It's human nature. Jim Zabel and Al Grady make no bones about their love for the Hawkeyes, and no one thinks any less of them for that.

Nothing bothers me more than unfair and inaccurate reporting about my players and coaches. I occasionally came down hard on members of the press who did that because I thought they should be corrected, and I let them know my feelings. That's just the way I am and the way I operate. I think it's a coach's responsibility to defend his team and his staff, and I've always done that.

As the years passed, I developed policies about how the press covered my teams. I understand and appreciate that the press has a job to do, but coaches also have responsibilities, such as doing their best to win. For instance, I learned early in my coaching career that you have much better practices if they are closed to the public and the press.

When I came to Iowa some coaches in the Big Ten scoffed at that policy, but one by one they closed the gates of their own practice fields. It was the same when we removed the artificial turf at Kinnick Stadium. They thought that was a mistake, but now most Big Ten stadiums have natural grass. When I recruited Jerry Levias at SMU other coaches in the Southwest Conference said they would never integrate their teams, but before long they were recruiting black players. So maybe I've done some things right.

I've enjoyed my relationship with members of the news media through the years. Many are my friends and most are fine people. I might have gotten mad at them from time to time, but I got it out of my system and moved on. I never carried a grudge. A wonderful thing happened when the news media opened its doors to women and minorities. That was a big step, one that needed to be taken, and I applaud the people who made it happen.

I'm sometimes asked if I have any connection with TV series called "Coach" that features a football coach named Hayden Fox, who works at Minnesota State. The answer is no, although the creator of the show, Barry Kemp, ran it by me before it ever went on the air. Barry's an Iowa grad and a Hawkeye fan and he didn't make it any secret that the name for his head coach was inspired by a certain coach back in the Big Ten. He offered me a royalty in the event the show made good—which of course it did—but I never accepted it. That was probably a mistake, because the popular show will no doubt be in reruns for many years.

I never appeared on the show, although I was invited, but I did three commercials to promote it. I have become a good friend of the star, Craig T. Nelson, who often played in the annual Amana VIP golf tournament on our University course. He's a really good guy, as is Jerry Van Dyke, who plays his assistant coach on the show. Jerry is even funnier in person than he is on the air. I'm not much of a TV viewer, but I've seen enough of "Coach" to understand why it became successful. I only wish my own life as a football coach was filled with as much humor as Hayden Fox's.

Title IX, the federal law that gave women the opportunity to participate in sports, is one of the best things to occur in my lifetime. It's been more than 25 years since the law was passed, and the growth of women's sports on the high school and college scene during that time has been remarkable. Athletic participation helps a youngster grow and mature, and that goes for girls as well as boys. It exposes them to discipline and teamwork and other things that will be of value in later life.

Most everything about women's sports is positive, except for the pressure it puts on football at schools like Iowa, where football is counted on to financially carry the women's programs. We've cut scholarships from 115 to 85 to help support the women's programs, and the decrease in scholarships has hurt football. It has hurt the quality of the game because it hurts practice and preparation. There is now a NCAA limit for the number of walkons for football. It's a bad rule that probably wouldn't stand up in court. At state schools like Iowa, every student should be allowed to go out for football.

Some schools, including many in the Big Ten, have dropped men's sports like baseball and wrestling to accommodate their women's programs. That's not right, and it has caused bitterness and divisiveness at those schools. We're fortunate at Iowa—as far as I know there has never been any discussion about dropping a sport for men.

When Title IX was enacted, I was at North Texas and it didn't take us long to develop a competitive women's program. All the sports for men and women were put under one athletic director, and I was that person. That worked well for us and I think it's best to combine men's and women's programs. When problems and conflicts surface, they are more easily and speedily resolved under one administrator.

Women's sports have flourished in the last 25 years. That's been wonderful to see and it shouldn't have taken a federal law to make it happen. Women should be granted to same rights as men in all things, including sports, but they should also accept the same responsibilities, and that includes financing their athletic programs. I hope they accept more of that responsibility in the coming years.

Chapter Thirty-five

1998 AND RETIREMENT

We came out of spring practice in 1998 with guarded optimism. I felt we could field a representative and competitive football team even though our personnel losses from the previous season were significant. We had just completed a three-year period that produced 24 victories and three bowl appearances, and we'd won two of those bowl games by big margins, beating good teams. The mood was upbeat even though we entered the season with a young and inexperienced team. But we couldn't afford any setbacks. We needed some good fortune to have a good season.

We had lost some tremendously gifted players, with nine of them signing NFL contracts as draftees or free agents. Tavian Banks had scored more touchdowns in a career and rushed for more yards in a season than any Hawkeye in history. Tim Dwight was Iowa's all-time leader in receiving and punt returns. Matt Sherman was a three-year starter at quarterback. We would be especially inexperienced at the skill positions.

After he considered skipping his senior year to play in the NFL, Jared DeVries lifted our spirits when he announced he would return to Iowa for his senior season. Although it was his decision, I joked that it was one of my best recruiting jobs. Jared's a great player and his presence would strengthen our defense considerably.

The bad news started when Tony Collins, our only wide receiver with any real experience, quit the team for personal reasons.
He was also the leading candidate to replace Dwight on punt returns. He would have been second to Dwight nationally in '97 but
he didn't have enough returns to qualify.

We got more bad news when two offensive linemen became
academic casualties in summer school. Chris Knipper had moved
from tight end to tackle, where he had a great spring, earning praise
from NFL scouts. Shalor Pryor was our best utility offensive lineman. Losing them for the season was a real setback to our offense.

Tragedy struck when sudden death took close relatives of
Randy Reiners and Travis Senters. Randy lost his sister, Natalie, just
before practice began, and for the first time in my coaching career,
we postponed press day so the team could attend a funeral. Travis
lost his father, Jerry, after our first game in which he started at linebacker because we had injuries at that position. Many in the Iowa
football family knew Natalie and Jerry, and their untimely deaths
were an emotional drain on the team and coaches.

Randy entered the season as our starting quarterback, but
grief as well as injuries diminished his performance. I hope he plays
his senior season without any more setbacks because he's a fine
leader with excellent ability. Travis came to Iowa as a walkon, earned
a scholarship and is also capable of making a strong contribution
to the team.

We had injuries all season at two important positions—quarterback and linebacker. We were never able to start the same quarterback more than two games in a row, with Reiners, Kyle McCann
and Scott Mullen in and out of the lineup. A team can't develop
consistency by playing musical chairs at quarterback, and our offensive production reflected that.

At linebacker, Vernon Rollins never recovered from his knee
injury of the previous season. Starters Matt Hughes and Raj Clark
missed games with various ailments. We wanted to redshirt freshman Aaron Kampman, an outstanding prospect, but he wound up
starting because of all the linebackers being injured.

Having your players get hurt is one of the toughest things
about being a football coach. When you watch them work hard to
become as good as they can be, and then get injured, it can be
devastating. Nobody worked harder than Vernon Rollins, and just
when he was becoming a great college football player he suffered
a knee injury that threatens his career. Some things in life aren't

fair. But injuries are part of football, and you have to learn to live with them or get out of the game.

Some players seem to be indestructible and are able to play with all kinds of ailments. Jared DeVries is a good example. He had three different injuries during the season that diminished his ability but he played courageously and often very well. Mark Bortz, who was in my first recruiting class at Iowa, was another defensive tackle who wouldn't let an injury keep him on the sidelines. He never missed a game, which is why he had such a long and productive career in the NFL.

As we entered the season, few people knew that Bob Elliott, our defensive coordinator, had a blood disorder that threatened his life. He had told me about it a few months earlier when he underwent chemotherapy. He knew the chemicals would affect his strength and energy, and he wanted to make me aware of it. By midseason, rumors were circulating about his condition, and he decided to tell his players and then the press, who made it public. I know it was a difficult thing for Bob to do, and his players took it very hard.

Bob is one of the brightest and most conscientious coaches I ever had. Although he was under great personal stress throughout the season, he put everything he had into his job and refused to slow down, although I urged him to do so. He is a highly competitive individual and has all the qualities to become a head coach. I pray that someday he gets the opportunity.

When it became obvious that we weren't going to a bowl game, I started thinking seriously about retirement. There had been speculation about when I'd quit coaching ever since I turned 60, and that was nine years earlier. Some schools were using my age against us, but I always told recruits I had no retirement plans, because I didn't. It was tempting to step aside after the 1995 season when we beat Washington in the Sun Bowl. My wife, Shirley, encouraged me to leave then and go out with my long-time buddy Bill Brashier, but I had promised some players that I would be at Iowa throughout their careers, and I wanted to honor that commitment.

Retiring after a bowl game wouldn't have been fair to Iowa and its fans, either. The University would have been looking for my successor in January, an awkward time to hire a football coach. A new coach needs as much time as possible to hire a staff and recruit. My decision to retire would impact the lives a lot of people, most of all, my coaches and their families, and they were a great concern to me. But I knew a decision would have to be made eventually and the earlier for the transition the better. Stepping aside in November seemed best to me.

The day after our last game of the season, I met with my coaches and told them I was leaning toward retirement, but that I wanted to do what was best for them, the team and the University. They encouraged me to do what was best for me. We had a long discussion, and I came away from the emotional meeting with the decision to retire.

The next day I held a press conference and announced that I was retiring after 47 years of coaching football. It was not an easy thing to do.

I was surprised and a little embarrassed by the reaction to my announcement. The response from the fans, coaches at other schools, former players and the news media was truly overwhelming. The fact that I was judged on my career rather than isolated games or seasons means a lot to me.

I've been asked about what legacy I leave at Iowa, and I'm not sure how to answer that. We recruited good young men who worked hard, won more than their share of games and played in a lot of bowls. They won the Big Ten three times and brought a lot of pride to the state. They were mostly good citizens and good students who earned degrees. I'm as proud of that as I am their achievements on the football field. We ran a program that was able to win pretty consistently over a 20-year period without breaking rules. If that's a legacy, then I'm proud to be leaving it.

I had a lot of great coaches and many are now running their own programs. One of them is succeeding me. I have every reason to believe Kirk Ferentz will be a successful football coach at Iowa. He's an outstanding person with a wonderful family. He was my assistant for nine years when we had some of our best teams. He developed and produced some great players. He knows the school, he knows the state, and he knows what it takes to win in the Big Ten. He also knows what great fans we have at Iowa, and I hope they will give him the same enthusiastic support they did me.

It was hard to win at Iowa when I arrived in 1978, but we were able to establish consistency beyond my wildest dreams. It's even harder to win today because academic requirements and admission policies have changed. The standards are higher, making the coach's job harder and winning more difficult. Iowa fans need to understand that.

It was hard to quit coaching football. It was the most difficult decision in my life. I coached for 47 years at some level—high school, Marines and college—and I loved everything about football, from preparation to practice to the games on Saturdays. I wish everyone could have the experience of standing on the sideline at Kinnick Stadium, as I did for 20 years, and feel the energy of 70,000 fans exploding with appreciation for an exciting play.

I'll miss that, of course, but most of all I'll miss the players and coaches. They are the ones who made my job special. They are the ones who make me get emotional when I think of all my years in the game. They gave me more than I could ever give them, and I am grateful.

I can't imagine anyone luckier than Hayden Fry. I'm blessed with a wonderful wife and children. I became a head coach at an early age and spent my life working in the game I love. Good health permitted me to coach longer than most men. There is very little about my life I would change.

The title of this book is a West Texas expression that means an exceptionally good time. That's a good way to describe my life. It has truly been a high porch picnic.

Appendices

Hayden Fry

Born: Feb. 28, 1929, in Eastland, TX
High School: Odessa (TX), 1946
College: Baylor, B.S. (Psychology), 1951
College Coaching Experience:
Baylor, Assistant Coach, 1960
Arkansas, Assistant Coach, 1961
Southern Methodist, Head Coach, 1962-72
North Texas State, Head Coach, 1973-78
Iowa, Head Coach, 1979-98

All-Time Record

Team	W	L	T
Air Force	1	3	0
Arizona	3	2	0
Arizona State	0	1	0
Arkansas	2	9	0
Army	0	1	0
Auburn	1	0	0
Baylor	7	4	0
Brigham Young	0	0	1
California	0	1	0
Cal Poly-Pomona	2	0	0
Central Michigan	2	0	0
Cincinnati	1	1	0
Colorado	0	2	0
Drake	4	0	1
Florida	1	2	0
Florida State	0	2	0
Georgia	0	1	0
Georgia Tech	0	1	0
Hawaii	2	1	0
Houston	1	0	0
Illinois	11	9	0
Indiana	11	5	0
Iowa State	16	4	0
Kansas State	2	0	0
Lamar	0	1	0
Long Beach State	0	1	1
Louisiana Tech	3	0	0

Louisville	1	1	0
Memphis State	2	3	0
Maryland	0	1	0
Miami (FL)	1	2	0
Michigan	4	12	1
Michigan State	11	5	1
Minnesota	12	9	0
Mississippi State	2	2	0
Missouri	0	2	0
Navy	2	0	0
Nebraska	1	3	0
New Mexico State	10	0	0
Northern Illinois	4	0	0
Northern Iowa	2	0	0
North Carolina State	1	2	0
Northeast Louisiana	1	0	0
Northwestern	18	3	0
Ohio State	3	14	1
Oklahoma	1	3	0
Oklahoma State	1	2	0
Oregon	0	3	0
Penn State	2	4	0
Purdue	12	6	2
Rice	8	3	0
Richmond	1	0	0
San Diego State	2	2	0
Southern Cal	0	1	0
Southern Methodist	1	2	0
Southern Mississippi	2	0	0
Tennessee	2	2	0
Texas	3	11	0
Texas A&M	6	5	0
Texas-Arlington	5	1	0
Texas Christian	5	6	0
Texas-El Paso	3	0	0
Texas Tech	5	7	0
Tulsa	3	3	0
UCLA	1	1	0
Virginia Tech	0	1	0
Wake Forest	1	0	0
Washington	1	2	0
West Texas State	5	1	0
Wichita State	1	0	1
Wisconsin	15	2	1
Wyoming	1	0	0

Achievements and Honors

Texas Sports Hall of Fame
Holiday Bowl Hall of Fame
1996 Robert R. Neyland Memorial Trophy
Distinguished Alumni, Baylor University
Johnny Vaught Lifetime Achievement Award
Texas High School Football Hall of Fame

NATIONAL MEDIA HONORS RECEIVED BY
HAYDEN FRY AT IOWA

The Sporting News Coach of the Year
ABC-TV Chevrolet Coach of the Year
Big Ten Coach of the Year three times
Midwest Media Coach of the Year
American College Football Coaches Association District Coach of the Year twice
United Press International Coach of the Week

THE IOWA HAWKEYES UNDER HAYDEN FRY

Three Big Ten championships
A school record 10 victories in 1985, 1987 and 1991
No. 1 national ranking during the 1985 season
Fourteen first division finishes in the Big Ten
Fourteen bowl game appearances in 17 seasons
Ten seasons of eight or more victories
Finished in the nation's Top 10 twice and Top 25 nine times

Year-By-Year Summary

At Southern Methodist

Year	W	L	T	Pct.
1962	2	8	0	.200
1963	4	7	0	.364
1964	1	9	0	.100
1965	4	5	1	.450
1966	8	3	0	.727
1967	3	7	0	.300
1968	8	3	0	.727
1969	3	7	0	.300
1970	5	6	0	.455
1971	4	7	0	.364
1972	7	4	0	.636
11 years	**49**	**66**	**1**	**.426**

At North Texas State

Year	W	L	T	Pct.
1973	5	5	1	.500
1974	2	7	2	.300
1975	7	4	0	.636
1976	7	4	0	.636
1977	10	1	0	.909
1978	9	2	0	.818
6 years	**40**	**23**	**3**	**.635**

At Iowa

Year	W	L	T	Pct.
1979	5	6	0	.455
1980	4	7	0	.364
1981	8	4	0	.667
1982	8	4	0	.667
1983	9	3	0	.750
1984	8	4	1	.654
1985	10	2	0	.833
1986	9	3	0	.750
1987	10	3	0	.769
1988	6	4	3	.577
1989	5	6	0	.455
1990	8	4	0	.667
1991	10	1	1	.875
1992	5	7	0	.417

1993	6	6	0	.500
1994	5	5	1	.500
1995	8	4	0	.667
1996	9	3	0	.727
1997	7	5	0	.583
1998	3	8	0	.273
20 years	143	89	6	.613

Career Totals

Years	W	L	T	Pct.
37 years	232	178	10	.564

Bowl Games Statistics (7-9-1)

1963 Sun: Oregon 21, SMU 14

1967 Cotton: Georgia 24, SMU 9

1968 Astro Bluebonnet: SMU 28, Oklahoma 27

1982 Rose: Washington 28, Iowa 0

1982 Peach: Iowa 28, Tennessee 22

1983 Gator: Florida 14, Iowa 6

1984 Freedom: Iowa 55, Texas 17

1986 Rose: UCLA 45, Iowa 28

1986 Holiday: Iowa 39, S. Diego St. 38

1987 Holiday: Iowa 20, Wyoming 19

1988 Peach: N.C. St. 28, Iowa 23

1991 Rose: Washington 46, Iowa 34

1991 Holiday: Iowa 13, BYU 13

1993 Alamo: California 37, Iowa 3

1995 Sun: Iowa 38, Washington 18

1996 Alamo: Iowa 27, Texas Tech 0

1997 Sun: Arizona State 17, Iowa 7

Winningest Iowa Coaches

Coach (years)	W	L	T
Hayden Fry (20)	143	89	6
Forest Evashevski (9)	52	27	4
Howard Jones (8)	42	17	1
Eddie Anderson (8)	35	33	2
Burt Ingwersen (8)	33	27	4
Alden Knipe (5)	29	11	4
John Chalmers (3)	24	8	0
Jess Hawley (6)	24	18	0

Order is based on total number of wins

Hayden Fry's Iowa Record

All games: **143-89-6**
    Home games: 77-38-3
    Away games: 66-51-3

Big Ten games: **96-61-5**
    Home games: 50-29-3
    Away games: 46-32-2

Non-league games: **47-28-1**
    Home games: 28-9-0
    Away games: 19-19-1

Games Coached, Division 1-A

1.	Amos Alonzo Stagg	548
2.	Pop Warner	457
3.	Bear Bryant	425
4.	Hayden Fry	420

Coach Hayden Fry's Lettermen
(1962 through 1998)

Over a span of 37 seasons as head coach in collegiate football, Hayden Fry had a major influence on hundreds of young football players. The following is a complete list of Coach Fry's letter winners at Southern Methodist University, North Texas State University and the University of Iowa.

**Southern Methodist University
(1962-72)**

Albright, Lewis, 1961, 1962
Allen, Randy, 1971
Armstrong, Michael, 1967, 1968, 1969
Arnold, Kelly, 1971, 1972, 1973
Berg, Douglas, 1970, 1971, 1972
Best, Rory, 1972, 1973, 1974
Black, Thomas, 1970, 1971, 1972
Blount, Ralph, 1972
Blount, Sherwood, 1969, 1970, 1971
Bobo, Keith, 1971, 1972, 1973
Bost, Robert, 1970
Bowles, Gerald, 1970
Bradley, Paul, 1970, 1971
Braugh, Roger, 1960, 1961, 1962
Brennan, Thomas, 1960, 1961, 1962
Brittain, Que, 1967, 1968, 1969
Brittain, Vic, 1968, 1969, 1970
Burke, Floyd, 1964, 1966, 1967
Campbell, Donald, 1961, 1962, 1963
Carey, Leonard, 1971, 1972
Carter, Gary, 1970
Caughran, Ronald, 1966
Caughran, Thomas, 1962, 1963, 1964
Chilton, Dan, 1966
Christopher, Truman, 1966
Clark, Rayford, 1971, 1972
Clarke, John, 1960, 1961, 1962

Clements, Fred, 1966, 1967, 1968
Cone, Rush, 1971
Corder, William, 1963, 1964, 1965
Cormier, Rufus, Jr., 1968,1969
Cosper, Ronald, 1961, 1962, 1963
Crenshaw, Robert, 1966, 1967, 1968
Crowder, Alton, 1962, 1964, 1965
Cude, Martin, Jr., 1961, 1962, 1963
Cupples, James, 1967, 1968, 1969
Curry, Patrick, 1969, 1970, 1971
Dannis, Charles, 1970, 1971
DeGrazier, Michael, 1961, 1962
Denbow, Donnie 1966
Derden, Max, Jr., 1962, 1963
Deweber, Donald, 1970, 1971, 1972
Dickerson, Joseph, 1970, 1971, 1972
Duncan, Brian, 1972, 1973, 1974
Duvall, Andy, 1971, 1972, 1973
Farris, James, 1972, 1973
Ferguson, Marvin, 1966
Ferguson, Michael, 1964, 1966, 1967
Fleming, Kenneth, 1968, 1969, 1970
Floyd, Robert, 1969
Fraser, William, III, 1967, 1968, 1969
Freeman, John, 1965, 1966, 1967
Gaiser, George, 1964, 1965, 1966
Gannon, William, 1961, 1962, 1963
Gholson, William, 1970, 1971
Gibson, Charles, Jr., 1964, 1965, 1966

Gibson, Robert, 1972, 1973
Gilder, Gordon, 1969, 1970
Goodrich, Robert, III, 1965, 1966, 1967
Gordon, Daniel, 1968, 1969
Goss, Randall, 1971, 1972, 1973
Goss, Randy, 1971, 1972
Graham, David, 1966
Graves, John, 1961, 1962, 1963
Gray, Jerrel, 1970
Green, Ray, 1960, 1961, 1962
Griffin, Jerry, 1964, 1965, 1966
Gross, Roger, 1962
Guthrie, Larry, 1969, 1970
Hackney, Clint, 1972, 1973, 1974
Hagle, James, 1965, 1966, 1967
Halla, James, 1965
Halpin, Lowell, 1967
Hammond, Gary, 1969, 1970
Hargrave, Harry, 1968, 1969, 1970
Harlan, William, 1962, 1963, 1964
Harrison, Kenny, 1972, 1973, 1974, 1975
Hart, William, 1968, 1969, 1970
Haynes, Michael, 1972
Haynes, Walter, 1968, 1969, 1970
Head, Albon, Jr., 1966, 1967,1968
Higgins, James, 1968, 1969
Hillary, Thomas, 1962, 1963
Hixon, Charles, Jr., 1968, 1969, 1970
Hodges, James, 1970
Holden, Samuel, 1967, 1968, 1969
Houghten, H. Dwight, 1969
Howell, Dennis, 1971, 1972
Hughes, John, 1961, 1962, 1963
Hutchinson, T.J., 1971
Irons, Richard, 1966
Jackson, Charles, 1966, 1967
Jackson, William, 1968, 1969, 1970
Janszen, Michael, 1965, 1966, 1967
January, Alan, 1963, 1964, 1965
Jernigan, Larry, 1963, 1965, 1966
Johnson, Edward, 1972, 1973
Johnson, H.B. 1969

Johnson, Hiram, 1969, 1970, 1971
Johnston, Fred, 1970
Johnston, James, 1968, 1969
Jones, Phil, 1972
Jordan, C. Michael, 1969
Jordan, John, 1968, 1969, 1970
Kelcher, Louie, 1972, 1973, 1974
Kimbrough, John, 1966, 1967
Knee, Gary, 1968, 1969
Knee, John, 1962, 1963, 1964
Krischke, David, 1972, 1973
Kuesel, George, 1970
LaGrone, John, Jr., 1964, 1965, 1966
Leitko, Mike, 1971, 1972, 1973
Lesser, Reid, 1968, 1969
Levias, Jerry, 1966, 1967, 1968
Line, Bill, Jr., 1968, 1969, 1970
Livingston, James, 1968
Livingston, Michael, 1965, 1966, 1967
Loyd, Paul, 1966, 1967
Maag, John, 1963, 1964, 1965
Magers, Harold, 1963, 1964, 1965
Mapps, Raymond, 1970, 1971, 1972
Maxon, Alvin, 1971, 1972, 1973
May, Terry, 1966, 1967, 1968
McAlister, Oran, 1962, 1963, 1964
McDearman, Rusty, 1971
McGinnis, Stephan, 1968, 1969
McLarty, Seth, 1970, 1971, 1972
McMillan, Marshall, 1968, 1969
Medlen, Norman, 1964, 1965
Medlen, Ron, 1964, 1965, 1966
Merritt, Ronald, 1963, 1964, 1965
Meyer, Johnny, 1970, 1971
Miller, Harry, 1962, 1963
Miller, Joseph, 1960, 1961, 1962
Mitchell, Mike, 1966, 1967, 1968
Moore, David, 1966
Moore, Jimmy, 1966, 1967, 1968
Moore, Michael, 1963, 1964, 1965
Moreman, Dan, 1966, 1967
Morris, Wayne, 1972, 1973, 1974, 1975

Morrow, William, 1964
Morton, Stephan, 1972, 1973, 1974
Motes, Kenneth, 1964, 1965, 1966
Mullins, Larry, 1964, 1965, 1966
Nady, Gary, 1972
Nekuza, Michael, 1968, 1969, 1970
O'Connell, John, 1967, 1968, 1969
Oefinger, Roy, 1964, 1965
Oyler, Robert, 1962, 1963, 1964
Parrott, G. Stephen, 1969
Partee, Dennis, 1965, 1966, 1967
Perez, Ines, 1966, 1967
Phillips, Jerome, 1964, 1965, 1966
Poirot, Rodney, 1966
Popelka, Robert, 1970, 1971, 1972
Portillo, Bruce, 1967, 1968, 1969
Poulos, Stanley, 1968, 1969
Pouncy, Gene, 1972
Pouncy, Joe, 1972
Raines, Arthur, 1962, 1963
Randell, Don, 1970, 1971, 1972
Ray, Earl, 1965, 1966
Reel, Ronald, 1963, 1964, 1965
Reinowski, Paul, 1964
Rhoads, Jack, 1960, 1961, 1962
Richardson, Harold, 1966, 1967
Richardson, Michael 1966, 1967, 1968
Richardson, Terry, 1969
Richey, John, 1961, 1962, 1963
Roan, Oscar, 1972, 1973, 1974
Robinson, James Lee, 1971, 1972
Roderick, John, 1963, 1965
Rogers, David, 1970, 1971
Rogers, Mack, 1971, 1972
Rollins, Arthur, 1970, 1971
Ryan, James, 1970, 1971, 1972
Savage, Randy, 1972, 1973, 1974
Schoenke, Raymond, 1960, 1961, 1962
Scoggins, Randy, 1971
Scott, Louis, 1970, 1971
Shaw, James, 1968, 1969
Shaw, Rufus, 1972
Shaw, Wanda, 1972

Shelton, Mike, 1971
Shelton, Michael, 1969
Sherwin, Thomas, 1961, 1962, 1963
Silverthorn, Kris, 1971-1972
Simmons, John, 1970
Sims, Steve, 1972
Smith, J. David, 1969
Smith, Michael, 1972, 1973, 1974
Smith, Robert, 1972, 1973, 1974
Smith, Steve, 1971
Standifer, Charles, 1964, 1965, 1966
Staples, Pelham, III, 1968
Stephens, Kenny, 1971
Stewert, Leslie, 1961, 1962
Stewert, William, 1964, 1965, 1966
Stier, Fred, 1964
Stringer, James, Jr., 1967, 1968, 1969
Stutts, Joe, 1968, 1969, 1970
Tabor, Michael, 1963, 1964, 1965
Taylor, James, 1963, 1964
Terry, Doug, 1972
Terry, Glen, 1965
Thomas, Bill, 1972, 1973, 1974
Thomas, Daniel, Jr.,1962, 1963, 1964
Thomas, David, 1969
Thomas, Guy, 1972, 1973, 1974, 1975
Thompson, Ted, 1973, 1973, 1974
Thornhill, Lynn, 1964, 1965, 1966
Tunnell, Larry, 1968, 1969
Upshaw, Jim, 1972
Valdez, Edward, 1967
Walker, Doyce, 1960, 1961, 1962
Walker, Ken, 1971
Weatherfornd, Billy, 1971
Weaver, Walter, 1965, 1970, 1971
White, Connie Mac, 1963, 1965, 1966
White Donald, 1966, 1968
White, Joe, 1969, 1970
White, Robert, 1972, 1973
Whitener, Charles, 1970, 1971, 1972

Wilmot, George, 1964, 1965, 1966
Wilson, David, 1963
Wilson, Jerry, 1966, 1967
Wood, Bill, 1972, 1973, 1974
Wood, James, 1966, 1967
Wright, William, 1968, 1969, 1970
Wyatt, Harry, 1970
Zaragoza, Christian, 1972
Zoch, George, 1970, 1971

North Texas State University (1973-78)
Arizaga, Nick, 1978
Armstrong, Tony, 1974
Babb, Frank, 1975, 1976, 1977
Bahner, Blake, 1978
Barnes, Nelson, 1977, 1978
Battle, Ron, 1978
Beaty, Mark, 1975, 1976, 1977
Bell, Bruce, 1975
Bowles, John, 1973
Broome, John, 1974
Brown, Jeff, 1975, 1976
Burkholder, Jimmy, 1973, 1974, 1975
Case, Jordan, 1978
Cecil, George, 1973
Chambers, Bruce, 1976, 1977, 1978
Champagne, Terry, 1976, 1977
Chapman, Walter, 1973, 1974, 1975
Clemmons, Charles, 1974
Cooksey, Mike, 1973, 1976
Collins, Milton, 1978
Cox, Billy, 1976
Croft, Jimmy, 1977, 1978
Cumby, Mack, 1974
Davidson, Greg, 1976, 1977, 1978
Davis, Frank, 1973
Davis, Melvin, 1973, 1974
Deaton, David, 1973
Dieb, Steve, 1977, 1978
Dilliard, Dennis, 1973, 1974, 1975
Dixson, Larry, 1976, 1977, 1978
Dooley, Mike, 1974, 1975
Dunlap, Don, 1973

Easley, Gary, 1974
Ende, Fred, 1973, 1974
English, Lee, 1978
Everest, Andy, 1974, 1975
Fechtman, Don, 1974, 1976
Ford, Tony, 1973, 1974, 1975
Fry, Kelly, 1975, 1976
Fry, Randy, 1975
Fry, Zack, 1973
Garrett, J.C., 1973
Glendenning, Rex, 1976, 1977
Golden, Sam, 1973
Gordon, Fred, 1977
Gosline, Ted, 1973
Green, Ollie, 1973, 1974, 1975
Hagan, Marvin, 1977, 1978
Hagerman, David, 1977, 1978
Hamm, Buddy, 1978
Hammit, Brad, 1975
Harrington, Lee, 1973
Harris, Sidney, 1974
Harvey, Pete, 1978
Henderson, Ralph, 1978
Henry, Mike, 1975, 1976
Hollins, J.T., 1974, 1975
Holman, Louis, 1973
Humbarger, Rex, 1973
Isaac, Warren, 1973
Jackson, Bernard, 1978
Jackson, Vance, 1973
Jenkins, Lavell, 1974
Johnson, Charles A., 1973, 1975
Johnson, Charles R., 1973
Jones, Malcolm, 1976, 1977
Jones, Michael, 1975, 1976
Kelley, Tom, 1978
Kerestine, Paul, 1978
Kervin, David, 1973
Khoury, Iseed, 1975, 1976
King, Donald, 1977
King, Garry, 1973, 1975, 1976
Kirk, David, 1973
Kuykendall, Les, 1973
Lark, Melvin, 1976, 1977, 1978
Lawrence, Clark, 1973

Lemming, Jim, 1977, 1978
Lemmons, Dennis, 1973
Lewis, George, 1976
Lewis, Glenn, 1977, 1978
Lewis, Reginald, 1975, 1976, 1977
Little, Bernie, 1974, 1975
LoCaste, Jim, 1977, 1978
Loftin, Tim, 1975, 1976
Marshall, Gordon, 1975
Martin, Paul, 1974, 1975, 1976
McCurin, James, 1977
McIngvale, Jim, 1973
Mitchell, Julius, 1976, 1977, 1978
Morris, David, 1977, 1978
Morris, Donnie, 1973
Morris, Pete, 1973, 1975
Morrison, Marty, 1976, 1977, 1978
Moss, Howard, 1973, 1974
Murray, Charlie, 1977
Newton, Jonathan, 1978
Norman, Levene, 1973
Odoms, Jimmy, 1975, 1976, 1977
Oliphant, Mike, 1976, 1977, 1978
Owen, Bobby, 1973, 1974
Pack, Sam, 1973
Pendarves, Shelton, 1973
Perry, James, 1978
Phillips, Rudy, 1977, 1978
Ray, David, 1975, 1976
Ray, Glen, 1975
Reece, Beasley, 1973, 1974
Ross, Richard, 1978
Shaw, Rick, 1973
Shepherd, John, 1974
Shotland, Phil, 1973
Shotwell, Paul, 1975, 1976
Sims, Walter, 1976, 1977, 1978
Smith, Charlie, 1978
Smith, Gary, 1975, 1976
Smith, Gary "Tex", 1974
Smith, John Thomas, 1974, 1975, 1976
Smith, Ken, 1975, 1976
Smith, Larry, 1974
Smith, Royce, 1973

Stevenson, Joe, 1978
Stout, Bob, 1973
Swierc, Sammy, 1974, 1975
Terrell, Darrell, 1978
Turner, Reggie, 1973
Varner, Les, 1973
Washington, Burks, 1975, 1976, 1977
Washington, Ken, 1974, 1975, 1976
Webb, Jeff, 1974, 1975
Wells, Steve, 1977, 1978
Wendler, Bill, 1973
West, Bernard, 1977, 1978
Whitaker, Danny, 1976, 1977, 1978
Wilkerson, Mike, 1973, 1974, 1975
Williams, Collin, 1974
Wood, David, 1978
Yarber, Jim, 1974
Young, Bill, 1973
Young, Charlie, 1978

University of Iowa (1979-1998)
Abraham, Ryan, 1994
Adams, Mark, 1987, 1988
Aegerter, Greg, 1988, 1989,1990
Alexander, Dave, 1983, 1985, 1986, 1987
Allen, Greg, 1991, 1992, 1994
Allen, Jeremy, 1998
Allendorf, Kevin, 1989
Alt, John, 1980, 1981, 1982, 1983
Anderson, Bill, 1986, 1987, 1988, 1989
Anderson, Tim, 1985, 1986, 1987, 1988
Andrews, Jeff, 1993
Angel, Kevin, 1985
Anttila, Jeff, 1990, 1991, 1992, 1993
Atkins, Plez, 1994, 1995, 1996, 1997
Bachman, Jay, 1983
Bailey, Bill, 1981, 1982, 1983
Baker, Jason, 1997, 1998
Baldwin, Marty, 1992

Montgomery, Marcus, 1995
Moritz, Dave, 1981, 1982, 1983
Morton, Rod, 1977, 1978, 1979
Mosley, Dennis, 1976, 1977, 1978, 1979
Mott, Joe, 1985, 1986, 1987, 1988
Mulherin, Mick, 1992, 1993, 1994, 1995
Mullen, Scott, 1998
Murphy, Dave, 1985, 1986
Murphy, George, 1986, 1987, 1988, 1989
Nelson, Jeff, 1990, 1991, 1992
Nemmersm Brett, 1994
Neuman, Scott, 1989
Nichol, Tom, 1981, 1982, 1983, 1984
Norvell, Jay, 1985
Oakes, Dave, 1978, 1979, 1980, 1981
O'Brien, Kelly, 1981, 1982, 1984, 1985
Odems, Demo, 1993, 1994, 1995, 1996
O'Hare, Cody, 1998
Olejniczak, Jason, 1990, 1991, 1992, 1993
Olejniczak, Lon, 1979, 1980, 1982, 1983
Oliver, Chris, 1998
Oostendorp, John, 1992
Ortlieb, Jon, 1994, 1995, 1996
Pace, Mario, 1976, 1977, 1978, 1979
Palladino, Sam, 1976, 1977, 1978, 1979
Palmer, Chris, 1992, 1993
Palmer, John, 1987, 1988, 1989
Pekar, Jim, 1980, 1981
Person, Nate, 1979, 1980
Peterson, Nate, 1979, 1980
Peterson, Hap, 1982, 1983, 1984, 1985
Peterson, Tariq, 1997, 1998
Petrzelka, Matt, 1977, 1978, 1979,

1980
Phillips, Eddie, 1980, 1981, 1982, 1983
Pipkins, James, 1987, 1988
Plate, Scott, 1990, 1991, 1992, 1993
Poholsky, Tom, 1986, 1987, 1988,1989
Polite, Eddie, 1984
Polly, Ed, 1988, 1989, 1990, 1991
Porter, Bo, 1992, 1993, 1994
Postler, Paul, 1978, 1979, 1980, 1981
Poynton, Jim, 1987, 1988, 1989
Price, Derek, 1994, 1995
Pryor, Richard, 1984, 1985, 1986
Pryor, Shalor, 1997
Puk, J.J., 1986, 1987
Purdy, Matt, 1992, 1993, 1994, 1995
Quast, Brad, 1986, 1987, 1988, 1989
Quest, Matt, 1992, 1993
Raitt, Travis, 1998
Reardon, Bill, 1993, 1994, 1995, 1996
Redman, Matt, 1997
Rees, Bob, 1990, 1991, 1992
Reid, Brad, 1977, 1978, 1979
Reilly, Jim, 1985, 1986, 1987, 1988
Reiners, Randy, 1997, 1998
Reischl, Matt, 1995, 1996, 1997, 1998
Renn, Tom, 1976, 1977, 1979
Ricciardulli, Tony, 1980
Richardson, Burt, 1991
Ridley, Sean, 1987
Rigtrup, Keith, 1997
Riley, Tom, 1980
Rinderknecht, Reed, 1991
Robertson, Cornelius, 1983
Robinson, Damien, 1993, 1994, 1995, 1996
Roby, Reggie, 1979, 1980, 1981, 1982
Rodgers, Matt, 1988, 1989, 1990,

1991
Roehlk, Jon, 1980, 1981, 1982, 1983
Rogers, Matt, 1998
Rollins, Vernon, 1995, 1996, 1997
Romano, Todd, 1992, 1993, 1994, 1995
Rose, Derek, 1996, 1997, 1998
Roussell, Mark, 1992, 1993, 1994
Rudolph, John, 1987
Ruhland, Matt, 1988 1989, 1990
Ryan, Ron, 1988, 1990
Saidat, Ed, 1998
Santos, Moses, 1988, 1989, 1990, 1991
Saunders, Mike, 1988, 1989, 1990, 1991
Schilling, Scott, 1978, 1979, 1980
Schmidt, Rick, 1984, 1985, 1986
Schmitt, Bob, 1987, 1988
Schuster, Joe, 1983, 1984, 1986, 1987
Schwind, Mike, 1992
Scott, Doug, 1991
Sennott, Tim, 1983, 1984, 1985
Senters, Travis, 1997, 1998
Serama, Ted, 1995, 1996
Sether, Scott, 1992, 1993
Shakoor, Damani, 1994, 1995
Shaw, Cedric, 1976, 1977, 1978, 1979
Shaw, Sedrick, 1993, 1994, 1995, 1996
Shay, Zach, 1998
Sheldon, Thad, 1998
Sherman, Matt, 1994, 1995, 1996, 1997
Sibert, Mike, 1992
Sims, Ken, 1983, 1984, 1985, 1986
Simonsen, Todd, 1978, 1979, 1980 1981
Sindlinger, Mark, 1983, 1984, 1985, 1986
Sistrunk, Dwight, 1986, 1987
Skillett, Jeff, 1988, 1989, 1990,

1991
Skradis, Bryan, 1977, 1978, 1979, 1980
Slattery, Joe, 1998
Slowik, Eric, 1991
Slutzker, Scott, 1992, 1993, 1994, 1995
Smiley, Keaton, 1985, 1986, 1988
Smith, Leroy, 1989, 1990, 1991
Smith, Robert, 1983, 1984, 1985, 1986
Smith Sean, 1988, 1990
Sobieski, Ben, 1997, 1998
Soliday, Jason, 1990
Spitzig, Kevin, 1980, 1981, 1983, 1984
Spranger, Mark, 1984, 1985, 1986
Station, Larry, 1982, 1983, 1984, 1985
Stemlar, Tom, 1981
Stewart, Tony, 1987, 1988, 1989, 1990
Stockdale, Matt, 1998
Stoops, Bobby, 1979, 1980, 1981, 1982
Stoops, Mark, 1987, 1988, 1989
Stoops, Mike, 1981, 1983, 1984
Strobel, Dave, 1981, 1982, 1984
Suchomel, Todd, 1980
Suess, Phil, 1978, 1979, 1980
Sullivan, Eddie, 1982
Swift, Jim, 1976, 1977, 1978, 1979
Taylor, Tyrone, 1986
Terry, Ryan, 1992, 1993, 1994
Thein, Rob, 1996, 1997, 1998
Thigpen, Eric, 1995, 1996, 1997, 1998
Thomas, Steve, 1986, 1987
Tippett, Andre, 1979, 1980, 1981
Titley, Michael, 1989, 1990
Trippeer, Kyle, 1998
Turner, Dave, 1988, 1990, 1991
Uhlenhake, Clay, 1979, 1980, 1981, 1982
Vang, Scott, 1990

Velicer, Ted, 1989, 1990, 1991, 1992

Verba, Ross, 1993, 1994, 1995, 1996

Vlasic, Mark, 1984, 1985, 1986

Vrieze, Jon, 1983, 1984, 1985, 1986

Wahls, Jason, 1995

Wanket, Tony, 1983, 1984

Ward, Tom, 1987, 1988

Watkins, Travis, 1987, 1988, 1989

Webb, Brad, 1979, 1980, 1981

Webb, Chris, 1993, 1994

Webb, Ivory, 1980, 1981

Weires, Bill, 1985

Weiss, Leven, 1976, 1977, 1978, 1979

Wells, Mike, 1990, 1991, 1992, 1993

Werner, Jon, 1991

Wessels, Ladd, 1989

Wester, Herb, 1984, 1985, 1986, 1987

Westhoff, Jeff, 1995

Wheatley, Austin, 1997, 1998

Whitaker, Matt, 1990, 1991, 1992

White, J.D., 1989

Wiegmann, Casey, 1993, 1994, 1995

Wildeman, Parker, 1993, 1994

Wilkes, Troy, 1989

Willey, Dan, 1977, 1978, 1979

Williams, Dwayne, 1979, 1980

Williams, Reggie, 1994, 1995

Willock, Richard, 1995, 1996, 1997

Wirth, Dan, 1984, 1985,1986, 1987

Wise, Brian, 1988, 1989, 1990, 1991

Woods, LeVar, 1998

Wozniak, Ben, 1978, 1979

Wright, Anthony, 1986, 1987, 1988, 1989

Yacullo, Mike, 1981, 1982

Yamini, Bashir, 1998

Yoder, Scott, 1997

Zdzienicki, Chris, 1997

Other Iowa Related Titles

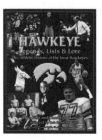